THE MEANING OF YIDDISH

Nostalgia Jewishness is a lullaby for old men

gumming soaked white bread.

J. GLADSTEIN, *modernist Yiddish poet*

CONTRAVERSIONS

JEWS AND OTHER DIFFERENCES

DANIEL BOYARIN,

CHANA KRONFELD, AND

NAOMI SEIDMAN, EDITORS

The task of "The Science of Judaism"

is to give Judaism a decent burial.

MORITZ STEINSCHNEIDER,

founder of nineteenth-century

philological Jewish Studies

THE MEANING OF YIDDISH

BENJAMIN HARSHAV

Stanford University Press • *Stanford, California*

Stanford University Press

Stanford, California

© 1990 by the Regents of the University of
California

First published in 1990 by the University of
California Press

Reprinted in 1999 by Stanford University Press

Printed in the United States of America

ISBN 0-8047-3575-1

LC 99-71318

This book is printed on acid-free paper.

Original printing of this edition 1999

to the memory of my mother
Dvora Hrushovski ("di lererin Freidkes")
principal of a Yiddish school in Vilna
1896–1985

Contents

Preface

> *Riding a train doesn't have to be dull if you manage to fall in with good company. You can meet up with merchants, men who know business, and then the time flies, or with people who have been around and seen a lot, intelligent men of the world who know the ropes. Such types are a pleasure to travel with. There's always something to be learned from them. And sometimes God sends you a plain, ordinary passenger, the lively sort that likes to talk. And talk. And talk. His tongue doesn't stop wagging for a minute. And only about himself, that's his one and only subject.*
>
> —Sholem Aleichem "The Man From Buenos Aires"[1]

Traveling with Yiddish is traveling not just with Yiddish. You look at the landscape of language, and in a wink it turns into culture, history, literature. You talk to it in Yiddish, and it responds with quotes in Hebrew, German, Russian. You cross worlds of geography and demography, Jewish history and modern transformations and, wherever you turn, you realize that you are crossing universal human spaces: the melting pot of language and cultural interactions, folk wisdom and modernization, national mentalities, and

1. Sholem Aleichem, "The Man from Buenos Aires," in: *Tevye the Dairyman and the Railroad Stories*, translated by Hillel Halkin (New York: Schocken, 1987), 166.

semiotics of discourse. The story of Yiddish becomes a parable for the human PLONTER, the tangle of words, beliefs, attitudes, traditions, experiences, and dialogues in the flux of culture.

Yiddish, no more the living language of a viable, intelligent society, still hovers over yesterday's horizon and evokes various anxieties: fear of identification, disparaging distance, or nostalgia. The issue, however, must not be seen as one of continuity or identity. Most great achievements of culture were created in languages of periods different from ours: the languages of Greek tragedy or of Hebrew poetry in medieval Spain are not alive today; the world of Shakespeare is certainly not our contemporary world. Closed chapters of history, they offer masterpieces of culture, relevant to us as fictional universes that enlarge our horizons of imagination and our sense of the past. Yiddish culture was one of the peaks of Jewish creativity in the last two thousand years. It may have no continuity in the future but it is interesting and rewarding for its own sake.

This book is a travel report: sometimes sketchy, sometimes selective, sometimes covering familiar terrain. It is an essay, attempting to rethink and present to the intelligent reader some of the basic aspects of the culture of Yiddish, the historical and social conditions that combined to mold the peculiar nature of its language, literature and life. My central question is: *Yiddish, what was it?* What kind of world was it? How can we read the intersections of meaning its texts seemed to provide? How did it lead in and out of Jewish history, moving between tradition and assimilation and between the internal Jewish world and the cultures of Christian Europe and America?

The book is not intended for the specialized scholar and may repeat issues known to the Yiddish linguist or Jewish historian. I surveyed the field in its broad contexts for readers who bring to it no previous knowledge except for curiosity. My goal was not to investigate new details or describe a few more facts but to rethink and analyze the issues in their full historical and cultural complexity, disregarding the boundaries between such different disciplines as linguistics, folklore, semiotics, literary criticism, and history. The book presents a series of constructs, which may be seen as hypotheses—to be accepted or refuted by others with counterexamples in hand. My goal is understanding things as they were, without apology or normativism. I do not argue specifically with other scholars or with sentimental popularizers; the specialist will understand the hidden polemics. And I focus on the centrality of discourse in human behavior and in Jewish culture in particular.

In the last millennium, the Yiddish language was the major original vehicle of internal communication developed by European, Ashkenazi Jews. It mediated between their daily lives and the Hebrew religious and educational heritage on the one hand, and the languages and beliefs of the surrounding, Christian world on the other. It was the cement of an extraterritorial enclosure which kept the separate social and religious network of the Jews within its own possible world. By the end of the nineteenth century, Ashkenazis constituted about ninety percent of world Jewry. In their powerful centrifugal movement from backward existence in impoverished, "medieval," small-town communities of Eastern Europe to the big cities, the West, the New World, or Israel, and to Modern Culture and Science, integration into technological societies, and assimilation, Yiddish fulfilled a vital role. It was both the vehicle of its own flourishing, though short-lived, culture and a hidden substratum for many transformations in the consciousness, ideologies, and languages of Jews and their descendants.

To be sure, not in all periods and not in all places of their dispersion did European Jews speak Yiddish. Throughout the centuries, they wrote in Hebrew and spoke Italian, French, German, Dutch, Czech, Polish, "Goyish" (used especially for Ukrainian), Russian, English, and other languages. We may never know exactly what proportions those languages occupied in each community or in the mind of each speaker in any given period. Be that as it may, Yiddish was the major linguistic creation of European Jewry and its extensions on other continents (North and South America, South Africa, and Australia). In its folklore world, Yiddish preserved the quintessence of the memories and perceptions of a people aware of its history, its "chosen," extrahistorical status, and its Diaspora predicament; a people remembering its Hebrew heritage and sensitive to the moods and moves of its dominant neighbors.

The civilization of Yiddish represented a fusion of lower-class attitudes with the pride and aspirations of a fallen aristocracy of the mind. It came of age as a cultural force in the last five hundred years and gave rise to a fascinating literature in the last hundred and thirty. The basic structure of the Yiddish language has features similar to other "Jewish languages" created in various linguistic milieus of the Diaspora—from Arabic through Persian to Spanish. Indeed, the new meeting ground of diverse diasporas in contemporary Israel called for a parallel interest in Ladino and other Jewish linguistic adaptations. But the richness of Yiddish culture and literature, its multilingual synthesis, and its independence from its source languages is unequaled among them.

The spectacular rise and fall of modern Yiddish culture is at the heart of the story of the secularization and modernization of the Jews in the last two centuries. Yiddish literature accepted the challenges of European literature and culture. At its best, it produced innovative works which harnessed the inimitable features of its language, folklore, fictional world, and character typology and confronted them with the whirlpool of the modern world and the challenges of modernist art. Yiddish literature flourished as part of what we may call the "Modern Jewish Revolution," the most profound change in Jewish history in the last two thousand years. The revolution was carried out by the internal, personalized responses of each individual to the trends, events, and possibilities of modern history and resulted in radical transformations in the geographic, professional, linguistic, and cultural existence of a whole people. In retrospect, modern Yiddish culture can be seen as a product of this period of transformation and, as such, it seems that it was destined to decline with its completion, when Jews had integrated into the languages and cultures of their new homelands, including the revived Hebrew in the state of Israel. In fact, however, history dealt it a deadly blow when the Nazis annihilated the centers of European Jewry and the Soviets stifled the last breath of Yiddish culture in Russia.

Like Jewish existence itself, the Yiddish language was never an automatic vehicle taken for granted. To many of its modern speakers or their children, Yiddish was the carrier of the memory of the recent past and, as such, either vigorously abandoned or nostalgically cherished, or both. Time and again, it has provoked deep, even violent responses: irrational hatred or emotional attachment. Today it has all become academic—in a literal sense as well: it has become the venerable object of academic study. As a living language, while in small circles it still clings to high literature, Yiddish has largely receded to its premodern, basically oral existence among its surviving speakers and in several orthodox religious communities.

Understanding Jewish history in Europe, the character of the Jews, and the world of the founders of the modern Jewish communities in the United States, Israel, the Soviet Union, France, England, Argen-

tina, and elsewhere involves understanding Yiddish. It is also a treasure
trove for the study of language and culture in general: cultural interaction, semiotics of cultural history, and languages in contact. And,
above all, it is interesting for its own sake, for its own ironies and
idiosyncrasies.

This essay does not claim to be comprehensive. I preferred the
discussion of several selected topics, showing the rich problematics of
the field, to the virtues of a general survey. The achievements of Yiddish linguistics and literary scholarship are my base of knowledge,
though I rarely quote them directly. In the heyday of structuralism,
Yiddish studies, too, moved from the popular sport of individual folk
etymologies to the discovery of "the rules of the game." But its major
scholars have always known that we must not separate the structural
analysis of language from the social forces and historical context which
permeated it, that language cannot be understood without its reflec-
tions in literature and culture, and that Yiddish cannot be understood
without its entanglement with Hebrew and vice versa.

There is still much in this field that should be researched and clar-
ified, corrected and argued. But, as we say in Hebrew, *lo aleynu ha-
melakha ligmor*, "It is not for us to finish the task."

Part One of this book discusses the major aspects of the Yiddish
language, its peculiar nature, and the semiotics of "Jewish" communication. It covers a broad historical context of Jewish history and
analyzes the nature of "Jewish discourse," flowing from the traditional
Hebrew library into Yiddish and from there to Kafka, Bellow, and
others. The chapters devoted to the nature of Yiddish begin, logically,
from the lower, linguistic elements and then proceed to the more semantic aspects of discourse and culture. I tried to present even the
most technical issues in a manner accessible to the interested layman,
explaining and illustrating the basic principles rather than covering the
whole grammar. All examples are translated and explained and no
knowledge of any component languages is required.

Part Two, *Literature in History*, discusses Yiddish literature in the
context of the broader movement of transformations of the Jews in
the last two centuries and the Jewish secular culture created in the
process—what may be called "the Modern Jewish Revolution." I end
with a brief survey of Yiddish poetry in the United States, focusing
on one Modernist trend, Introspectivism, which emerged in New York
in 1919. And, finally, a glance at some motifs of Glatshteyn's poetry

takes us to the lament on the Holocaust of the Yiddish language that became a central theme in Yiddish poetry itself.[2]

This book emerged as a byproduct of my work on *American Yiddish Poetry*.[3] The reader will find in AYP a large selection of Yiddish poetic texts (in their original and in English translation) and some typical examples of literary theorizing by Yiddish poets, to support generalizations made here. Several chapters of this book were used, in part, for the introduction to that anthology but were expanded here.

All translations of texts quoted in this book (unless specifically mentioned otherwise) are by Barbara Harshav and myself. Their primary intention here is to be as close to a literal translation as possible, in order to bring the reader to the modes of thinking and imagining in the original, rather than to provide a substitute in the language of the translator's own modern world.

Acknowledgments

This book was written at the Institute for Advanced Study in Berlin in 1984–85. To the unforgettable two years at that noble institution and to its staff I owe the great opportunity for creative brooding, outside of history and daily duties. For a short time, in the 1920s, Berlin was one of the major centers of Yiddish literature in the world. That ghost was still palpable to me, if to hardly anyone else. In Berlin I felt like Erich Auerbach in World War II Ankara writing a book (*Mimesis*) on the essence of what seemed to him the disappearing culture of Europe. Like Auerbach, without the benefit of a proper scholarly library in this field, I was trying to understand some essential aspects of what seemed to be an almost extinguished culture and to do it through a close analysis of telling examples.

For the chapters on language, I used many ideas and illustrations from the masterpiece that synthesized the work of modern Yiddish linguistics: Max Weinreich's (1894–1969) closely argued and pro-

2. Several studies on the forms of Yiddish versification were collected in my book, *Turning Points: Studies in Versification*, Porter Institute for Poetics and Semiotics, Tel Aviv University, 1990.

3. Benjamin and Barbara Harshav, *American Yiddish Poetry: A Bilingual Anthology*, (Berkeley, Los Angeles, Oxford: The University of California Press, 1986). Henceforth quoted as: AYP.

fusely documented life-work, *History of the Yiddish Language.*[4] In a way, my chapters on language try to popularize some of the central notions of that detailed and difficult study, though my conceptual framework differs from it. To the landmark scholarship and unforgettable friendship of Max Weinreich and his son, my childhood friend Uriel Weinreich (1925–1966), Professor of Linguistics at Columbia University, I owe my attraction to the serious research and thought on the inimitable world of Yiddish.

The perspicuity and ideas of Itamar Even Zohar and Khone Shmeruk's conception of Yiddish literary history fed my understanding of this field in ways I probably cannot account for.

I am grateful to Marvin Herzog, Chana Kronfeld, and David Roskies, who read the manuscript and made valuable remarks. Ruth Gay was the ideal "intelligent reader," whose fine ear and alert mind guided me in preparing the final version of the manuscript. Personal thanks are due to my inveterate reader and editor, Barbara Harshav, and to the openness and encouragement of my friend and publisher, Stanley Holwitz.

The book is dedicated to the memory of my mother, mathematics teacher and early feminist, principal of an experimental Yiddish secular school ("Sophye Markovne Gurevich Shul") in prewar Vilna, who saw in elitist Yiddish culture the dignity of her people and the pride of her personal revolution. She was the Yiddish pillar of my bilingual childhood on a vanished planet. She died in peace in Haifa at the age of ninety, speaking Hebrew, speaking Hebrew.

A Note on Transcription

The transcription of Yiddish into the Latin alphabet in this book usually follows the standard system devised by the YIVO, with some simplifications, to make it as lucid as possible for the contemporary nonlinguist reader. Yiddish, like English and other languages, allows for various realizations of each vowel in different dialects. What follows is not a phonetic guide to the language but a schematized reading of standard literary Yiddish. The general principle

---

4. Max Weinreich, *History of the Yiddish Language,* (Chicago: University of Chicago Press, 1980) (earlier published in the original Yiddish: *Geshikhte fun der yidisher shprakh,* [New York: YIVO, 1973]), vols. 1–4.

is a direct correspondence between the Latin letters and the sounds of standard Yiddish (i.e., more like French and German than like English). The main pronunciations to keep in mind are:

s - like *s* in English *sad*
z - like *z* in English *zebra*
sh - like *sh* in English *shoe*
tsh - like *ch* in English *chair*
ts - like *zz* in *pizza*
kh - like *ch* in *Chanukah* or *chutzpah*
y - like *y* in English *yes*
a - like *a* in English *father*
e - like *e* in English *get*
o - like *o* in English *dog*
u - like *oo* in English *book*
i - like *i* in English *fill*
ey - like *ay* in English *day*
ay - like *uy* in English *guy*
oy - like *oy* in English *boy*

It is important to note that some Yiddish syllables have no vowel letters. At the end of a word (and before a suffix), a cluster of two or three consonants ending in *l* or *n* constitutes a syllable. Thus, the Yiddish MEY-DL has two syllables (like the English *ped-dle*), whereas its English counterpart, *girl*, is monosyllabic. The same is true of MA-KHN (to make), LA-KHN (to laugh), A SHTI-KL (a piece), GE-KE-STL-TE (checkered), or TU-ML-DI-KE (tumultuous, noisy).

In most Yiddish words, the stress falls on the first syllable; whenever this is not the case, I capitalize the stressed syllable: MESHENE ("of copper," stress on first syllable) but: meSHUGE ("crazy," stress on second syllable). Yiddish poetry does not capitalize the beginnings of verse lines; I follow the same principle in the English transcriptions of Yiddish verse, so as not to confuse it with capitals marking stress.

In the English text itself, however, I have deviated from the rules whenever there is a commonly accepted English spelling of familiar Yiddish words. For example, the usual transcription CH for the guttural sound of CHANUKAH, CHUTZPAH, or CHALLAH came to English from the spelling of Jewish names in German or Polish and is, indeed, misleading to an English reader. Nevertheless, I yielded to custom and wrote CHUTZPAH, CHALLAH, and SHOLEM ALEICHEM in the English text. I have also accepted several commonly used compromises between the Hebrew and Yiddish spellings of Jewish religious concepts and the double *d* in the word "Yiddish" itself. But in transcriptions of Yiddish quotes, the transliteration was kept consistent: KHUTSPE, KHALE, YIDISH.

Furthermore, Yiddish words are transcribed here according to their "standard" or "literary" pronunciation, as codified by the YIVO, though the dialects of most speakers deviated from this unified norm. The same holds for the Hebrew elements within Yiddish, which were actually pronounced and read in a whole range of contractions and dialect variants but are represented here in "standard" Yiddish. Nevertheless, when Hebrew expressions are quoted or explained independently (or for the sake of comparison with their Yiddish form), I took the unusual step of representing Hebrew too according to a standardized norm, namely the modern Israeli pronunciation. I did it to avoid the problem of the many changing readings of Hebrew words throughout history and geography, often unknown to us, as well as to make the quote more immediately intelligible to contemporary readers who may know some Israeli Hebrew. To avoid confusion between various Hebrew pronunciations, I did not mark the place of stress in Hebrew words proper.

PART ONE

The Yiddish Language

1

Language and History

A Language New and Old

By the beginning of the twentieth century, both Yiddish literature and the Yiddish language—then spoken by the majority of Jews around the world—were well-established vehicles of communication and culture, mediating to their readers masterpieces of world literature as well as modern ideologies and political and social events. Yiddish was seen by its adherents as "the language of the people" in a populist atmosphere, as the bearer of the genuine values and vitality of the "people." It represented to them the proud stand against self-denial and "careerist" assimilation on the one hand and the "fossilized" straitjacket of orthodox religious behavior on the other.

When the young men and women who eventually became Yiddish-American writers arrived on the American shore, determined to start a new life in the free and difficult new country, and went on to write poetry and to create new poetic modes, it was art in that language and innovation in the framework of that literature that they strove to achieve. Most of them left their mothers and fathers behind "on the other side of the ocean." They carried with them an internalized admiration for an ideal world of books—a secular extension of the traditional authority of "the fathers"—and warm feelings for the intimate and flexible MAME-LOSHN, Yiddish. The expression MAME-LOSHN ("mama-language") is a typical Yiddish compound of Slavic and Hebrew roots, connoting the warmth of the Jewish family, as symbolized by mama and her language, embracing and counteracting the father's awesome, learned Holy Tongue. (This popular nickname of the Yiddish language is diametrically opposed to the sociological term used in modern Yiddish, the cold, Germanizing, MUTER-SHPRAKH, "mother-tongue").

Paradoxically, the Yiddish language was very old and very young at the same time, rich in emotive expressions and poor in denotations of "realia," specific objects in everyday life and nature. As Max Weinreich pointed out, it had few names for flowers but three words for "question": FRAGE (derived from German), KASHE (from Aramaic) and SHAYLE (from Hebrew). The same holds for Yiddish literature: it was perhaps seven hundred years old and still seemed to lack beauty in comparison with the literatures of Europe, and sublimity in comparison with biblical Hebrew. Yiddish writers of the last hundred years experienced the frustrations—as well as the elation—of having to create and enrich both their language and their literature as if they were just beginning. True, unlike Hebrew, until recently merely a language of texts, Yiddish carried the cadences and emotive connotations of a spoken language. But an enormous effort had to be invested—by writers, teachers, essayists, journalists, and political activists—to enrich its vocabulary and expand it to cover new domains of politics, knowledge, nature, industrial cities, poetry, and human experience. Yiddish literature had to discover and work out for itself the very genres in which it was writing; novelists had to invent narratives fitting their peculiar society; poets had to mold Yiddish words into the supple lines and phrases of European-type verses. And at the same time there loomed the constant double menace that Yiddish culture might be trivialized and the language disappear altogether. Indeed, the beginning and the end of his language often ominously crossed the horizon of a single Yiddish writer in the course of one lifetime.

Modern Yiddish literature sprang out, as deus ex machina, from contemporary European literature rather than evolving from its own heritage. It was only from the strength of this newly developed culture and its creative explosion in the twentieth century that scholars came to rediscover and reconstruct a linguistic tradition and a literary history.

The History of Yiddish and Jewish History

According to Max Weinreich's reconstruction, Yiddish, like a number of other European languages, emerged around the year 1000. Weinreich locates the cradle of the language in the cities on the middle Rhine in the ninth or tenth century, in the Carolingian realm. There are only a few vestiges of the early centuries of "Yiddish" (as it was to be called much later) since it was a predominantly oral language and, in the course of Jewish expulsions and migrations, few documents in this non-holy tongue were preserved. Yet, it is possible to reconstruct some of its early features from the sounds of words and proper names and from analyses of later texts.

Jews appeared in Europe from the beginning of the Christian Era; they came to Cologne with the Roman Legions in the first century. A new and significant migration to the Rhine area around the tenth century originated in Northern Italy and France. The immigrants spoke what was called in Hebrew "LA'AZ" (Weinreich's LOEZ, "the language of a foreign people"). Actually, those were two variants of spoken Latin preceding the oldest "French" and the oldest "Italian," infused with Hebrew elements. On this basis, they absorbed parts of the vocabulary and syntax of the spoken dialects of their Germanic neighbors, selected through their own linguistic and semantic filter. With time, the new amalgam became an indigenous Jewish language, used separately by Jewish communities and written in a separate, Hebrew alphabet. A further step of independence occurred when Yiddish speakers moved outside of the German domain: to Italy, the Netherlands, the Slavic countries, and the Americas, where their language was entirely set off from the languages of their neighbors.

ASHKENAZ, the Hebrew name for Germany, became the name for most of European Jewry and, later, for their descendants in Israel, the United States, and elsewhere. It is distinguished from SEPHARAD, the Hebrew name for Spain, which came to indicate Jewish communities that dispersed around the Mediterranean (Greece, Turkey, Italy, North Africa) after the Spanish Exile. The label, "Ashkenazi," does not necessarily mean that all Ashkenazi Jews came from Germany but that they adopted the cluster of Ashkenazi culture which included the specific Ashkenazi religious rite and the German-based Yiddish language. Thus, it is plausible that Slavic-speaking Jewish communities in Eastern Europe (which existed there from early times) became dominated in the sixteenth century by Ashkenazi culture and adopted the Yiddish language. At various times, the language was spoken in Germany, Bohemia and Moravia, Poland, Lithuania, and the Ukraine, as well as in Amsterdam, Venice, Strasbourg, Riga, Jerusalem, Safed, Melbourne, Moscow, New York, and Los Angeles.

The end of the first millennium and the early centuries of the second millennium of the Christian Era were a busy period in the formation of Ashkenazi Jewry. At that time, the Ashkenazi prayerbook and liturgy—brought from Italy to the Rhine area around the tenth century—were consolidated in their basic forms. And so were all aspects of life: from a detailed code of daily behavior, service, and education based on the classical canon of Judaism, to the law of monogamy, formulated here in the tenth century. Rashi's (1040–1105) precise and detailed commentaries on the basic Jewish religious texts, the Bible and the Talmud, were composed in France in the eleventh century and became a cornerstone of Ashkenazi culture; eventually they became semicanonized on the pages of the printed Bible and Talmud and have remained key tools of Jewish education to this day. Famous yeshivas (academies) grew up in France and Germany, raising generations of Talmudic scholars and religious poets and shifting the center of Jewish learning from Babylon to central Europe. Here, the concept of dying for KIDDUSH HA-SHEM, for one's faith, was forged during the Crusader slaughters of Jewish communities, and here the early "Hassidic" movement emerged in the twelfth and thirteenth centuries. Yiddish imbibed the atmosphere and style of this intensive collective work and life. It became its oral vehicle. As Max Weinreich puts it, "the history of Yiddish and the history of Ashkenaz are identical in more than a chronological sense" (p. 41).

From the fourteenth and certainly by the sixteenth century, the center of European Jewry had shifted to Poland, then one of the largest countries in Europe, comprising the Grand Duchy of Lithuania (including today's Byelorussia), Crown Poland, Galicia, the Ukraine and stretching, at times, from the Baltic to the Black Sea, from the approaches to Berlin to a short distance from Moscow. At the same time, between the thirteenth and the fifteenth centuries, the Jews were expelled from the major Western European countries—England, France, most of Germany, Spain, and Portugal. (Smaller Jewish communities survived, however, in Holland, Alsace, some German areas, and Italy; and a major center developed outside the Christian world, in the Ottoman Empire around the eastern Mediterranean.)

By the sixteenth century, according to some estimates, about two-thirds of world Jewry lived in the vast Kingdom of Poland and Grand Duchy of Lithuania. Jews played an important role in developing the cities and in settling the new eastern areas (notably, today's "Ukraine"), mediating between the ruling Polish aristocracy on the one hand and the peasants of various nationalities in this vast "bread-basket of Europe" on the other. They lived, managed agricultural estates, and traded among people speaking minority languages (or dialects) and communicated with the landowners in Polish. In sixteenth- and seventeenth-century Poland, there was a Jewish autonomous "state within a state," epitomized by the "Assembly of Four Lands," a kind of Jewish parliament responsible for the imposition of law among Jews, centralized tax collecting, and coordination of all internal affairs of the Jewish communities. A strong network of Jewish education and learning developed. In this area, the Hassidic movement emerged in the eighteenth century and it was here, too, that most Jewish political movements—from Socialism to Zionism—and the new Hebrew and Yiddish literature flourished from the end of the nineteenth century on. Indeed, this was the home of the Yiddish-speaking Jewish masses before the Holocaust.

Toward the end of the eighteenth century, however, the great Kingdom of Poland and Lithuania was dismembered by its neighbors, Russia, Austria, and Prussia (later Germany). The Jewish population was carved up with the territories and incorporated in these states, most of them in the Russian Empire. In Russia, they were confined to the formerly Polish territories, the "Pale of Settlement," a huge geographical ghetto in the western parts of the Russian Empire, including what is today the Ukraine, Byelorussia, and Lithuania, as well as the heart of Poland proper, "Crown Poland." Thus, when we speak of "Russian" Jews, we must remember that most of the Jews under Russian rule before the Revolution of 1917 did not live in Russia proper but in the former Polish territories. The Jews of Galicia, however, also a former part of Poland, found themselves separated from their cousins and living in the Austro-Hungarian Empire, where the state language was German. (Hence, most "Polish" Jews immigrating to America before World War I were considered either "Russians" or "Austrians.") And many of the so-called German Jews, notably the Jews of Berlin in the twentieth century, actually descended from Posen, Krakow, Silesia, and other formerly Polish areas. From the eighteenth century on, considerable Jewish populations emerged in

Hungary and Rumania, mostly as overflow from the former Polish domains.

Neither in the Russian nor in the Austrian Empire, where the masses of Jews were concentrated, did the majority live among speakers of the state language. Rather, they found themselves in the midst of various minorities: Poles, Ukrainians, Byelorussians, Lithuanians, Latvians, Germans, Czechs, Hungarians. This fact enhanced the preservation of Yiddish—and of Jewish cultural autonomy in general—in the densely populated Jewish small towns or city quarters. With time, many of the rich and the intellectuals mastered the languages of state and "culture," German or Russian respectively and, whenever permitted, they moved to the capital cities of Vienna, Moscow, Petersburg, Berlin (and, farther away, to London, Johannesburg, Montreal, New York, Chicago, or San Francisco). In the nineteenth, and especially in the twentieth century, a similar process occurred in the emerging smaller nations, where Jews became prominent in the new cultural life and languages of Poland, Hungary, Lithuania, and Rumania.

The Jewish population in Eastern Europe grew immensely, both in numbers and in poverty, throughout the eighteenth and nineteenth centuries. Millions migrated overseas. In 1700, there were about one million Ashkenazi Jews in the world, while on the eve of World War II (in 1939) their number was over fifteen million (as compared with over a million Sephardic and Oriental Jews in the world at that time).

A Language of a Polylingual Society

What is the nature of Yiddish?

We could describe it under three headings: bilingualism, fusion, and the semiotics of Jewish communication. Essentially, it means that:

1. Yiddish was spoken by people in a bilingual (or multilingual) context.
2. The language is a fusion of elements from several source languages, which are still used as living components of an open language field.
3. Yiddish was the carrier of a second level of social "language," a peculiar semiotics of Jewish communication.

We shall devote separate chapters to each of these aspects.

In today's world, bilingualism is a well-known phenomenon. His-
panics in the United States learn English as well as Spanish; Soviet
minorities learn their own language and the dominant Russian; black
Africans speak their tribal languages and use English or French in state
institutions and to communicate with one another. In Europe, even
before the rise of the nation-state, this was not the norm.[1] The Jews
in Europe, however, were a bilingual—actually, polylingual—people
par excellence. Their polylingualism was of two kinds, internal and
external.

Internal Polylingualism and the Tradition of Jewish Learning

The separateness of European Jewry rested both on laws
prescribed by the Christian powers and on an intensive internal social
and cultural organization, dominated by a religious conceptual framework. The opposition "Christian" vs. "Jew," central to the conception
of both religions, cemented this separation. The Jews had their own
community institutions, schools, courts of law, hospital and burial societies, welfare and professional organizations, scribes and publishing
houses, synagogues and cemeteries. This separate institutionalized organization of a social group, perfectly acceptable in a pluralistic, feudal
society, separated the Jews and their mental world from their Christian
neighbors as profoundly as did the laws of discrimination, ghettos,
hatred, and persecutions. It thrived on an intensive intrusion into the
personal lives of its participants: the order of the day and its required
prayers; mandatory learning and valorized personal studies and reading; cooking and preparation of food; sexual life and interaction; garb
and language; the talk at synagogue and at home; the habitual interpretation of daily events and of encounters with strangers—all were
permeated by Jewish norms, language and ideologies.

1. True, there were discrepancies between local dialects and the "language of the
king," but most people did not have to master both and there was nothing like the
contrasts between the German-based Yiddish, its Semitic Hebrew components, and the
surrounding spoken Slavic languages.

It was a social structure implemented in Ashkenaz in three internal languages, all written in the same Hebrew alphabet: Yiddish, Hebrew, and Aramaic. Hebrew was, of course, the language of the Bible and the language of Eretz Israel, the Holy Land. Aramaic was the "Yiddish" of a previous millennium, the *mediating language* serving Jewish communities and institutions—including study, explication, and teaching of the Hebrew Bible—in the Middle East, especially in Palestine and Babylon until the Arabic conquest. With its demise as a spoken language, it too became a Jewish language of texts. Unlike Greek (used in the Septuagint, the classical translation of the Bible), Aramaic was not shared with other, dominating cultures and hence became the language of the domesticated and canonized Jewish translations of the Bible (*Targum*); it was also the frame-language of the Talmud and the language of the *Zohar*, the classical book of the Kabbalah. But unlike Yiddish in a later time, Aramaic (in several dialects and historical layers) was subsequently preserved and canonized as part of the "Holy Tongue" and as a major vehicle of what we may call the "Jewish Library." From a language of daily life, discussion, and learned dialogue, it too became a frozen text, to be studied and interpreted.

A Jewish male is supposed to pray at least three times a day; prayer requires each man to read Hebrew texts by himself. Religious Jews have no mediating priest and thus each person is responsible for communicating directly with his God and learning His teachings. In addition, there are blessings to be said on many occasions and long sessions of praying and reading the Bible in the synagogue on Sabbath and holidays. All these texts are in the "Holy Tongue" (LOSHN-KOY-DESH), a general term covering several historical layers of Hebrew and Aramaic. The Holy Tongue—especially in its Hebrew-based form, replete with Aramaic expressions—was the written language of Jewish theology, philosophy, poetry, law, and communal societies. Throughout the ages, it continued to serve as the main language of official documents, community annals, letters, books, international correspondence, liturgical and historical poems, even rhymed inscriptions on gravestones (we can still find a rhymed Hebrew poem on the back of the German tombstone of the Neo-Kantian philosopher, Hermann Cohen, in the Weissensee cemetery in East Berlin).

The consciousness of Judaism was molded, basically, by two conceptions: a historical one and a transhistorical one. The holy text—which also served as the ultimate authority for all later texts, ranging from religious law to secular Hebrew poetry—was the "Book of Books," the Bible ("Old Testament") and its core, the *Torah* (Pentateuch), handed down to His people by God at Mount Sinai. The Bible presented a historical perception of the Jewish people, located in the past. It began with the creation of the universe and closed with the Book of Chronicles, listing the chain of generations. The historical narrative served as a framework and as a backbone pattern for all other genres embedded in this polyvalent anthology, including law, stories, history, poetry, prophecy, and wisdom. The nature of the Jewish people, their relation to God, the messages of the prophets, the religious laws, and even the Ten Commandments were all revealed in historical, narrative contexts.

With the Second Destruction, however (the fall of the Second Temple in Jerusalem to the Roman army in 70 A.D.), and the loss of an independent Jewish state, the Bible was closed and canonized. Now, in Jewish perception, *history was over.* The whole universe of Jewish consciousness and beliefs was rethought and reformulated in Mishnah, Midrash, Talmud, and a vast religious literature in which the Judaism that we know today was crystallized. From then on, the Bible was read as a *repository of law and language*, as a text with suspended narrative order, according to the precept: "EYN MUKDAM U-MEUḤAR BA-TORA" ("there is no 'earlier' or 'later' in the Bible"), that is, all its verses and chapters are equivalent and simultaneous. Christianity, adopting the same attitude, saw the stories of the "Old Testament" as prefigurations of events in the life of Christ. Judaism saw the biblical text as a treasure of overt and hidden laws and as contextual evidence for the semantics of complex words.

Thus, postbiblical religious literature—with the *Talmud* as its core (closed in Babylon around 500 A.D.), the *Shulḥan Arukh* as the code of daily behavior (written in Safed, Palestine, in the sixteenth century), the prayer books and liturgical poetry, and a vast, open-ended library of other texts and commentaries—transposed the historical myth of the Bible into a transhistorical perception of an "Eternal People" (AM OLAM), bound by a complex network of timeless and interdependent codes of law, belief, legend, and behavior. But OLAM means both "eternity" and "the universe." Hence, AM OLAM, "The Eternal People," also means: "the World People," that is, a people living in all time and in all space—actually, outside of any specific time and space, any concrete history and geography.

The prayerbook, stratified according to the days, weeks, and holidays of the year, connected each Jew and his family directly to both the historical narrative, turned into a symbolic myth (notably, in the Passover *Hagadah*), and the transhistorical code of Judaism as a behavioral guide and a living experience.

To master this literature, to preserve the laws, beliefs, and myths dominating Jewish life in its grand moments and in all its minutiae, learning was imperative. Jews were the only people in medieval Europe who had compulsory education, at least for men. Prayer was not enough, however: ideally, each individual was supposed to understand the teachings of the faith, and study the sources, commentaries and arguments, thus keeping the Torah alive by learning. Preservation of the Torah—meaning both the *text* and the *learning*—was as important as preservation of the race. From an early age, Jewish boys in Eastern Europe in recent centuries (the focus of our discussion) spent long days studying, if possible, until their marriage; and, if the bride's parents were rich—or if the wife was an EYSHES KHAYIL (a "woman of valor," literally "a woman soldier") and worked or tended the store and could support the family—men studied all their lives.

No doubt, not everyone was a scholar, and there was a great deal of ignorance among Jews, but practically every man could read at least two languages, Hebrew and Yiddish. More important, scholars constituted the most prestigious group in society and learning was required for the continuation of Jewish existence. Since the Jewish religion had no central administrative authority, the regulation of life emanated from the source of knowledge, guided by those who understood it (hence the governing role of the rabbi in the Jewish community, even when his position depended on the sources of economic power). Learning also provided the justification for the unusual predicament of the Jews among their neighbors. The Yiddish proverb says: TOYRE IZ DI BESTE SKHOYRE ("learning is the best merchandise"), thus translating the two mythological ideals of Jewish Diaspora existence—learning and trade—into each other's language. A rich man would select a poor "genius" (ILUY) studying in a yeshiva, often in another town (where he was fully supported by the community), as a husband for his daughter (thus "wealth" was matched with "wisdom"). Even busy or uneducated men, such as Sholem Aleichem's Tevye the Milkman, would devote some time to daily study, each according to his level of literacy.

It must be pointed out that many women, too, could read, as in-dicated by the Yiddish texts and religious books written for them. Many girls, even the poorest, were literate in Yiddish and were able to read and write letters and read the religious and entertainment books for women (the Yiddish poet H. Leyvik's father was a poor Yiddish teacher "for servant girls"). Girls in well-to-do or enlightened families were given an education in Hebrew and in other languages as well. This, however, was a voluntary matter since girls did not have the obligation to study or pray and could be taught only when a private tutor was hired: the school system was strictly for boys (until the modern girls' schools, both secular and religious, were opened in the twentieth century). Hence, Jewish women in modern times were free to study the languages of country and culture and often excelled in them. The institutionalized school system, however, was exclusively for boys, and it was at least trilingual.

The texts taught in elementary school, the KHEYDER (also tran-scribed as CHEDER or HEDER), were predominantly Hebrew: the To-rah, commentaries, the weekly portions of the Bible. Every child at-tended KHEYDER from the early age of three or four, sometimes five. Here he learned to read Hebrew and absorbed the images, stories, places, and characters from the heroic past of his people (further elab-orated in oral transmission), which served as the basic myth of Jewish society.

The higher school, YESHIVA, emphasized independent study and, in addition to Hebrew, taught texts in Aramaic (a language cognate but quite different from Hebrew and unintelligible to Hebrew speak-ers). The yeshiva prepared its students to "swim" in "the sea of the Talmud."[2] The Talmud became the most important book of Diaspora Judaism. It is a bilingual multivolume text, written in a complex but controlled mosaic of Aramaic and Hebrew and comprising bodies of "Law" and "Legend," presented in the form of recorded oral argu-

2. Typically, deriving from this metaphor and connoting the infinite scope of learn-ing, the Hebrew word A YAM ("a sea") came to mean in Yiddish: "the largest number," "an uncountable quantity" or simply "a lot." It is used in such expressions as A YAM MIT TSORES (translating the European "sea of sorrows" into Yiddish with Hebrew words) as well as in daily matters: KH'HOB A YAM TSU TON ("I have a sea of things to do," i.e., I am flooded with work). The original Hebrew phrase is also transformed in a Yiddish rhymed proverb: DER YAM ON A BREG—DI TOYRE ON AN EK ("The sea has no shore, learning has no end"), which is echoed in the title of Chagall's painting: "Time Is a River Without Shores."

ments. In addition to the classical, canonized texts, the scholars studied commentaries and books written throughout the ages, up to their own time. All these were not just "religious books": within an all-embracing religious framework, they included elements of history, legends, hagiography, stories, prophecy, mysticism, poetry, behavioral guidance, life wisdom, and moral teaching, as well as law and theology.

Hebrew books and manuscripts were holy. In Yiddish, the Hebrew word SEYFER was used for religious books in the Holy Tongue, whereas the Germanic-derived BUKH, or slightly disparaging BIKHL, denoted Yiddish, secular, or foreign language books. Damage caused to a copy of the Torah was a sin to be expiated by the whole community. Torn books and fragments with Hebrew letters—SHEYMES (from the Hebrew word for "names," i.e., potentially including God's name)—were to be saved and buried. Thus, for example, in the great "Cairo Genizah," a repository of Hebrew manuscripts discovered in the early twentieth century in a small synagogue in Egypt, thousands of texts and fragments from almost ten centuries were preserved, including legal and trade documents, numerous manuscripts of Hebrew poetry, and the important fourteenth century "Cambridge Manuscript" of Yiddish verse.

Judaism was thus located in an ever-expanding library, containing a self-reflexive world of rules, beliefs and anecdotes, separated from any realistic, geographic, historical or personal context. It had to be constantly studied, interpreted and applied to actual circumstances. It provided the raison d'être of Jewish existence as such, absorbing its followers in the magic of an intense, "escapist" universe of discourse. The conceptual world of the Jews was molded to a large degree by the images, terms, and phrases of this literature, written in Hebrew and Aramaic and often retold, simplified, and folklorized in Yiddish.

Education itself, however—we are focusing on the last centuries in Central and Eastern Europe—was conducted in Yiddish. It was done in two distinctly different and complementary manners:

1. The Hebrew text of the Bible was taught from early childhood through word-by-word translation into Yiddish: each Hebrew word of the original text was followed directly by its Yiddish equivalent (mostly from the Germanic component, to make clear that it is a translation). For example, the first verse of the Bible, "In the beginning God created," was read thus (Hebrew words are in "quotation marks," Yiddish in italics):

"BEREYSHIS"—*in onfang*, "BORO"—*hot baSHAfn*, "ELOKIM"—*got*, and so on.

2. Talmudic learning (in Aramaic and Hebrew), as well as later and contemporary writings and topical issues, were reunderstood, rephrased, explained, juxtaposed, challenged, and argued in Yiddish dialogues, lectures and sermons. Yiddish provided the syntactical frame for each sentence and the dialogical framework for the discourse as a whole; it served as the conversational setting in which all those treasures—an immense imaginary vocabulary—were embedded.

The central book of this learning tradition, the multivolume Talmud, called "the oral teaching" (TORA SHE-BE-AL-PE), was itself written as an edited synopsis recording five centuries of discussions, analyses, questions and answers, arguments and counterarguments on the laws of Judaism and its basic texts. The explicit structure was a sentence-for-sentence commentary on the second century codex of legal precepts, the *Mishnah*, but the deep structure was an interpretation of God's Bible as a legal and theological system. It seems that only God and His biblical prophets could address a monologue to the people. Subsequent human generations could only interpret and argue the meanings and intentions of the Holy text. In most cases, theirs was only a place in a dialogue.

The Bible itself favored the monologue form of narrative and poetry. The typical biblical discourse is a narrative monologue by an anonymous speaker (or God) describing things in the third person or in the past (in which short dialogues and scenic presentation may be embedded). The narrative may recede into the background to make room for poems, laws, and finally for the books of the prophets—all monologue genres in their own right. True, these monologues can be seen as a series of texts strung on a dialogical tension between God and His chosen people: every event, every seemingly trivial love affair, acquired its depth in light of this historical-moral-existential tension. Furthermore, many of the important monologues by individual voices—God's words or the prophets' "Word" to the people—are delivered in a dialogical situation, while the other side responds mostly with actions rather than with words. Nevertheless, the constitutive form of the discourse itself is a monologue.

With the canonization of the Bible, the prevalent mode of Jewish discourse changed. Dialogue became the dominant form: actual dialogue between human beings and timeless dialogue between alternative positions. Historically, the legal-theological literature provided a three-tier dialogical structure: (1) The Sages conducted dialogues and arguments on the detailed rules of Judaism and on the meanings of the Biblical texts invoked. Those were actual dialogues, located in a specific time and situation. (2) The Talmud, then, presented a second-level dialogue, textually fixed, a dialogue between alternative positions on any given issue, compiled and selected in a timeless framework, for which it quoted voices from the historical, first-level dialogues between sages of various generations in the past. (3) In the processing of Jewish law and learning throughout time and space, *this second-degree dialogue—canonized as a text* (the Talmud)—was then embedded in a third, reopened, dialogue-frame, in which whole libraries found their place. On this third tier, latter-day scholars could challenge or re-argue and re-apply the arguments of the Talmud and of later "Halachic" (legal) literature, as if it all were one synchronic presence.

What was canonized in Judaism was the biblical *text*, not necessarily its specific *meanings*. The meanings were reinterpreted and semi-canonized in further, mutually controlling texts. It is interesting to note that the basic behavioral precepts and rules in Judaism were much more conservative throughout history than matters of ideology, theology, and world view (as the innovations of Kabbalah and Hassidism may illustrate).

This three-tier dialogue structure employed two interlaced and interdependent dialogical forms which we may call "horizontal" and "vertical." A horizontal dialogue is essentially synchronic, juxtaposing two or more positions on an issue, quoting from texts, statements, or dialogues of different periods as if they were co-present, that is, disregarding their distance or order in time. A vertical dialogue is diachronical, analyzing the language of a biblical or other canonized prooftext, or telling an exemplary story, and reading the meanings of the source from the perspective of the current context and vice versa. The horizontal dialogue is essentially argumentative, the vertical, interpretive. In the Hebrew Library, neither form existed without the other: every text is an intersection between a vertical and a horizontal perspective. But there are distinct generic differences.

The Talmudic text subordinates the vertical dialogue to the horizontal, the quotation to the argument, since the topic at hand is the organizing principle of the text. The composition of Talmudic chapters has no narrative backbone, no direction. The narratives that appear in the Talmud are short and anecdotal. Embedded in the argument, they serve to illustrate a point of meaning, to tell an emblematic case, or to illuminate the character of one of the speakers quoted in the text, rather than to relate a plot or advance the text in time. The Talmud is organized thematically. But each chapter does not present one unfolding, logical, or hierarchical argument; it is conceived as a series of analyses of sentences from the *Mishnah*. But the *Mishnah* itself is built as a long string of generalized statements, a taxonomy of rules, often representing several differing positions on a given rule. Thus, the structure of the Talmudic text is *additive* rather than *directional*. It has neither the direction of plot, of a chain of events in time, nor the direction of a hierarchical logical argument as practiced in European philosophy and science. In compensation, however, the smallest unit of the text—not harnessed to any logical or narrative chain—is related to the universe of discourse as a whole. Hence, the reified importance of the small unit, the weight of interpretation of each point and word presented as a knot in this double, entwined, horizontal and vertical dialogue.

Of a different nature are the written and oral texts in what may broadly be called the *sermon* (DERASHA) tradition, including published collections as well as sermons and anecdotal explications by a *maggid* (a wandering preacher), a Hassidic *rebbe* (dynastic leader of a sect), a rabbi of a community, or a bar-mitzva boy. Such texts take off from a specific biblical passage (often, the chapter of the week) and ostensibly subordinate the horizontal to the vertical dialogue. A sermon purports to explicate the biblical passage but it actually invests the biblical text with meanings and messages topical in the immediate environment of the speaker and his audience. A Hassidic book like *Noam Elimelekh* (a collection of sermons by the nineteenth-century rebbe Elimelekh of Lizensk) has an overall coherent ideology, which may be reconstructed from its text, but the form of presentation lies not in any systematic or analytical argument but in individual actualizations of biblical passages. Another example comes from a religious radio program recently broadcast from New York: the interpreter condemned King David's lenient attitude toward his son as the cause of the son's revolt, which resulted in thousands of casualties; he then immediately harnessed this explication to a protest against the closing of a kosher cafeteria at Brandeis University, as if this is what the Bible were talking about.

A biblical chapter is not usually organized topically but as a succinct narrative. In the new reading, its real, narrative structure is suspended for moralizing and interpretive purposes, that is, every sentence, scene, or expression is read for its abstracted "meaning" or "moral" rather than as an event in a chain of events. Hence every sentence or expression may be used separately, for the purpose at hand. Furthermore, meanings extrapolated from such a text will dance all over the place, as opposed to the more disciplined, thematical clusters of the Talmud. The mode of thinking is associative, both because the thematic chain of the original text is alogical and because of the exigencies of actualizing it, of pulling it in any topical direction and wandering off on a tangent.

In these two kinds of Hebrew discourse, the legal-Talmudic and the sermon type, the unity of the text is saved by a total universe of discourse to which all meanings and interpretations are subordinated. And, by the same token, though every scholar and preacher is respected for his individual contribution, they are all subordinated to a total, collective universe of rules and mythology, in which "all Israelites are responsible for each other." Without the disciplines of narrative and logic, the text became an associative chain of brilliant explications and anecdotes. When such patterns of discourse were absorbed by the language of conversation, Yiddish, which did not even have the responsibilities of religious dogma and written text, a mode of talkative behavior emerged in which association reigned supreme, analogy was paramount, and anything could be symbolic for anything else.

Narratives proper, based on Talmudic or Hassidic anecdotes liberated from their larger, didactic context, were absorbed in the Yiddish oral tradition, along with stories from European folklore sources. But this mode, naturally, consisted of short texts, convenient for oral transmission, and often employed as allegories or parables embedded in a wider discourse frame. Narrative hardly ever became the constitutive, compositional force of a larger text.

The only genre that approaches the pole of pure vertical dialogue is a direct commentary on the Bible. But here, too, we can discern a horizontal perspective. Rashi explicates the Bible with an eye to what the Talmud says. And in Abraham Ibn Ezra's commentary on the fifth chapter of Ecclesiastes, we find an excursus on the controversy about the comparative merits of Spanish and Palestinian norms of Hebrew rhyme to be used for writing Hebrew poetry in Italy.

Thus the prevalent discourse of Jewish thought was radically different from the monological forms of lecture courses, which molded many texts of German philosophy, or of the discursive writing, typical of the English "Essay" tradition. Indeed, most Hebrew texts written in Ashkenaz in the last millennium in the religious tradition were dialogical texts: sermons or commentaries upon commentaries of earlier texts. Of course, there were some systematic books in the Jewish library as well, for example, the monological writings of Maimonides, working in a rational, Aristotelian tradition of Arabic philosophy and science. But the religious library included those in the mega-dialogue: you could either object to the rationalist Maimonides or exclude him from the reading list altogether. On the margins of this culture, there was the monological, individualistic, and secular Hebrew poetry developed in Spain and Italy, but it did not enter religious education or the spoken discourse.

This double-directed dialogical network of Jewish religious discourse was also a fascinating tool to captivate sharp minds and enmesh its students as partners in a dialogue with an invisible interlocutor residing in an immense, open-ended library. The method was not to dictate to but to engage the student as an active partner in a process of understanding. There were two conditions: the prescribed answers could not be finally undermined and you could not lose interest in the topics themselves (as did the "relevance"-minded pupils of European enlightenment). The method is alive and well to this day, as can be seen from the following story: a commentator on New York's WEVD radio (formerly, a Socialist station named after Eugene V. Debbs and now broadcasting orthodox religious programs) explained in Yiddish the gist of the Lubavicher rebbe's last Saturday talk; quoting a sharp challenge the rebbe raised to a Talmudic passage (at a distance of fifteen hundred years), the commentator asked the listeners: "MEYNT IR AZ DER TALMUD VET ZIKH MISBALBL VERN?" ("Do you think that the Talmud will get discombombulated [from the rebbe's challenge]?") No, the Talmud pulled "himself" together and found an answer, thus providing the substance of the day's sermon.

The Hebrew fiction writer, M. Z. Feierberg, in his story *Whither?* (1899), vividly described the struggles in a bright student's mind when he is confronted with this huge library:

He studied for three hours straight, the problem was extremely hard and complex, the "attendants" [of the Talmud, i.e., its interpreters] wage the war of the Torah with courage and determination—one is a "Mount Sinai" in his proficiency, another is "Upheaving Mountains" in his acuity—and how pleasant and dear is this war to him! His sorrow dispersed, his heart expended tremendously, he delights in the depth of the Torah. Now, he succeeded in raising by himself the challenge posed by the *Pney yehoshua* [xviii c.] and responding to it with the interpolation of the *Maharsha* [xvi c.]. His soul overflowed joy and pleasure: another victory, and another victory, another bastion topples to the ground! . . .

The protagonist studies by himself, by way of internalized dialogue. He makes vertical forays into the library to discover positions supported by various commentators and place them in a horizontal "battlefield" in which a sixteenth-century scholar can respond to a challenge posed by an eighteenth-century author.

Dialogue within dialogue within dialogue was the name of the game. A large part of the learning process proceeded in a similar way, embedding the written Hebrew and Aramaic dialogues in a new, oral and interpretive frame-dialogue in Yiddish. Especially since the ascendancy of the *Pilpul* method of teaching (originating in Germany in the sixteenth century), a good student was not simply one who knew the answers but one who could question an accepted position, find a difficult or weak point, challenge a written argument, bring later writings to bear against the text, and offer counterarguments (to be explained away in the end). Studies in the yeshiva proceeded in pairs: after the teacher's *shiyur* ("lesson") two students would immerse themselves in the text and clarify its arguments in a dialogue with each other. In addition, there was the method of *sikhas khulin* ("casual conversation"), when the teacher would take a student for a walk and discuss with him or examine him on the topic of study.

A flexible language of conversation in a direct speech situation was desirable for this purpose. Aramaic fulfilled that role in Talmudic times but became a holy and foreign text to be explicated in its turn. Yiddish took over this role as *the final, fourth-level discourse-framework*. "The Yiddish language also soared linguistically because it was the study language: it became the means of expression of a complicated juridical-moral-philosophical universe of discourse long before German, Polish, and the like were used for similar purposes" (M. Weinreich, p. 255).

Naturally, in spite of its overt Germanic garb, Yiddish absorbed a great deal of the phraseology, vocabulary, conceptual world, conversational modes, and intonations of the Hebrew and Aramaic texts. It also influenced them in turn. Furthermore, a special style, the language of scribes and public announcements, used a mosaic of Hebrew and Yiddish fragments in one text, even in one sentence, overlaying each language with the modes of the other.[3] To this day, Yiddish can be filled to the brim with Hebrew. The five-hour televised sermons ("FARBRENGEN") of the Grand Rebbe of Lubavich, carried by satellite from Brooklyn to England and Australia, are nominally in Yiddish but as much as eighty to ninety percent of the text may consist of quotes and phrases from the holy texts—Yiddishized in their grammar and pronounced in the Lubavicher's Lithuanian Ashkenazi dialect. Yiddish proper serves here as the syntactical vehicle, including conjunctions and basic expressions of communication (such as, "what does it mean?" "and then they will see the light," "as you know," and the like). In spite of the predominant Hebrew-Aramaic vocabulary, this is still Yiddish: there are no independent Hebrew words or free word combinations, only quotations and set phrases. But this is Yiddish at its uttermost Hebrew limit, oriented toward a polylingual scholarly audience, hence wide-open to incorporating bodies of Hebrew and Aramaic texts. It is not like Latin, used for learned purposes only: the same Yiddish language, with the same grammatical structure and basic vocabulary, served the mundane purposes of the same people in their family lives; there was a direct flow of expressions and discourse patterns and gestures between the two domains of life, study and home.

In sum, Yiddish was the language of education, debate, preaching, community meetings, legal advice, court procedures, trade, storytelling, family life, and all other forms of oral communication. Yiddish also became the lingua franca, the wireless international network linking Jews of distant places, when they met in trade or wandering and resettlement. It is no accident that the term for "negotiation," MASE-U-MATN ("give and take," literally: "carry and give," from Talmudic Hebrew), applies to trade as well as to a dialogue analyzing a problem. In persecution as in wandering from one country to another—for the sake of study, trade, artisanship, or immigration, or for moral preaching and, in recent times, for cultural and political propaganda—Jews, who were not allowed to own any real estate, could carry with them two "unreal estates," two sign-systems, money and language.

Thus, a functional relationship held Yiddish and the Holy Tongue interlaced in one polysystem (in I. Even-Zohar's term). Yiddish served primarily as the oral vehicle of communication with Hebrew and Ar-

3. See Uriel Weinreich, "The Hebrew-Yiddish Style of Scribes" [in Hebrew], *Leshonenu* 22 (1958): 54–66.

amaic supplying and multiplying the library of texts. At the same time, and in a similar manner, since Yiddish contained Germanic and Slavic components, it could also serve as a bridge to and from the external, Christian world and as a channel for the absorption of concepts and images from the Gentile milieu. Of course, this was not a rigorous, religious, and legal system and was absorbed in the lively and fluid forms of folklore and popular beliefs. The structural unity of the Yiddish language thus served as a junction, a noisy marketplace where "internal" and "external" languages and cultures met and interacted. It was the coherent floor of a schizophrenic existence.

We must remember that Hebrew was not a "dead" language in the full sense of the word; it was continuously studied and written throughout the ages. But Hebrew remained an unspoken language until its revival in modern Palestine at the end of the nineteenth century. There was no question of the primacy of Hebrew: Hebrew was the language in which the Torah was given. Most prayers are in the Holy Tongue; the Hebrew texts of the Bible and the Mishnah are taught and explicated again and again to grasp the meaning of existence, Jewish history, and daily behavior. Indeed, a most frequent expression in both Hebrew and Yiddish is: "as it is written" (or its equivalent, "as it is said," for the Talmud is considered a mere record of speech), serving to support any observation or argument with a quotation from an authoritative book. It appears in the *Hagadah*, read every Passover, in private letters, in prefaces to books, as well as in daily conversation. It is prominent in the Yiddish questioning form: "VU SHTEYT ES GESHRIBN?" ("Where is it written?" i.e., "Who says it should be like that?" "Who forbids me to do the opposite?") A semi-ignorant village Jew, Tevye the Milkman, uses it constantly, referring to various classical Hebrew (or mock-Hebrew) texts as his authority.

As Max Weinreich pointed out, the same rabbis who conducted their oral discussions in Yiddish conducted their correspondence on the same subjects in Hebrew. The institution of Questions-and-Answers, mediating between the world of learning and daily events, was bilingual and socially stratified: a simple woman would ask the rabbi a "Question" (whether her chicken was "kosher," for example) and get her "Answer" in Yiddish, but the written "Questions-and-Answers" (*Responsa*) were basically in the Holy Tongue. The Hassidic rebbe, Rabbi Nakhman of Bratslav, told his symbolic stories in Yiddish but his scribe, Nathan, knew to "write them down" in Hebrew as well.

Religious education and scholarship were predominantly for men; schools and study-houses were exclusively for men; teachers and preachers were male; boys accompanied their fathers to synagogue and absorbed expressions in Hebrew and Aramaic. Thus, the Holy Tongue became associated with the male world. Its expressions flowed into Yiddish through this channel. Yiddish books were ostensibly printed for women though read by men as well. Yiddish was the language of home, family events, and intimacy.[4] It was the "mama-language," with all possible connotations, negative and positive, which this division implied. Subdivisions of a language into social and professional idiolects are a general phenomenon; but here, two differently balanced idiolects—the world of learning and the world of home and trade—met in one family. (Indeed, in Christian medieval societies, much of the Latin learning was located in a separate class, often in monasteries.) And in modern times, the Western world of ideology and culture broke into this same universe, this time marking the younger generation vis-à-vis the old.

In the processing of texts which gave life to this quite "unreal" society, there was a hierarchical structure: the basic text of the Bible was read in Hebrew, accompanied by Aramaic translations and Hebrew commentaries, expanded by "Midrash" and legends (both written and oral), and translated and explained in the mediating language, Yiddish. Yiddish was thus the final, actualized stage of an open-ended, written series.

Though most areas of the religious world were embodied in Hebrew and Aramaic texts, for less weighty occasions, such as Purim, weddings, or family life, Yiddish plays and poems were acceptable (as suggested in the historical studies of Khone Shmeruk[5]). Yiddish also extended the open series of the Hebrew religious-cultural network in

---

4. The "femininity" of traditional Yiddish literature was explored in S. Nigger's 1919 pamphlet, "Yiddish Literature and the Female Reader." Title pages of Yiddish texts would make this humble point. Often, however, the dedication in the book itself was expanded to read: "for women and men" or "for women and men who are like women, that is, uneducated." Such formulas look like dedications for "children of eight to eighty years." There is no doubt that many Yiddish texts were not only written but also read and enjoyed by men albeit as a peripheral or secular genre.

5. Khone Shmeruk, *Yiddish Literature: Aspects of its History* [in Hebrew] (Tel Aviv: The Porter Institute for Poetics and Semiotics, 1978).

the forms of Jewish cooking, play, and behavior, which were as important to the preservation of Jewish identity as the upper rungs of
this series. The proverb, "He means the KNEYDLAKH not the HAGA-
DAH," refers to the well-structured family ceremony of the Passover
Seder, consisting of two parts: food and the reading of the text; the
text ("Hagadah") is in Hebrew, the food is represented by the Yiddish
term (derived from German) indicating the beloved "kneydlakh." An
eighteenth-century rabbi, Ḥatam Sofer, warned: a Jew is distinguished
by his language [= Yiddish], his garb, and his beard [BI-LSHONO, BI-
LVUSHO U-BI-ZKANO], that is, if you shed those, if you cut off your
beard or your Yiddish language, as some Maskilim demonstratively
did, you lose your Jewish identity.

Yiddish was, furthermore, a repository of a folklorized and ho-
mogenized "world" of Jewish myth, lore, attitudes, and world views,
based on an amalgam of concepts from the Hebrew texts with beliefs,
stories, and images absorbed from Christian and even pagan (folklorized) traditions. The European cat, for example, lives on as a magical
figure in Yiddish folklore and, through it, in Bialik's Hebrew poetry.

But Yiddish did not remain a mere oral vehicle of discourse. For
centuries, it developed a written literature of its own, employing European genres or continuing Hebrew genres, and addressing both religious and secular themes. Furthermore, within the oral domain itself,
a rich folklore literature was created and transmitted in Yiddish, in
such formalized genres as stories, anecdotes, songs, proverbs, riddles,
and plays, all generating autonomous oral texts, separated from the
casual flow of conversation. All those were *new* texts, independent of
the interpretations of the classical library.

This unique internal equilibrium made Yiddish not simply an independent language of daily life but part of a complex, polylingual
communicational system. Intersecting with it, we find the external
polylingualism, which was every bit as open and dynamic as its internal
counterpart.

External Polylingualism

Medieval Jewish communities were small; in Germany,
they often consisted of a narrow street along the walls of a city, the
"Judengasse" (later transformed in Yiddish literature into a proud im-

age of our internal world, *Di yidishe gas*, "the Jewish Street," as A. Sutskever, emerging from the Holocaust, called his book.) Even in Eastern Europe, when many Jews inhabited predominantly Jewish small towns or "ghettos," quarters in larger cities, the Jews were a minority in every land. Many ties of trade, finance, neighborly relations, legal and administrative problems, the weekly fairs in Jewish towns attended by Christian peasants, the work of Jewish craftsmen and peddlers in Gentile villages, and of Gentile maids and servants in Jewish houses—all these linked them to the Christian world. Few medieval Jews read the Latin alphabet. Their knowledge of other languages was oral and varied widely in scope. But they at least had access to the spoken language of the surrounding population and often to several languages of different language groups. Jews were exposed to French and German in Alsace; to Czech and German in Bohemia and Moravia; to Ukrainian ("Goyish," the language of the peasant population) and Polish (the language of the landlords) or Russian (the language of the state) in the Ukraine; or to Russian (the state language), Polish (the surrounding language), and German (the language of culture and of the Leipzig fairs) in nineteenth-century Russian-governed Poland. Their economic function in the external world was, by and large, to form a bridge between center and periphery, ruling languages and minorities, aristocrats and peasants, East and West. Their culture lived and thrived in the interstices between nations, tongues, religions, and empires.

Intelligent Jews were truly polylingual. Elye Bokher (in Hebrew, Eliyahu Bakhur, known by Christians as Elia Levita, 1469–1549), born in Germany and active in Italy, taught Hebrew and the Kabbalah to Christian humanists and to a Catholic cardinal in Rome; he wrote a Hebrew grammar, treatises, and poetry (both in Sephardic and Ashkenazi Hebrew); he composed a Latin-German-Hebrew-Yiddish dictionary and wrote epic romances, influenced by Italian sources, in German-based Yiddish and in perfect *ottava rima* stanzas.[6] In later centuries daughters of bourgeois families, exempt from Hebrew studies, typically learned French and the languages of state and culture: German, Russian, and Polish.

6. See Benjamin Hrushovski, "The Creation of Accentual Iambs in European Poetry and their First Employment in a Yiddish Romance in Italy (1508–09)," in Lucy S. Dawidowicz et al., eds., *For Max Weinreich on his Seventieth Birthday: Studies in Jewish Languages, Literature and Society* (The Hague: Mouton, 1964), 108–46; reprinted in Benjamin Harshav, *Turning Points*, Porter Institute, Tel Aviv University, 1990.

Naturally, not everyone in the community knew all those languages equally well. There were marked differences in the knowledge of the Holy Tongue between male and female, scholars and simple men, inhabitants of a Jewish town and individual Jews scattered in the countryside ("Yishuvniks"). The varying degrees of contact with outside society, too, entailed considerable differences in the knowledge of those languages. Nevertheless, in the community as a whole, there was a sense of the sounds, intonations, vocabulary, and grammar of several languages. Since most of those languages (or their linguistic families) had a foothold in Yiddish proper, it was relatively easy to move out of Yiddish to any of them or to bring new elements back to Yiddish from the outside. As a result, in its semantics, syntax, and folklore, Yiddish is very much a European language. For readers sharing a similar, European universe of discourse, it would be superfluous to demonstrate this aspect here.

Thus Yiddish, a language of fusion like English, was much more directly aware of its composing languages, since it lived among them— among Hebrew texts and German and Slavic neighbors—and kept relatively open and wavering boundaries. In modern times, when individual Jews were not only capable of communicating in other languages but adopted them as their own and entered the social, cultural, and economic institutions shaped by them, the balance was tipped and eventually, the separate Jewish languages faded from active use in the Diaspora. Hebrew became the state language of one country, Israel. The attempts to achieve the same for Yiddish—in Birobidjan, the Crimea, Surinam, or elsewhere—failed, and Yiddish, the "World Language," lost its social base.

2

The Nature of Yiddish

A Language of Fusion

The vocabulary and grammar of English are derived from several stock languages, primarily Germanic dialects ("Anglo-Saxon"), Danish, French, and Latin (with a few sprinklings of others, including Yiddish). The balance between these components has changed throughout the history of English and is different in different genres of writing. It is a relatively stable language now and, though Wallace Stevens claimed that all French words are part of the English language, it is possible to distinguish between a French word that has merged into English and one that is merely quoted or borrowed ad hoc. For the native speaker, the English language appears as one system and the etymology of words does not concern him unless his attention is called to it or he is confronted with a bilingual situation (for example, while visiting Paris).

In this respect, the nature of Yiddish is similar to English. The main components of Yiddish derive from German, the "Holy Tongue" (Hebrew and Aramaic), and several Slavic languages, and can still be recognized as such. At its roots, it also had a small Romance component ("La'az") and, in modern times, it absorbed a considerable layer of so-called "Internationalisms," as well as English and modern Hebrew words.

Though observed for centuries, the fully developed theory of Yiddish as a *language of fusion* is Max Weinreich's contribution to Yiddish linguistics. It was promoted in a period when Yiddish culture was still apologetic vis-à-vis the strong majority cultures inviting assimilation. Yiddish had to defend itself against the double accusation of being a "jargon," a distorted and poor form of German, and an unprincipled hodgepodge of words stolen from various languages. Indeed, the language was called "ZHARGON" in Russian and in Yiddish well into the twentieth century, even, lovingly, by its own masters, Peretz, Sholem Aleichem, and Dubnov. It was also a period of immense normative efforts, made by Yiddish schools, writers, teachers, linguists, and such academic institutions as the Yiddish Scientific Institute, YIVO, founded in Vilna in 1925 and headed by Max Weinreich. Embroiled in the "War of Languages" (between Yiddish and Hebrew) on the one hand, and facing mass assimilation on the other, the Yiddishists took the normative road deriving from the neighboring young national state cultures (and ultimately from the French academy rather than from the lenient English-American tradition). It seemed important to elevate and standardize the language, modernize and unify its spelling (against the centrifugal forces of the many Yiddish dialects), and purify it of "foreign" expressions ("Germanism," "Slavisms," "Hebraisms," "Americanisms," and other unwelcome weeds), thus asserting its particularity and refining its treasures.

Max Weinreich convincingly foregrounded the fusion structures and processes which made Yiddish into a unified language. It is important to stress, however, that in the actual life of the language, the opposite tendency worked too: Yiddish always was an *open language*, moving in and out of its component languages and absorbing more or less of their vocabularies, depending on the group of speakers, genre of discourse, and circumstances. For Yiddish was, almost by definition, a language used by multilingual speakers. They were always aware of the component languages of their speech: they lived among those languages and recognized their imprint. It is precisely because the very problem of fusion was at the center of Yiddish language consciousness and the components did not really fully melt, that openness and overstepping the boundaries into another language were a viable option. It is the most typical habit of Yiddish conversation—by simple and learned people alike—to borrow expressions from beyond the language border and to shift for a while from Yiddish proper to pieces of discourse in other languages and back.

With this double-directedness in mind, we may now address the theory of fusion: elements from the stock-languages combined in Yiddish and fused with each other in various aspects of vocabulary and grammar. According to Weinreich, this happened at the very inception of the language: "Owing to a special—we can safely say one-time—constellation, some parts of the raw material began to melt" (p. 29).

Actually, we may add, there was a second "moment" of this kind, the meeting of Yiddish with the Slavic world. No doubt, the basic grammatical structures of Yiddish were by then well established but the internal balance had changed, the "flavor" of the language was transformed. A new, major partner joined the fusion. Yiddish has absorbed words and expressions from Czech, Polish, Ukrainian and Russian.[1] It is even possible that Slavic-speaking Jews, living in the Slavic countries for centuries, provided the substratum for their newly adopted German-Jewish language with the waves of Ashkenazi immigrants from the West.

This meeting with the Slavic world generated a profound reshuffling of Yiddish and Yiddish culture, to the extent that, in several respects, it became a Slavic culture with a German-based language living in a Hebrew library. Hassidism was steeped in the Slavic world. Yiddish literature and the language we know are unimaginable without it. Modern Yiddish (and, for that matter, Hebrew) poetry was a Russian-oriented European poetry with a Jewish cultural background. This second moment has dramatically separated the so-called Eastern Yiddish, which developed in the Slavic lands and invaded Romania, Hungary, the United States, and other countries overseas, from Western Yiddish, almost devoid of Slavic elements, which thrived in medieval Central and Western Europe and survived in some enclaves in Alsace, The Netherlands, Switzerland, and Southern Germany until the twentieth century.

Furthermore, this move to the East gave Yiddish its full independence as a language. In German-speaking territory, Yiddish could be seen in two ways: from the inside, as a separate, Jewish language, written in its own alphabet and practiced by an isolated society of

1. Jews spoke Czech in Bohemia and Moravia in the beginning of the second millennium, as they spoke a Romance language in France. Indeed, some of the early traces of the Czech language were found in Jewish texts, as were the early traces of French and Spanish. Czech was called "Canaanite" (from the "Canaanite slave," i.e., Slavic). See: Roman Jakobson and Morris Halle, "The Term *Canaan* in Medieval Hebrew," in Roman Jakobson, *Selected Writings* (The Hague: Mouton, 1985), Vol. VI, 858–86.

coreligionists; from the outside, as merely another German idiolect. It also repeatedly absorbed elements of German and, in some genres, notably in European-type medieval epics written in Hebrew letters, it approached the condition of slightly modified German. Furthermore, at various times, individuals and groups of speakers moved out of Yiddish into German proper (Yiddish itself lived on in Germany, where Yiddish books were written and published, until the end of the eighteenth century, and survived as a partial, spoken family language in some areas until the twentieth century).

The independence that Yiddish gained in non-German-speaking territories as an extraterritorial social vehicle, transmitted from generation to generation and totally different from its neighbor languages, was the final test of its viability and made it the special language it became. For awhile, Yiddish flourished in northern Italy (see the colorful figure of Elye Bokher, mentioned above), but it was a language of German immigrants with no transmission to further generations. The same fate met Yiddish later in the United States, Canada, Argentina, Australia, and other immigrant countries. It seems that only the particular historical and sociological position of the Jews in Eastern Europe, especially in Poland and in the Russian Pale of Settlement, the critical mass of their numbers and the autonomous network of their social and cultural institutions, guaranteed the independent life of the language—and of the culture developed in it—over more than one generation.

And there was a significant third "moment": the encounter of Yiddish with American English from the 1880s on. This third fusion was relatively short-lived and was violently opposed by the immigrant intellectuals and the purists in Europe. Indeed, it endangered the worldwide unity of the Yiddish language, since "Europe" could not possibly accept it, and threatened with a rift similar to the one between Western and Eastern Yiddish. In the twentieth century, a strongly ideological Yiddish culture, literature, and school system flourished in Eastern Europe and determined the norms of a standard Yiddish language, while America was seen as a primitive and vulgar "diaspora" from the European cultural center. Thus the Americanization of the Yiddish language was left in the hands of the uneducated masses and the mass-circulation newspapers (led in this ideological battle by Abe Cahan, the brilliant and willful editor of the New York Yiddish newspaper *Forverts* [*The Daily Forward*]). For a short while, the new fusion, coined in the manner established in Yiddish for ages, had markedly

affected the language of American Yiddish-speakers, newspapers, realistic fiction writers such as Yoyseph Opatoshu, and excellent poets
such as Morris Rosenfeld and Yehoash. It was, however, so maligned
and constantly purged by the purists that—aside from scorn—no
proper studies have been made of this new fusion, the quarrel between
Americanisms and Slavisms within it, and the interesting encounter
of old Germanic elements coming from both traditional Yiddish and
English.

A similar process of Russification and Sovietization of Yiddish
could be observed in the Soviet Union after 1917. But both in the
United States and the Soviet Union, the opportunities for assimilation
in the twentieth century were such that Yiddish as a mass language
disappeared before it was transformed again. In neither of those two
dynamic societies was there a territorial and social base for an autonomous Jewish minority culture and for a new chain of transmission
to future generations.

Absorption and fusion never stopped in Yiddish but the basic grammatical structures of these processes were established relatively early
to allow the formation of a socially accepted "sense" of what Yiddish
was. Let us now observe specific phenomena.

On the face of it, Yiddish often looks like German. Compare, for
example:

Yiddish:	IKH HOB A HOYZ.	MAYN NOMEN IZ BINYOMEN.
German:	ICH HABE EIN HAUSE.	MEIN NAME IST BENJAMIN.
English:	I HAVE A HOUSE.	MY NAME IS BENJAMIN.

In these sentences, all lexemes are identical in the three languages
(including the Hebrew name, "Benjamin"). The differences in pronunciation between Yiddish and German are explained by the fact that
Yiddish drew on an old stage of German (mostly Middle High German), and especially on its spoken southern dialects, and then separated from it and did not participate in either the development of
New High German after Martin Luther or in the modern intellectual
literary language. Like English, Yiddish developed as the language of
an oral culture and underwent an internal evolution, especially outside
of Germany, in the Slavic East. Nevertheless, the German element in
Yiddish is close enough to modern German to be recognized as such
(much as English has many words easily recognized as "French"). It
is also sufficiently dominant in the basic vocabulary and morphology

to enable a Yiddish speaker to "Germanize" his speech, that is, to drop all recognizably non-German words and change the pronunciation (e.g., from "o" to "a": Yiddish IKH HOB is turned into German ICH HABE) to make his speech sound German—which he cannot do in any of the other components.[2]

This is, of course, a one-sided example. If you take a sentence like: ER IZ SHOYN KEYNEHORE A BAR-MITSVE BOY (literally: "he is already, no-evil-eye [should see it], a bar-mitzva boy," meaning: "the boy grew almost as big as an adult"), we see *boy* from English, BAR-MITSVE from Aramaic and KEYNEHORE (or KEYNEYNORE) as a compound of the German KEIN ("no") and the Yiddish EYN HORE (from Hebrew AYIN HA-RA, "the bad eye"). KEYNEHORE means literally: "no-evil-eye" but, in addition, it always means something positive: "big, grown," "beautiful," or other positive features which are so good that they have to be guarded by some such linguistic amulet. The German element appears here only in secondary words and as the syntactical framework of the sentence.

The exact proportion of the components of Yiddish may differ considerably in various texts. Leo Wiener, a Harvard professor of Slavic who in 1899 published (in English!) the first history of Yiddish literature, claimed that Yiddish consisted of "70% German, 20% Hebrew, 10% Slavic." This may be true for many written texts (or was true in Wiener's time). In daily use, however, the proportion of German-stock words is normally higher. What makes it Yiddish is the crucial role the non-German components play in coloring the style and semantics of Yiddish and their fusion in one linguistic system.

The most radical characteristic of fusion lies in the interinanimation (to use I. A. Richards's term) of elements from different source languages in one word. For example, Hebrew suffixes may be used with words of other origin: DOKTOYRIM ("doctors") has a European root (DOKTER) and a Hebrew plural suffix, -IM.[3] Similarly, NARONIM ("fools") is coined from the German "Narr" with the Aramaic/Hebrew

2. Such "Germanizing," however, results in the poorest kind of language, confined to the limited number of those German words that are known in Yiddish and lacking the semantic "salt and pepper" of the non-Germanic expressions and the stylistic effects of their interaction in Yiddish; it is ridiculous to the German ear and has been used as a grotesque device on stage and in fiction.

3. There is also a typical Ashkenazi Hebrew vowel change: the second "o" in the original European "DOKTOR" becomes "oy" in plural as if it were of Hebrew origin. Cf., KHAMOR—KHAMOYRIM, "donkey(s)," and in Lithuanian Yiddish: KHA-MEYRIM—DOKTEYRIM.

suffix -ONIM, just as RABONIM is the Aramaic plural of the Hebrew component ROV ("rabbi"). And TAYVOLIM, the plural of TAYVL ("devil"), from German, is treated like MESHOLIM, the plural of MOSHL ("parable"), derived from Hebrew.

Conversely, German suffixes are attached to roots from all other sources. Thus, Yiddish ROD ("wheel") takes the plural by changing the root vowel and adding the suffix -ER: ROD-REDER (as in the German RAD-RÄDER). The same German pattern is applied to the Slavic SOD-SEDER ("orchard")[4] and the Hebrew PONIM-PENIMER ("face"), which have no such suffixes or vowel changes in their stock languages. Similarly, the German infinitive suffix -EN, as in NEMEN ("to take"), is applied to: LEYENEN ("to read") with a Romance root, SHEMEN ("to be famous") with a Hebrew root and NUDZHEN ("to nudge") from Slavic. In these cases, we have a unified grammatical system of the new language, Yiddish, applied to words of various sources, precisely as English uses the plural suffix -s for words of German or French origin alike: NAME-S and INTENTION-S. The same can be observed in the German forms of the Yiddish verb system which applies similarly to roots from German, Hebrew, or Slavic: IKH BIN KRANK GEVORN ("I got sick," with a German root) and IKH BIN NISPOEL GEVORN ("I was amazed," with a Hebrew root and with disregard for the fact that the Hebrew word is already in the reflexive form), IKH BIN FARNUDZHET GEVORN (with a Slavic root, NUDZH, embedded in a German completed verb form, FAR——T).

As soon as the principles and patterns of the fusion were established, they acted as productive grammatical categories do and absorbed new words, concepts and expressions in the same manner. Thus, the Slavic suffix -NIK may be combined with roots from any origin, especially to designate a kind of person. For example, NUDNIK from Slavic ("a pest," compare the American Yiddishism, "to nudge"); SHLIMEZALNIK ("shlemiel," literally, "a person of bad luck") from German (SCHLIMM, "bad") plus Hebrew (MAZAL, "luck") plus Slavic (-NIK, a nominalizing suffix); OLRAYTNIK from American (a successful social climber, one who is "doing all right"). From Yiddish, this pattern entered Israeli Hebrew (KIBUTSNIK, PALMAKHNIK, KOLBOYNIK) and American English (BEATNIK, REFUSENIK).

---

4. SOD itself comes from the Polish SAD, with a typically Yiddish change of "A" to "O." Its homonym, SOD, meaning "secret" (from Hebrew), takes a Hebrew plural form, SOD-SOYDES.

Thus the whole language, irrespective of origin, was treated as one field, in which patterns *could* cross boundaries of source languages. But still, some groups of words did cling to their original patterns, reinforced by the openness of the language; for example, strong verbs remained primarily in the German stock (as in English) while Hebrew words mostly kept their original plural form (as some Latin words in English kept the Latin plural: DATUM—DATA, FORMULA—FORMU-LAE).

In the same way, on a higher level, proverbs, idioms, and collo-cations in Yiddish employ all components of the language. Sholem Aleichem's folk character, Tevye the Milkman, "quotes" sayings and wisdom from Ukrainian folklore as well as from the Bible and the prayerbook, in line with the Hassidic dictum, A GOYISH VERTL IS LeHAVDL A TOYRE ("A Gentile proverb is, with all due distinction, [like] a teaching of the Torah").

In the sentence, ER HOT GeSHEMT OYF DER GANTSER VELT ("he was famous far and wide," literally: "he was famous in the whole world"), the root "shem" is the only Hebrew component (embedded in a German past participle form, GE——T). But in Hebrew, SHEM denotes primarily "name," whereas in Yiddish it means "fame," derived from specific Hebrew phrases, such as SHMO HOLEKH LEFANAV (lit-erally: "his name goes before him"). This is a typical Yiddish percep-tion of Hebrew not as a language with an autonomous vocabulary but as a repository of texts and phrases. The meaning of a Hebrew word in Yiddish is often determined by a context from which it was borrowed rather than by any independent lexical denotation. Further-more, since Yiddish uses Hebrew from the world of learning and prayer, it often reflects postbiblical developments in Hebrew.

Sometimes, the source languages are represented on different levels of a Yiddish text. The proverb A BEYZE TSUNG IZ ERGER FUN A SHTARKER HANT (literally: "an evil tongue is worse than a strong hand") is of purely German components but makes little sense in Ger-man. Indeed, the proverb has a subtext in two Hebrew phrases: LASHON HA-RA (literally: "language of the bad" or "evil tongue," meaning: slander) and YAD KHAZAKA (literally: "strong arm," mean-ing: force or enforcing, high-handed); thus, the general meaning of the proverb is: "slander is more damaging than violence." In the id-iom, ES SHITN ZIKH IM PERL FUN MOYL (literally: "pearls pour out of his mouth," meaning: "his speech is precious, exquisite, full of wis-dom"), all words are of the German component but in the background hovers the Talmudic idiom, PE SHE-HEFIK MARGALIOT (literally: "a mouth producing pearls"). In many cases, two source languages clash in one utterance. BeMOkem sheEYn ish/ iz a hering oykh a fish ("Where there is no man, a herring, too, is a fish") is a typical Yiddish rhymed proverb. The first half is in pure Hebrew, the second is basic Yiddish of the German stock. The Hebrew part contains no word used independently in Yiddish but is a well-understood quotation from the popular book, *Pirkey avot* (in Yiddish: *Pirkey oves*, "Ethics of the Fathers"), and an allusion to its context: "In a place where there are no men, strive to be a man" (or, in plain Yiddish, "be A MENTSH"). The structure of the proverb follows the regular learning or quoting pattern: a Hebrew phrase is followed by its Yiddish (German-stock) translation or elucidation. Here, however, we get a surprising twist. The second part of the proverb, though using only Germanic words, is related to a Russian proverb that is often quoted in Yiddish too: NA BEZRYbye I RAK RYBA (literally: "In fishlessness, a crab too can pass for a fish"). But the idea is translated into the Yiddish world of imagery, in which a crab is not kosher and is unknown as a kind of food, whereas a herring is a major character. A herring—poor people's food—cannot be a "fish"; the Yiddish speaker is not concerned with the herring's biological category, but with its function in the religious culinary custom: you cannot make "gefilte fish" for the Sabbath out of herring. In a Yiddish text, if you quote this same idea in Russian proper, you don't pay attention to the literal meanings of individual words and accept the total meaning of the Russian proverb. But translating the idiom into Yiddish words exposes the unacceptable denotata of single words (such as the non-kosher "crab") and requires a transposition of the same situation into terms domesticated in the Jewish world.

The rhyme in the "herring" example is a genre marker: it indicates that this is a proverb rather than a mere translation of the first clause. The rhyme brings the two components of the proverb together, ironizing their juxtaposition while reviving and undermining the traditional dictum at the same time. Placed as it is, after a Hebrew phrase and parallel to it, the second clause looks like a translation or explication of the first; but it actually opposes the emphatically "simple," "coarse," and smelly herring to the lofty and moralistic Hebrew style. Substituting for the original "man," the herring becomes a metaphor for whomever is the object of this sentence ("small fry"), degrading or ironizing him. Indeed, it is often used as a self-effacing gesture by

the speaker himself. The clash between meanings occurs not just between individual words but works on a second level as well: the world
of the herring barrel as a substitute for the *Ethics of The Fathers.*

This is what Yiddish is all about: the individual words may be very
simple but their interaction—involving pieces of texts and divergent
languages and cultural situations rather than mere lexical denotations—makes it rich, ironic, plurisignifying.

In Yiddish, the casual family language, expressions from religious
texts are *secularized*: they are used as a *situational language* outside
their original, specific religious meaning. Hence, they essentially function as metaphors, linking meanings from the lofty, religious domain
to secular situations. Thus TOYRE in Yiddish may, indeed, denote the
"Torah" (in its original sense) as well as any teaching, belief or theory.
S'IZ NISHT AZA GROYSE TOYRE ("it is not such a difficult theory")
may apply to something as secular as learning to cook a certain dish
and actually means: "It is not such a big deal." OYF TISHE NAYNTSIK
KAPORES is literally: "for nine/ninety kaparot,"[5] deriving from the
custom of discarding a chicken on Yom Kippur which would expiate
a person's sins. The idiom means, however, "good for nothing" in
general. At the same time, KAPORES by itself can denote the original
religious function when used in a limited context. Similarly, OPSHPILN
A KHASENE (literally: "to play [the music] at a wedding") is generalized outside of its original context to mean: "to raise hell," "to make
someone a big scandal," "to dress him down in public."

The same holds for concrete descriptions drawing on a mythol-
ogized "Jewish" world: in proverbs and idioms they become generalized, individual objects serving as a general language. The codified
areas of religious and daily behavior become sources of situational
imagery, a language to understand the world. Here lies the secret of
the emotive power Yiddish speakers feel when using such simple
words as HERING, KASHE, BORSHTSH, or MEGILEH outside of their
realistic context—and in today's culinary world they are always outside
of their natural context—that is, they are marked as an import from

5. Note: in this idiom, the "nine[ty]" appears twice, in Hebrew and in a Yiddish
[mock-]translation, as some holy teaching would. The mismatch in the numbers indicates the loss of the specific Hebrew grammatical value and makes the Hebrew word
sound like Yiddish, as in the beginning of another idiom, OYF TISH UN OYF BENK
("On tables and benches," i.e., "much to do").

a different "world" and carry the connotations and values they had in that world in addition to the figurative effect of the transfer itself.

Another example is the seemingly simple collocation: TSEZEYT UN TSESHPREYT ("scattered and dispersed," "sown to the wind"). It may be used to indicate a person's scattered family, his disorderly clothes, or his books published in various places. But the underlying allusion is to a central image of Jewish historical consciousness, the dispersion of the Jews. The subtext is in the Book of Esther (3:8): "There is a certain people scattered abroad and dispersed among the peoples in all the provinces of the kingdom." The two Hebrew verbs in the source, MEFUZAR U-MEFURAD (scattered and dispersed), are linked by morphological and sound parallelism. When read in the Ashkenazi pronunciation, they sound like two Yiddish words with a Germanic alliteration of their stressed, initial root consonants: MEFUzer UMEFUred. The original Hebrew collocation itself may be used in Yiddish, especially in a "lofty" style, but it has also been transposed into Yiddish words of German origin: TSEZEYT UN TSESHPREYT ("sown and spread far and wide"). This pair is, again, parallel in sound and morphology but, instead of alliteration, it uses end-rhyme, a form favored in Yiddish folklore. In a statistical count of Yiddish lexemes, the phrase would be registered only for its German components, but its actual subtext is Hebrew and its semantic substance is specifically Jewish.

And now the matter becomes even more complicated: this Yiddish idiom is often augmented to TSEZEYT UN TSESHPREYT OYF ALE SHIVE YAMIM ("scattered and dispersed over all the seven seas"), ostensibly adding a "Jewish" tone by the addition of an emphatically Hebrew phrase, SHIV'A YAMIM ("seven seas"). Indeed, these Hebrew words are not used in normal Yiddish: "seven" in Yiddish is ZIBN and the plural of YAM ("sea") is YAMEN (the proper phrase would be: OYF ALE ZIBN YAMEN). By using a phrase in real Hebrew rather than in the Hebrew that merged in Yiddish, the impression of an authoritative quotation is achieved. But, in reality, this Hebrew phrase is absent in the Bible and is, paradoxically, coined from the European collocation, "seven seas."[6] The vocabulary and semantics of the German and He-

6. A similar phrase, "SHIV'A YAMIM" appears several times in the Bible; but it is a quasi-homonym, meaning "seven days" (and pronounced in Yiddish "SHIVE YOMIM"),

brew components in each part of the larger idiom have thus been reversed: semantically, the Germanic words have a Hebrew subtext, and Hebrew words a European one.

Many Yiddish expressions have such a subtext in a classical text or in collocations of the other stock languages. VOS BAY A NIKHTERN OYF DER LUNG/ IZ BAY A SHIKERN OYF DER TSUNG (literally: "what a sober man has on his lung, a drunkard has on his tongue"; that is, the drunkard spills out what the sober man would hide) might have derived from a rhymed German proverb. But the Yiddish proverb has a Talmudic subtext in Hebrew: NIKHNAS YAYIN YATSA SOD ("enter wine, exit secret"). The original Hebrew phrase can appear in Yiddish speech too (albeit merely as a "quotation," since the first three words are not used independently in Yiddish). It also has a further subtext which is part of the Yiddish culture: in the system of GEMATRIYA (from the Greek "geometry"), the combined numerical values of the Hebrew letters that compose the word SOD ("secret") is 70: $S+O+D = 60+6+4 = 70$ (a mysterious number in itself) and so is the letter count of YAYIN ("wine"): $Y+Y+N = 10+10+50 = 70$. Thus, "wine" = "secret"; one can be transformed into the other, and the puzzle is explained: when you take in wine, you give out secrets. This is not abstruse mysticism but daily Yiddish folklore usage and a common children's game. From the surface of the German-looking rhymed proverb which uses only one, domesticated Hebrew word (*shiker*), it is impossible to tell the cultural depth of this expression.

This peculiar nature of Yiddish was seen, though in a distorted mirror, by the German professor, Johannes Wagenseil, describing the Yiddish language in 1699: "[The Jews have given the German language] an entirely foreign tone and sound; they have mutilated, minced, distorted, the good German words, invented new unknown [words], and mixed into German countless Hebrew words and phrases; with the result that he who hears them speak German must conclude that they speak nothing but Hebrew, practically no single word comes out intelligible" (quoted in M. Weinreich, pp. 103–4). The same would have to be concluded by a person listening to Dutch speech and assuming that he "hears them speak German." Furthermore, in this early account, based on Western Yiddish, the crucial

whereas our proverb implies the plural of YAM = "sea" rather than of the Hebrew YOM = "day," which is only marginally used in Yiddish.

Slavic element was still missing; modern Yiddish is even further removed from High German.

Yiddish made wide use of its fusion nature. The extraordinary richness of the language felt by its native speakers is heavily based on this
characteristic. The vocabulary of Yiddish is rather poor in comparison
with English or Russian, but each word has an aura of connotations
derived from its multidirectional and codified relations not just within
a semantic paradigm, as in other languages, but to parallel words in
other source languages, to an active stock of proverbs and idioms, and
to a typical situational cluster. Yiddish speakers speak not so much
with individual referring words as with such clusters of relations,
ready-made idioms, quotations and situational responses. Since each
word may belong to several heterogeneous or contradictory knots,
ironies are always at hand. It is precisely the small vocabulary of the
language that makes the words more repetitive and more dependent
on their habitual contexts, hence weightier in their impact (like the
words in the limited vocabulary of the Bible). It is not the range of
denotations that the language covers but the emotive and semantic
directions of the hearer's empathy. In this mode of discourse, the overt
clash, ironic or clever, between words of different stock languages in
one sentence is a major source of meaning, impact, and delight.

Often, differentiations of meaning and style are based on the separation of synonyms derived from various stock languages. English
has "end" and "extremity," "find" and "discover," "name" and "term,"
"fancy" and "imagination." And Yiddish: BUKH—SEYFER ("secular
book"—"religious book"); POSHET—PROST ("simple"—"coarse");
BITE—BAKOshe—PROSHEnye ("request," derived from German,
Hebrew and Russian, respectively; the first means asking a favor, the
second is a special plea, the third is a humble and formal written
petition to authorities).

The examples of fusion, however, must not obstruct our view of
the fact that Yiddish words are marked with the sign of their source.
The role of the various stock languages changes from case to case. As
one might expect, the Hebrew stock synonym often connotes a loftier
matter or a higher style. Thus, BUKH ("book") indicates a secular
book, splitting the semantic field with the Hebrew SEYFER, meaning
"religious or Hebrew book." DOS HEYLIKE ORT ("holy place") is a
cemetery, while its Hebrew counterpart, MOKEM KOYDESH, is a synagogue. (In contemporary Hebrew, MAKOM KADOSH means neither
"cemetery" nor "synagogue" but simply a holy place or a religious

site, often Islamic.) MOKEM (literally: "place") indicates the (non-Jewish) town and became a favorite nickname for Amsterdam, in Yiddish and in Dutch (MOKUM). However, the Hebrew-derived EYNAYIM ("peepers") is coarser than the Germanic OYGN ("eyes"), RAGLAYIM than FIS ("legs"), NEKEYVE ("a loose woman") than FROY ("woman"), all perhaps coming from the language of the underworld, where Hebrew was used to conceal messages from the Gentiles. And the usual Yiddish SHO ("hour," Hebrew: SHA'A) is simpler than the high rhetorical or poetic SHTUNDE (from German STUNDE).

This play with components is often ironized in Yiddish itself. Thus, the proverb, DI BESTE KASHE OYF DER VELT IS KASHE MIT YOYKH (literally: "the best KASHE [challenge] in the world is KASHE [porridge] with chicken soup) puns on the homonyms: (a) KASHE from Aramaic (KUSHIYA), meaning a query, a Talmudic question raising a difficult point in an argument; and (b) the popular, Slavic food, KASHA (buckwheat porridge); in other words: staple food is better than any problematic puzzlement. Another example: DI MAYSE FUN DER GESHIKHTE IZ AZA MIN HISTORYE ("the story of this history is a tale in itself"), where the word for "(hi)story" is repeated thrice, in synonyms from three stock languages: Hebrew, German and French via Slavic. The proverb is used to introduce a speaker's account of events and is also a mock expression for verbose storytelling.

Yiddish literature developed a profound grasp of this interaction and play of components and used it as a major source of semantic and stylistic variation and impact.

The Components of Yiddish

In Yiddish as we know it today, we can still recognize a few Romance elements, such as BENTSHN ("to bless" from "benedicere"), LEYENEN ("to read," a pre-French form derived from "legere"), KREPLAKH (compare the French "crêpe"), TSHOLNT ("cholent," warm Sabbath dish, cf., the old French "chalt," "warm") or certain personal names, such as YENTL (from "Gentile"), BUNEM (cf., French "bonhomme"), SHNEYER ("Senior"), FAYVL or FAYVUSH (from Latin "Fabius" or "Vivus"), or BEYLE (cf., "Belle" in French or "Bella" in Italian), from which the later SHEYNE derived.

One interesting old French influence, according to Weinreich, is the plural suffix -s, adopted by English and Yiddish but rare in German. For example, BOBE—BOBES ("grandmother[-s]," while in Slavic it is: BABA—BABY); VIBORES ("elections," from Russian VYBORY); BEKHER—BEKHERS ("goblet"), VEYLER—VEYLERS ("voter" while in German it is BECHER—BECHER, WÄHLER—WÄHLER); KLEZMER—KLEZMERS (also: KLEZMOrim, KLEZMEYrim, "musician[-s]," while in Hebrew it is: KLI ZEMER—KLEY ZEMER). It seems that the productivity of this plural suffix in Yiddish is due to its convergence with the Hebrew plural suffix -OT, pronounced in Yiddish -ES. If it were only a Hebrew suffix, however, it would not have covered all the components of the language as -S does (the more common Hebrew plural -IM is applied to only a few words outside of the Hebrew component); moreover, in Yiddish (as in English) in most cases, only the consonant -S remained. By a coincidence, a second convergence occurred: in Hebrew, the suffix -OT usually (though not exclusively) indicates a feminine noun: KHALA—KHALOT, in Yiddish: KHALE—KHALES ("challah," Jewish festive bread). At the same time, Yiddish has many feminine words ending in unstressed -E, derived from different languages and all using the plural -S:

1. The Slavic feminine ending -A becomes -E in Yiddish:
   SHMATE—SHMATES ("rag"),
   KHATE—KHATES ("hut"),
   ZHABE—ZHABES ("frog"),
   PODLOGE—PODLOGES ("floor"),
   BARKE—BARKES ("barge").

2. International words, coming via the Slavic pattern:
   VIZE—VIZES ("visa"),
   REKLAME—REKLAMES ("advertisement"),
   GIMNAZYE—GIMNAZYES ("gymnasium, high-school"),
   REKOMENDAtsye—REKOMENDAtsyes ("recommendation"),
   DYUNE—DYUNES ("dune").

3. German feminine nouns in -E:
   BITE—BITES ("request," in German: BITTE—BITTEN),
   HILE—HILES ("cover," in German: HÜLLE—HÜLLEN).

4. The Hebrew feminine ending -A (Ashkenazi O, "*kamats he*") be-
   comes -E in Yiddish; it takes the same plural -s but in this case
   it is spelled in Yiddish too with the Hebrew spelling, -OT:[7]
   TSORE—TSORES ("trouble"),
   MEGILE—MEGILES ("scroll" or "long list, long talk"),
   DAYGE—DAYGES ("worry"),
   KALE—KALES ("bride"),
   KHOKHME—KHOKHMES ("wisdom, wit").

5. Hebrew masculine words, ending in Yiddish with -E and turned
   feminine:
   REGE—REGES ("moment," Hebrew plural: REGA'IM),
   MAKHNE—MAKHNES ("horde"),
   MAYSE—MAYSES ("story" or "event"),
   BOREKHABE—BOREKHABES ("greeting," in Hebrew: BA-
   RUKH HA-BA—BRUKHIM HA-BAIM).

As a result, we have similar Yiddish words such as SIBE—SIBES
("cause"), LIBE—LIBES ("love"), GLIBE—GLIBES ("clod of earth")
from Hebrew, German, and Slavic respectively, all unified by this
French-Hebrew, predominantly feminine plural. The same holds for
KURVE—KURVES (from Slavic) and NAFKE—NAFKES (from Hebrew),
both indicating a "whore."

If, however, the word denotes a masculine person, the gender is
masculine: TATE-S, ZEYDE-S ("father," "grandfather"). Words ending
with a consonant are rare with this plural suffix and are usually masculine: VAGON—VAGONES ("train car"), LERER—LERERS
("teacher"), SHRAYBER—SHRAYBERS ("writer") (in all of these examples, the -s is optional).

Notwithstanding such curiosities, the bulk of the Yiddish language
consists of lexical material derived from three language groups:

7. It is important to note that the ending -s in Yiddish represents several different
Hebrew endings and often causes their confusion: (1) -OT for plural; Hebrew: TORA—
TOROT, Yiddish: TOYRES ("systems of learning"); (2) -UT and -IT as suffixes of feminine
nouns; Hebrew: GALUT, TA'ANIT, Yiddish: GOLES, TONES ("Diaspora," "a fast"); (3) -
AT for the connected genitive; Hebrew: MEGILAT ESTER, Yiddish: MEGILES ESTER ("the
Scroll of Esther"). Hence, SIMKHES in Yiddish may be a connected noun: SIMKHES
TOYRE ("the Feast of the Torah") or a plural: LOMIR ZIKH ZEN OYF SIMKHES ("let us
meet at festivities"); in Hebrew: SIMKHAT, SMAKHOT, respectively.

THE HOLY TONGUE — GERMAN — SLAVIC

In Yiddish, none of these languages is represented in its pure form or in its full range. What we have in Yiddish is a *slanted selection* from the source languages. For example, it is not German syntax per se that dominates Yiddish sentences but those German syntactical *components* which entered the Yiddish language. The syntax of Yiddish derived from spoken, rather than written German, and has limited its options mostly to what seems acceptable in Hebrew or Slavic. Thus, Modern Yiddish uses a straightforward word order, with the complete verb phrase in the second place of each sentence rather than with one part of the verb at the end of a long sentence, as in literary German.

The "Holy Tongue," as seen from the perspective of Yiddish, includes biblical, Mishnaic, Midrashic, and medieval Hebrew as well as several sources of Aramaic. Slavic components range all the way from some Czech and old Polish lexemes absorbed long ago to Ukrainian and modern Russian. Sometimes, the specific Slavic source language may be traced but often it is hard or impossible to tell, hence the general "Slavic" category.

In spite of the pervasive fusion, the German component seems to be in the center, to dominate the Yiddish text and to provide its "floor," as it were—its basic morphology, syntactic framework, and the bulk of its vocabulary—with the other two coloring it in a variety of ways. Indeed, it is possible to make a Yiddish text exclusively of the German lexical component but it is impossible to do so with any other component. A Yiddish text may use a whole sentence in Hebrew, Russian, or English but it can become part of Yiddish discourse only when embedded in a larger text or dialogue with Germanic-based syntax, and its status remains that of a quotation or a proverb.

There is, however, a flexible stylistic requirement, changing in different contexts, which can be formulated thus: for a text to be Yiddish, it must be sprinkled with Slavic and Hebrew elements. Those, however, must not be overdone, that is, you are encouraged to use Slavic or Hebrew expressions, even those that are not normally acceptable in Yiddish, provided you don't overload the text with them and don't overstep their minority status. This rule works both on the level of the sentence and on the level of the discourse as a whole. Its specific implementation, however, changes from genre to genre and may be used either for effects of the refined and exquisite or the humorous and grotesque.

There is no one-to-one relationship between any component and a thematic or ideological intention, but there are socially perceived tendencies of this kind. On the whole, the Holy Tongue is felt to add a tone of Jewishness to a text, or a "juicy" flavor, whereas the Slavic often adds either something concrete, from nature, something intimate and sentimental, or something Eastern European or lower class, even coarse. But for every component, some elements exhibit stylistic functions in other directions as well. Thus the Yiddish layer that permeated German underworld and city slang was predominantly of the Hebrew stock. As mentioned previously, Jewish underworld characters used the Hebrew component to avoid being understood by Gentiles, and it was precisely this that became understood and adopted in other languages. Modern German still uses MESHUGE, MAKE, GANOVE, PLEITE, and TOHUWABOHU. Such words in Yiddish have nothing lofty about them, rather something earthy and slangy. Similarly, English may use MESHUGAH, MAVEN, SHMOOZ, CHUTZPAH, MEGILLAH.

German elements came to Yiddish from various regions and periods and melted into the Yiddish system. To be sure, entire semantic fields of the German vocabulary were absent in Yiddish (courtly life, agriculture, most names of flora and fauna, military, administrative, and juridical terms, etc.). In part, they were occupied by the Hebrew component (e.g., religious or legal terms), and in part by Slavic terms (names of trees and foods). But to a large extent, the Jewish perceptual world was a deficient system in which certain areas of nature and civilization were not observed and had no linguistic correlates.

Furthermore, many words and forms that look like German were developed independently in Yiddish or took on a different meaning in Yiddish under the influence of Hebrew or Slavic patterns. TSU-ZAMENFOR ("conference") was coined in a period of emerging political parties, modeled on the Russian "syezd" (literally: "to come together," deriving from French like the English "convention"); the word is made of German lexemes but is not a borrowing, for in German itself, "Zusammenfahren" means "collide, crash, recoil, startle." Similarly, IBERSHRAYBN ("to copy," literally: "to re-write") is like the Russian "perepisat'," whereas the equivalent German word, "überschreiben," means "to write over" or "superscribe." Or, such a popular expression as FARFALN ("lost," "regrettably irreversible") is more like the Russian "propalo" (literally: "fallen through") than like the German "verfallen," meaning primarily "decline, decay." The idiom, ALE MONTIK UN DONERSHTIK ("very frequently," literally: "every Monday and Thursday"), though German-looking, would make no special sense in German; indeed, it is based on Jewish religious custom connected with these two days of the week (as one of Agnon's characters says: "If I did not fast every Monday and Thursday, I would die of hunger").

Yiddish is known for its profusion of diminutive and endearing suffixes added to any noun or name. Those may be used to convey the relative smallness of an object or person. But the same diminutive may be used for an object or person that is not small; in that case, it expresses the speaker's attitude to the object or person, indicating that he finds them lovely or familiar or, on the contrary, despised and scorned. Some of these suffixes came from German dialects (-L, -LE) but are used with a Slavic abundance in Yiddish. For example, M. L. Halpern's poem, "The End of the Book," is built around a long chain or rhyming diminutives: BIKHELE—TIKHELE—SHIKHELE—TSIKHELE—KIKHELE—PLIKHELE—SHMIKHELE ("cute little book, handkerchief, shoe, pillow case, cookie, baldness, shmaldness". Indeed, "little" is not a good translation of the diminutive, which expresses here not smallness but rather a warm, emotional relation of the speaker to the object, as if he were saying "my sweet baldness.") Here is a transcription of the poem (all DIMINUTIVES are in SMALL CAPITAL LETTERS, their stresses are on the first syllable) followed by an English translation:

freg ikh bay mayn liber froy,
vi azoy tsu farENdikn dem roMAN
in mayn BIKHELE—
zogt zi: dos glik zol aVEK mit der ban,
un tsuRIKvinken mit a TIKHELE.
zog ikh: TIKHELE—SHMIKHELE—
zogt zi: BIKHELE—SHMIKHELE—
un fregt mikh, tsi vil ikh nisht beser
kave mit a KIKHELE.
zog ikh: KIKHELE—SHMIKHELE
un heys mir oyftsiyen oyf mayn kishn
a TSIKHELE.
zogt zi: TSIKHELE—SHMIKHELE.
un heyst mir aRAYNtrogn tsum shuster
ir SHIKHELE.
zog ikh: SHIKHELE—SHMIKHELE.
vert zi broygez, un vayzt mir
az kh'hob shoyn a PLIKHELE—

zog ikh:
PLIKHELE—SHIKHELE—TSIKHELE—KIKHELE—TIKHELE—BIKHELE—
SHMIKHELE.
ken zi nisht zogn azoy gikh vi ikh, azoy gikh vi ikh,
PLIKHELE—SHIKHELE—TSIKHELE—KIKHELE—TIKHELE—BIKHELE—
SHMIKHELE.
hobn mir inEYnem geLAKHT—
inEYnem geLAKHT.
biz zi hot mir di oygn farMAKHT—
di oygn farMAKHT.
un mikh ayngevigt mit dem lid funem regn,
mit dem lid funem regn,
vos men zingt fun kleyne kinders vegn.

[So I ask my dear wife
How to finish the affair
Of my little booky—
Says she: Let happiness leave on a train
And wave back with a hanky.
Says I: Hanky-panky—
Says she: Booky-shmooky—
And asks me whether I'd like
With my coffee a cooky.
Says I: Cooky-shmooky—
And tell her to put a case on my pillow
And not to play hooky.
Says she: Hooky-shmooky.
And tells me to repair her shoe
By hook or by crooky.
Says I: Crooky-shmooky.
So she jumps up, and points at my head:
I am bald and spooky.
Says I:
Spooky-crooky-hooky-cooky-hanky-panky-booky-shmooky.
But she cannot say it as fast as I can:
Spooky-crooky-hooky-cooky-hanky-panky-booky-shmooky.
So we laugh together—
Laugh so nice.
Till she closes my eyes—
Closes my eyes.
And rocks me with a song of rain and light,
Rain and light,
That you sing to little children at night,
Children at night.
                              —AYP, 429]

Another such Slavic grammatical challenge is the system of aspects used in Slavic verbs indicating the state of completeness of a process. Yiddish found substitutes for this purpose, using words of the German component. Again an example from Weinreich: IKH SHRAYB ("I write") has a whole chain of further possibilities: IKH GIB A SHRAYB ("I write in a jiffy"), IKH TU A SHRAYB ("I jot down, I write something hastily"), IKH HALT IN EYN SHRAYBN ("I keep writing and writing"), IKH HALT BAY SHRAYBN ("I am about to write"), IKH HOB GE-SHRIBN ("I have written"), IKH HOB ONGENSHRIBN ("I completed writing [something]"), IKH HOB SHOYN OPGESHRIBN ("I am finished writing"), and, we may add: IR ZOLT ZEY BASHRAYBN FUN KOP BIZ DI FIS ("may you write them up from head to toe," as a woman character, Gitl Purishkevitch, demands of Sholem Aleichem, playing on both meanings of the word BASHRAYBN, "to describe" and "to cover [something] with a text").

To demonstrate the role of Slavisms in Yiddish, we may take the following example: PAVOLYE, PAVOLINKE, PAVOLITSHKE, and PAMELEKH all mean "slowly, little by little," but with different degrees of softness and different attitudes of speaker to hearer. PAMELEKH is the most casual word, describing an objectively slow process, while PAVOLYE is used more as an admonition—"take it easy"—and has the ring of a "foreign," Slavic word. PAVOLINKE is addressed as to a child: "do it slowly, but take it easy, be careful"; PAVOLITSHKE conveys roughly the same idea, but more emphatically, perhaps with an implied addition of "my dear" (the two suffixes make it doubly Slavic; they are usually applied to personal names, thus qualifying not the verb but the person to whom the admonition is addressed). PAMELEKH is the most neutral synonym because the Slavism is hardly felt (the German "allmählich" merged with the Polish "po-malu"), whereas the conspicuously Slavic suffixes in the second and third synonyms have a pronounced emotive tone, untranslatable in another language.

Unlike their normal, automatic use in the stock languages, the effect of Slavic expressions in Yiddish is especially strong and striking, precisely because they are estranged in their new context: they do not constitute the prevalent vocabulary of the text but stand out as a minority layer, contrasting conspicuously in sound and word length with the usual, run-of-the-mill Germanic component and, quite often, can be turned on or off. Hence, to the inherent meaning of the word, there is an added meaning, signaling a special use, to be interpreted specifically for each case and context.

Stylistically, there are various kinds of Slavic elements in Yiddish. From the point of view of their integration in Yiddish, we may distinguish three groups, which we may call *basic*, *merged*, and *extension* layers of the language. The boundaries between these kinds are neither fixed nor stable, which does not diminish the sociolinguistic validity of the typology itself.

1. Slavic words, suffixes and particles that are part of the *basic* language, are entirely absorbed in Yiddish, usually have no substitute from another source and are mostly short: NEBEKH, TAKE, PA-MElakh, aBI, KHOTSH, MALE-VOS, NU, ZHE, MASKE, KHATE, KASHE, KRETSHME, KHREYN. (The words mean roughly: "poor soul, nebish," indeed, slowly, if only, though, no matter what, "nu," "so," mask, hut, porridge, inn, horseradish.)

2. Slavic words *merged* in Yiddish but outstanding in their sound combinations and differing conspicuously from their Germanic environment (notably, with sibilant and affricate consonant clusters), especially multisyllabic words: BORSHTSH, SHTSHAV, SHMATE, PI-ROSHkes, ONGETSHEPET, SHTSHEPETILNe, DZHEGAKHTS, PODLOge, STATETSHne, TSEKHRAStet, STRASHIDle, SMAR-KATSH, VINTSHEVAnyes (borsht, schav, rag, piroshky, stuck on or hooked on [as with many hooks or thorns] or sticking to someone, subtle and touchy, wheel grease, floor, dignified, with open shirt, scarecrow, nasty brat [literally: "running nose"], congratulations).

3. Slavic words and expressions felt to be borrowings or *extensions* rather than organic parts of Yiddish and used by various speakers in varying degrees but nevertheless widespread and well understood: DUSHA NA RASPASHKU, PREDSEDATYEL, NATSHALSTVE, VIBORES, PSHEKUPKE ([a Russian] open soul, chairman, the authorities or managers, elections [all from Russian], small saleswoman [from Polish]). This group, consisting primarily of late-comers to Yiddish and hence felt to be loan-words (such as Polish cultural terms and Russian administrative or literary expressions), was censured by the purists but used in popular speech and in Soviet Yiddish. *Beyond* it, there is the large stock of the foreign language itself, available for further borrowing whenever needed.

A parallel tripartite division may be observed in both the German and the Holy Tongue components. With *basic* Yiddish words, one is hardly aware of their origins. For example, KHOTSH, AFIle, TSI, TAKE,

EPES, VEYS-IKH-VOS, MEYLE, MAYLE, MALE-VOS, KHAY-GELEBT, ABI-GIZUNT, FRISH-GIZUNT-UN-MISHUGE (though, even, whether, indeed, "something," "who knows" ["nonsense!"], never mind, virtue, whatever [one may think or say], the good life, "the main thing is health," "fresh-healthy-and-crazy"). Words of the second kind are *merged* in the language and are perceived as fully and authentically Yiddish, but the speakers are *component conscious* about them. Words of the third category are not fully legitimate or domesticated in Yiddish but are still widely used and understood (as we saw with some of the Hebrew quotes in Yiddish proverbs above). There is no defined limit to this extension; indeed, it opens the doors to three compendious verbal stocks outside of Yiddish proper, three languages and cultural worlds within a speaker's reach that he may use to enlarge the potential of his expression, either as adopted Yiddish words, borrowings ("foreign words"), or ad hoc quotations. It is only the linguistic tact of the speaker or the genre and context of his discourse that will limit the proportions of such "sprinkling" devices.

This hierarchy of degrees of merging offers, on the one hand, the feeling that there is a basic core of Yiddish, a domesticated, unified, intimate language of fusion, composed of elements from all stock languages and absorbed in one structural system of grammar; and guarantees, on the other hand, the *openness* of Yiddish toward its component languages, the easy way its native, plurilingual speakers may enrich its vocabulary whenever new semantic fields are acquired. As those languages have permeated Yiddish, so Yiddish can spill over into their domains while enlarging its own field of usage, either on a permanent or an ad hoc basis. We may have a hard time deciding which of those elements are part of Yiddish and which are mere temporary borrowings not to be included in a Yiddish dictionary; the sociolinguistic fact, however, of their appearance in Yiddish texts is undeniable, as can be profusely documented from Yiddish literature and newspapers.

We could represent this sociolinguistic situation in the following diagram:

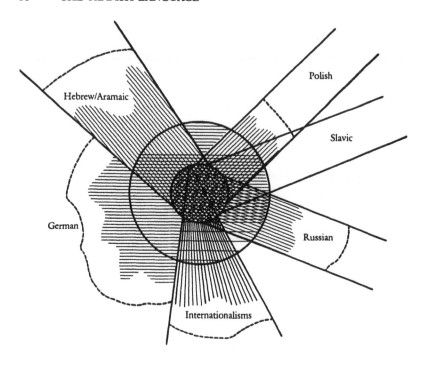

The inner circle is *basic* Yiddish; the central circle represents the domain of *merged* Yiddish (the shaded lines indicate merely the source of the components, without showing their mutual interpenetration). Outside the circle, discontinuous boundaries mark areas of *extension*; dotted lines represent areas open for further borrowing from the adjacent languages.

The Slavic impact on Yiddish is much more pervasive than one might assume from the German-derived vocabulary. There are Slavic influences on Yiddish pronunciation, grammar, fairy tales, magical beliefs, food, and songs, as well as on the architecture of Eastern European synagogues and the poetics of Yiddish poetry in Europe and America. Even Hassidic folk songs on religious themes often used "macaronic verse," combining Hebrew and Slavic fragments. The "foreign" (non-Germanic) elements deautomatize the flow of speech and enhance its emotive value. In the following couplet, the first verse is a perfect Russian phrase, made of words not merged in Yiddish; the second verse is a ready-made pure Hebrew phrase:

MY PIYOM, MY GULYAYEM/ VEATO MEYLEKH KHAY VEKAYEM!

("We keep drinking, we make merry [Russian]/ And you are the King Who lives forever [Hebrew]").

In the whole couplet there is only one word, MEYLEKH, that can be used independently in Yiddish (the collocation KHAY-VEKAYEM appears only in frozen idioms but its individual words do not function separately). Both phrases are extensions into Russian and Hebrew, perfectly understood by the polylingual Hassidic speakers. The effect is enhanced by the fact that the couplet contains not a single word of German origin, thus avoiding the main body of Yiddish vocabulary and syntax.

The surprising Hebrew/Russian rhyme and the use of trochaic tetrameter, popular in Slavic folk songs, are effective in bringing together surprisingly disparate elements: the two extreme components of Yiddish (Slavic and Hebrew), two extreme styles (peasant talk and religious hymn), two poetic traditions (Slavic folk song and Hebrew liturgical song), and two morally extreme values (the "un-Jewish" drinking and God's eternal existence). Only a component-conscious audience can savor the full impact of this little masterpiece constructed of such seemingly simple elements.

Just as metaphor works by juxtaposition of two terms representing two disparate semantic domains, so does the clash and interaction of various linguistic components, still felt as such in Yiddish, create stylistic tension and semantic density unique to this language.

Ashkenazi Hebrew and Hebrew Merged in Yiddish

The crucial component of Yiddish, what gives it its "Jewish legitimation," is Hebrew. The Hebrew alphabet establishes a final boundary around any Yiddish text and separates it clearly from German and any other non-Jewish language. Indeed, there were various attempts to write Yiddish in the Latin alphabet, in order to open it up to any European reader. If that had succeeded, perhaps Yiddish literature would be more available to the non-Yiddish reader, more continuous to literature in other languages, though it might have been at the cost of sacrificing the raison d'être of the culture's Jewishness. The Zionist leader Jabotinsky and others tried to do the same—with no lasting success—for Hebrew, which might have undercut the link of contemporary Hebrew to the classical texts. (Indeed, Itamar Ben-Avi, the son of the founder of modern spoken Hebrew, Eliezer Ben-Yehuda, published a Hebrew newspaper in Jerusalem in the Latin alphabet.) Moses Mendelssohn in his time understood the value of the alphabet for fencing a text within or without a culture: when he set out to translate the Bible into pure German that would, in his view, replace the "contorted" language, Yiddish, he still published it in Hebrew letters.

But from inside the culture, alphabet is not enough: it becomes automatic; in the spoken language, it is rarely relevant. Hence, internally, Hebrew words are essential ingredients for any text to be marked as Yiddish. Max Weinreich, in his own linguistic writings, using a scientific language based almost exclusively on German and international terminology, went out of his way to saturate his discourse with Hebrew expressions (on the level of rhetoric rather than of the science itself).

By 'Hebrew' we mean not just Hebrew proper but the Holy Tongue (LOSHN KOYDESH), including all layers of Hebrew and Aramaic that entered the spoken language as if they were of one source. The *Yiddish Dictionary Containing all Hebrew and Chaldaic Elements of the Yiddish Language*, composed in Denver, Colorado, by Dr. Charles Spivak and Sol. Bloomgarden (the Yiddish poet, Yehoash) and published in New York in 1919, announces in the Preface: "All Jews of the whole world, from the Babylonian exile to this day, no matter what language they used, have always employed in their daily intercourse with each other, some more and some fewer, Hebrew words." This dictionary and other collections list about five thousand Hebrew and Aramaic ("Chaldaic") expressions used in Yiddish. As we have seen in many cases above, Hebrew is a profound substratum of Yiddish; it has influenced the coinage of words and phrases made of other stock materials as well. Hence its impact is much greater than the statistics of surface lexical items would suggest. But the statistics themselves belie the superficial view of Yiddish as yet another German dialect.

Hebrew was read and pronounced in Ashkenaz very differently from the way it is in contemporary Israeli Hebrew. Unlike the spelling of other languages, Hebrew spelling was extremely conservative and has hardly changed throughout the ages. But most written Hebrew texts did not use vocalization and represented the consonants only, hence the same spelling could be vocalized and stressed differently in different historical and geographical contexts. For those texts that were vocalized, especially the Bible and the piyutim (liturgical poems), different readings of the same vowel-signs were practiced by different communities. Scholars assume that from about 1300 (or later),[8] a special Hebrew pronunciation was developed in Europe (or brought with some wave of learning from elsewhere), known as "Ashkenazi Hebrew." It is different from Sephardi and from contemporary Israeli Hebrew and actually consists of a whole group of subdialects, parallel to the dialects of Yiddish and the geography of other languages (Dutch, Byelorussian, Hungarian). Ashkenazi Hebrew was used throughout the ages in Hebrew writing and reading and it was the language of the modern revival of Hebrew literature in Europe between the eighteenth and twentieth centuries and of the new Hebrew education in Europe and America until the recent influence of the Israeli (quasi-"Sephardic") dialect.

Since most readers today are more familiar with contemporary Israeli Hebrew, we shall describe the Ashkenazi pronunciation in comparison to it. Ashkenazi (here, we have in mind a neutral, "standard" Ashkenazi, rather than its various dialects, see below) differs from the "Israeli" pronunciation in several respects:

1. In Ashkenazi, the accent in most words falls, *if possible, on the penultimate syllable of the basic word*, whereas the Israeli stress falls in most words on the last syllable.[9] For example we have Ashkenazi: isROEl, TOYro, meDIno vs. Israeli: israEL, toRA, mediNA ("Israel, Torah, State").

   Naturally, if a word has only one syllable, it is equally stressed in both dialects: KOL ("voice"), GOY ("Gentile"), SOF ("end").

8. The exact reason for the shift from what looks like "Sephardi" Hebrew (where both *patah* and *kamats* are pronounced a), employed in Ashkenaz before that time, to the later Ashkenazi dialect is not clear. What concerns us here is the accommodation Ashkenazi Hebrew found with Yiddish (or the Yiddish influence on it).

9. Israeli Hebrew also has a small and well-delimited group of words with a penultimate stress, such as DEgel, REgel, NA'ar, and words with several morphological suffixes, such as the feminine present verb and adjective: koTEvet ("she writes"), shoMEret ("she watches") and past verb forms: aMARti, aMARnu ("I said, we said"). In all these cases, the stresses in Ashkenazi and in Israeli are identical.

Stress cannot fall on a traditional "half-syllable" (represented in writing by a *shewa* or *ḥataf*). If the penultimate syllable was historically short, the stress recedes: Israeli MA-A-LA ("virtue") becomes Ashkenazi MA-A-LO; but in short words, the stress can move only forward: TE-HOYM ("abyss"), ḤA-LOYM ("DREAM"), A-NI ("I"). However, Yiddish knows no half-syllables, the *ḥataf* is either deleted or raised to a full syllable. Hence in Yiddish the same words read: MAY-LE, T'HOM, KHO-LEM, A-NI.

Auxiliary syllables at the beginning of a word (which are separate words in European consciousness: articles, prepositions, conjunctions), such as HA- ("the"), VE- ("and"), BE- ("in"), LE- ("to"), are not stressed in Ashkenazi: HA-YOM ("the day"), HA-ISH ("the man"), BE-SOD ("in secret"). However, in Yiddish, Hebrew grammar did not count, hence the auxiliary was often felt to be part of the word and was stressed: OYLEM-HAZE ("[joys of] this world," instead of the Ideal Ashkenazi: HA-OYLOM HA-ZE), ADAYEM or AD-HAYEM ("until now," instead of AD HA-YOM).

2. Every vowel sign in the canonical Bible (except for the length of half-vowels) has a sound equivalent in Ashkenazi, thereby creating eight vowels and diphthongs, whereas Israeli Hebrew has only five: both Ashkenazi "O" and "A" are pronounced "A" in Israeli Hebrew; "E" and "EY" are pronounced "E", and so on. For example, BORUKH ATO ADOYNOY (in some dialects: BUR-IKH ATU) ("Blessed Art Thou, Oh Lord") is pronounced in Israeli Hebrew: BARUKH ATA ADONAY. The Ashkenazi New Year, ROSH-HASHONO, is ROSH HASHANA in Israeli Hebrew.

The Ashkenazi diphthongs -OY and -EY (when represented by one vowel sign) are reduced in Israeli to simple vowels, O and E: MOYSHE, TOYRO, and MEYLEKH are MOSHE, TORA, and MELEKH in Israeli Hebrew.

3. The soft "th" ("tav") is pronounced T in Israeli and s in Ashkenazi. For example, the holiday of "Succoth" (Tabernacles) is pronounced SUKOT in Israeli but SUKOYS in Ideal Ashkenazi and SUKES in Yiddish. Letters of the alphabet are OYSIYOYS in Ideal Ashkenazi, OYSYES in Yiddish (or EYSYES in Lithuanian Yiddish) and OTIYOT in Israeli.

4. However, Hebrew words that merged in Yiddish underwent further adaptations to the fusion language. Since, in Ashkenazi,
Hebrew stress moved from the last to the penultimate syllable
(in all bi- or multisyllabic words), the syllable following the
stress was weakened; all vowels at the end of those words were
reduced to one neutral vowel (usually pronounced as an unstressed E), as in the rest of Yiddish. Thus, Ashkenazi SIMKHAS
TOYRO (the "Joy of the Torah" holiday) is in Yiddish:
SIMKHES TOYRE. Ideal Ashkenazi MOKOYM KODOYSH
("Holy Place") is in Yiddish MOKEM KOYDESH. In the ceremony, bridegroom and bride are KHOSON and KALO but in Yiddish: KHOSN—KALE.

The Yiddish saying, OYLEM—GOYLEM ("stupid crowd," literally: "the 'world' [= "the masses"] is a Golem") derives from
Ideal Ashkenazi OYLOM—GOYLEM (in Israeli Hebrew:
oLAM—GOLEM). But even the national Hebrew poet, Bialik,
rhymed these two words in his Hebrew poetry, that is, pronounced them in the "Yiddish" manner.

A special case are final syllables that end in a consonant +
N or L and have no vowel-letter in Yiddish: MEY-DL, MA-KHN,
ZO-GN. Hebrew words, too, follow this rule: Israeli MEYVIN,
SEKHEL, GIMAL, and KHATAN are in Ashkenazi: MEY-VN,
SEY-KHL, GI-ML and KHO-SN ("maven," "intelligence," "the
letter G," "bridegroom").

In the actual use of Hebrew in Ashkenaz, we may distinguish three
major ways of pronouncing Hebrew words:

1. *"Ideal Ashkenazi Hebrew,"* that is, a reading that would actualize
properly all sounds of the Hebrew text, assigning a constant
sound-value to each consonant and vowel sign of the written
text. It was supposedly used for the careful and solemn reading
of vocalized Hebrew, especially for reading the Torah in the synagogue and was artificially revived in Ashkenazi Hebrew schools
in the twentieth century.

Though every Jewish child was aware of the sound-values of
all vowels, the actual scope of such careful reading is not quite
clear. Even the Hebrew poets of the modern literary revival in
Europe, though highly conscious of their language and striving
to purity, often "mispronounced" the written words, as we can
see from their rhymes; that is, they pronounced them in the

manner of their Yiddish dialect. For example, Y. L. Gordon (1830–1892) or David Shim'oni (Shimonovich) (1886–1956) could rhyme what in Israeli Hebrew reads KOSOT—BEREY-SHIT, and in Ideal Ashkenazi KOYsoys—beREYshis, because in the Lithuanian Yiddish dialect they read: KEYses—BE-REYses (soft T = s = sh). Thus, a "Standard Ashkenazi Hebrew" may never have existed, and if we do reconstruct it, it is really an extrapolation from the effort of creating an inter-dialectal, "Standard Yiddish" coupled with an assumption that pronunciation faithfully followed the written signs.

2. *"Hebrew Merged in Yiddish,"* that is, Hebrew and Aramaic expressions absorbed in Yiddish. Some of them changed considerably, for example, Hebrew YOM TOV ("holiday") became in Yiddish YONTEF; Hebrew KRIYAT SHMA ("saying the 'shema' "), in Ideal Ashkenazi KRIyas shma, became in Yiddish KRISHme (indeed, Bialik pronounces it so and counts it as two syllables even in his Hebrew verse).

As an organic part of Yiddish, Hebrew words were further differentiated by Yiddish geographical dialects.[10] Does one say MISHPOkhe or MISHPUkhe ("family"), TSOres or TSUres ("trouble"), BALEBOSte or BALEBUSte ("home maker, house wife")? The first of each pair is in "Lithuanian" (or "North-Eastern") Yiddish; the second, in "Polish" ("Central") and "Galician" and "Ukrainian" ("South-Eastern") Yiddish.[11] As far as Hebrew within Yiddish is concerned, this is the major dialectal divide; there were further differences in pronunciation and many

10. See Uriel Weinreich, "Ashkenazi Hebrew and the Hebrew in Yiddish: their Geographical Aspect" [in Hebrew], *Leshonenu* 24 (1960), 242–52; 25 (1961), 57–80, 180–96.

11. Hebrew vowels are pronounced variously in the different Ashkenazi dialects. While the full list is too ramified to go into here, we may indicate, schematically, the major distinctions (the first sound represents Lithuanian Yiddish, the second, Polish and Ukrainian):

kamatz = O/U, *patakh* = A (Israeli: A);

tseyre = EY/AY, *segol* = E or EY/AY (Israeli: E);

kholam = OY (Israeli O);

shuruk and *kubutz* U/I (Israeli U);

khirik I/Y (Israeli I);

Two vowels with a mute consonant (spelled ayin, alef) between them create a diphthong: AY/AA (Israeli A'A). In Israeli Hebrew, diphthongs do not represent simple signs but may result from a combination of vowel + Y (DAY, LAYLA).

subdialects and variants, as well as the quite different Hebrew dialects of *Western Yiddish* (Dutch, Alsatian, Southern German, etc.), not discussed in this framework.

3. *"Practical Ashkenazi Hebrew,"* used while reading, studying and quoting Hebrew texts proper. Though not part of Yiddish, it seems that it, too, followed in the main the spoken, Merged Ashkenazi Hebrew and its dialects, however keeping closer to the written text.

Thus, as we indicated earlier, all vowels in the last, unstressed syllable of a word were reduced to a neutral E: the holiday *Succoth* is pronounced SUKES though in ideal Ashkenazi it is SUKOYS. The Israeli Hebrew SHALOM (peace, greetings, or a man's name) is in Ashkenazi SHOLEM or SHULEM rather than the ideal SHOLOYM (cf. the spelling GERSHOM SCHOLEM, while in Hebrew he spelled his last name SHALOM).

For this reason, all Hebrew suffixes ending with a "tav" (T) are often blurred: Israeli -AT, -OT, -UT, -IT are all pronounced -ES in Ashkenazi (see note 7) and are often misspelled in religious books and on posters written by orthodox Jews in Jerusalem (e.g., DVEYKES for Hebrew DVEYKUT, SIMKHES for both SIMKHAT and SMAKHOT, MITSVES for both MITSVOT and MITSVAT). This is the way the Lubavicher rebbe quotes Hebrew and Aramaic to this day. A commentator on a Lubavicher radio program argued recently that King David was KHEYSEKH SIVTEY ("sparing his whip," in Israeli Hebrew HOSEKH SHIVTO, pronounced in the Lithuanian Ashkenazi dialect). Such "distortions" of pure, grammatical Hebrew were a target of ridicule by the Maskilim of the eighteenth and nineteenth centuries.

Nevertheless, while reading a Hebrew text proper, contractions of Merged Hebrew words would be avoided: BALAS HA-BAYIS rather than the Yiddish BALEBOSTE.

Here are some examples of the major kinds of Hebrew pronunciation:

Merged Hebrew (Lithuanian/Polish dialect)	*Ideal Ashkenazi*	*Israeli Hebrew*
SHOlem/SHUlem	SHOloym	shaLOM ("peace, greetings")

NAkhes	NAkhas	NAkhat ("satisfaction")
KOved/KUved	KOvoyd	kaVOD ("honor")
DOvid/DUvid	DOvid	daVID ("David")
baleBOSte/baleBUSte	BAlas haBAyis	ba'aLAT haBAit ("housewife")
mishPOkhe/mishPUkhe	mishPOkho	mishpaKHA ("family")
TSORes/TSUres	TSOroys	tsaROT ("troubles")
ROSHeshone/ rosheSHUne	rosh-haSHOno	ROSH hashaNA ("New Year")
KEYles/KOYles	KOYloys	koLOT ("voices")
miSHUge/miSHIge	meSHUga	meshuGA ("madman")
MEYvn/MAYvn	MEYvin	meyVIN ("maven")
YONtef (pl.: yonTEYvim/yonTOYvim)	YOM TOYV (YOmim TOYvim)	[YOM TOV ("holiday"[12]) (yaMIM toVIM)]

In spite of its domestication in the fusion language, the Hebrew component remained different from the rest of the Yiddish language and stood out in any context. In writing, this is clear: Hebrew was the more prestigious writing system and its careful spelling was a key element of preserving the religious tradition; therefore, Hebrew words in Yiddish were spelled as in Hebrew texts, while the rest of Yiddish developed toward a European-type vernacular spelling, including letter representations of vowels, and was also less consistent. In many Yiddish texts, the Hebrew words were even printed in a typeface different from the surrounding Yiddish and enclosed in brackets, to separate the holy from the mundane (or the masculine from the feminine). In speech, many merged Hebrew words may have sounded as other Yiddish words: SIBE—SIBES ("cause-s," from Hebrew) is like LIBE—LIBES ("love-s," from German); SHIKER ("drunkard," from Hebrew) is like SHLEPER ("bum," from German); MESHUGENER ("madman," from Hebrew) is like TSEFLOYGENER ("absent-minded," from German). But, in grammar, a Hebrew memory was preserved: the plural has SHLEPER—SHLEPERS but SHIKER—SHIKURIM (as in Hebrew); TSEFLOYGENER—TSEFLOYGENE but MESHUGENER—MESHUGOYIM (as in Hebrew).

Furthermore, Hebrew words are marked as different from the rest of Yiddish by their stress. In Yiddish, stress is governed by two complementary principles: (1) stress normally falls on the first syllable of

12. In Israeli Hebrew, "Yom tov" means simply "a good day," the word *khag* is used for "holiday."

a word: NA-RISH, ZIN-GEN, VEY-NEN, MEY-NEN, MEY-DE-LE, VE-ZN-TLEKH, OYS-GE-TRAKHT; (2) This principle is overruled by fixed morphological patterns: specific prefixes or suffixes are inherently stressed or unstressed, for example, FAR- is unstressed: FAR-BEY-GN ("to fold; to overlook"), FAR-FA-LN ("lost cause"); A-RUN-TER- is stressed on the second syllable: A-RUN-TER-GEYN ("to walk down"), A-RUN-TER-NE-MEN ("to take down"). In some cases, stressing or unstressing a prefix makes a difference in meaning: TSE-VAR-FN ("to scatter, break up") but TSU-VAR-FN ("to throw in"). On the other hand, some suffixes place the stress at the end of the word: AD-VO-KAT ("advocate"), DOK-TO-RAT ("doctorate"); EKSTAZ ("ecstasy"), MIRSHAS ("nasty woman"), MISHUGAS ("craziness"), BARDAS ("wise person"), MEDITSIN ("medicine"), MASHIN ("machine"); or on the penultimate syllable: SOCIALIZM ("Socialism"), TSIYONIZM ("Zionism"); NATSYE ("nation"), PROFANATSYE ("profanation"), LEGITIMATSYE ("legitimation" or "I.D."). "Foreign" or international words too are a special case (see below).

Ashkenazi Hebrew kept its separateness from the rest of the Yiddish language by a differently conceived first rule. As we saw, in Ashkenazi Hebrew, stress falls, whenever possible, on the penultimate syllable: MEY-LEKH ("king"), SEY-FER ("book"), NA-KHES ("satisfaction"). If the word is bisyllabic (as in the above examples), the stress coincides with the beginning of the word, but not otherwise: for example, O-MAR ("he said") but O-MAR-TI ("I said"); ME-SHU-GE ("crazy"), BE-NE-MO-NES ("truthfully"), A-VEY-DE ("loss"), A-VOY-DE ("religious work"). In sum, the shift from the "Sephardi" or "biblical" stress to the Ashkenazi, penultimate stress brought the Hebrew component close to, but separate from, the rest of Yiddish.

The second principle of Yiddish stress, however, governs Hebrew roots too; that is, if a Hebrew word is included in a Yiddish morphological pattern, stress is decided by that pattern: in A-ROYS-GE-GAN-VET ZIKH ("snuck out [of a place]"), the Hebrew root GANEV is embedded in a Germanic verb pattern, stressed on the second syllable (which is here the fifth from the last!). The same is true for KHO-SHEV—KHO-SHE-VER ("distinguished" as adverb and adjective), ME-SHU-GE—ME-SHU-GE-NER ("crazy"), with Yiddish suffixes that require stress on the third-to-last syllable. But when Hebrew grammar is employed, stress moves to the penultimate syllable, as in Ashkenazi Hebrew; the same words in plural are penultimately stressed: KHA-SHU-VIM, ME-SHU-GO-YIM. Sometimes a Yiddish word may not remember its Hebrew source: KHA-SE-NE ("wedding," Hebrew: KHATUNA) is stressed as any Yiddish word with the suffix -E-NE (like YI-DE-NE, "Jewish woman"), though here it is not a suffix at all; KHA-NI-KE ("Hanukah," Hebrew: ḤANUKA) rather than KHANUKE. God, however, kept his old Hebrew end-stress even in Yiddish: ELOKIM, ADOYNOY.

In many cases, Hebrew words and expressions are contracted in Yiddish into one. For example, the Bible is called SVARBE in Yiddish, from ESRIM VE-ARBA, "twenty-four" (the number of books in the Old Testament). The reading of the Shema is called KRISHME (Ashkenazi Hebrew KRIYAS SHMA, Israeli KRIAT SHMA); a musician is a KLEZMER (from the Hebrew KLEY ZEMER, "instruments of music"). In Yiddish, auxiliary words merged with the basic word into one, penultimately stressed unit: OYLEM-HAZE, OYLEM-HABE ("this world; that world") should be HA-OYLOM HA-ZE, HA-OYLOM HA-BO in Ideal Ashkenazi. HAKL-BAKL-MIKL-KOL ("everything including all details") should be HA-KOL BA-KOL MI-KOL KOL (literally: "all in-all from-all entirely").

The meaning of such expressions may also be different. In Hebrew, KLEY ZEMER are musical instruments, while the Yiddish KLEZMER are musicians. In Hebrew, BA'AL HA-BAYIT denotes "the owner or the master of this house"; in Yiddish, BALEBOS is a "boss" in general, whoever rules a house, a situation, a department, or a factory and, with this meaning, it returned to spoken Israeli Hebrew. Often, the Yiddish usage of a Hebrew word distilled in that word the meaning of a whole phrase: A MEKHAYE ("a pleasure, refreshing") is abbreviated from MEKHAYE NEFASHOT ("[he] revives the souls") while in Hebrew, MEKHAYE is simply "he revives"; MIYES ("ugly") derives from MUKTSE MEḤAMAT MIYUS ("not to be touched because of its loathsomeness") while in Hebrew, MAUS is "loathsome." The meanings of Hebrew words in Yiddish have changed in the course of the centuries or have inherited and canonized postbiblical Hebrew meanings and, in this changed form, often entered the new Israeli Hebrew (though the purists, going back to the Bible, fought hard to eliminate all Yiddish traces from the revived Hebrew language).

Here we may point out that contemporary Israeli Hebrew is not fully "Sephardic" but has Ashkenazi influences as well. As the late linguist Chaim Blank showed, all the sounds of contemporary spoken Hebrew (except for the glottal stop) existed in Yiddish, all the rest (e.g., the gutterals) are actually suppressed by most speakers. The phonetics of spoken Hebrew is not "Sephardic" but is based on the least common denominator of all dialects: the vowel system is reduced, as in Sephardi, and the consonants are reduced, as in Ashkenazi. There is also a predilection for an "Ashkenazi" penultimate stress in first names (PNINA, MOYSHE, RINA, SARA, even ITAMAR) and in various slang expressions (BIMKOM is "instead" but BIMKOM in kibbutz parlance is "an alternate dish").

A curious concomitant of the Holy Tongue as a mixed language of texts is a number of Greek words which came into Yiddish with it, stemming from the Hellenistic culture in ancient Palestine: SIMEN ("sign," as in the English word "semantics"), GEMATRIYE (letter counting, cf. "geometry"), ANDROYGENES ("hermaphrodite," cf. "androgynous"), EPIKOYRES ("heretic," from Epicurus), A POYTIKE ("large fortune," cf. the French "hypothèque"), APETROPES ("guardian"), PRAKMATYE ("merchandise"), the Passover AFIKOYMEN ("epicomen," the end of the meal). This layer provides an easy transition to the modern influx of "Internationalisms." Thus, DUGME ("example"), which came from Greek via Talmudic Hebrew, has its counterpart in DOGME ("dogma," as in "dogmatic"), arriving from modern European culture.

The Openness of Yiddish

Linguists like Max Weinreich and purist Yiddish educators or writers, like the Introspectivist poets in New York in the 1920s and 1930s, emphasized the independence of Yiddish from its source languages, its fusion character, and its whole, systemic function as one integrated language in one Jewish society. The opposite, however, is also true: Yiddish is a uniquely open language.

English has also had periods of openness toward French or Latin vocabulary (e.g., in the time of Chaucer). Yiddish, however, was radically more open because it lived among or close to its stock languages and was constantly reminded of their full extent and contemporary, casual or "correct" form. The bridgehead which those languages held within Yiddish enabled an easy enlargement of their share in the language (as shown in our diagram above). This did not endanger the nature of Yiddish since its basic grammatical framework, the patterns of fusion and of absorbing new words, were well established. But the boundaries of its vocabulary were ill-defined and shifting. There is nothing easier than taking a word from any number of languages into this flexible frame, experienced with Romance, East and West Slavic, German, English, Hebrew, and Aramaic expressions.

Thus, with the rise of German literacy among East European Jews in the nineteenth century, Yiddish speakers were confronted with written German and a strong Germanizing tendency ensued among intellectuals as well as among the masses. Shomer's (1846–1905) melodramatic novels of love and adventure—he wrote dozens of them—were very popular; he used a whole layer of directly German words, "daytshmerish," against which Sholem Aleichem launched his great battle for a pure and rich Yiddish. Similarly, the Yiddish "proletarian" poets in America at the end of the nineteenth century, popular among Jewish workers, used an array of lofty German words to poeticize the language of their verse and to lift the spirits of the sweatshop AP-REYTERS ("operators," from American): the poetic MOND ("moon," from German) substituted for the everyday Yiddish leVOne; MEER ("sea," from German) for YAM; ZEL ("soul," from the German SEELE), for the Yiddish neSHOme; and its conventional rhyme counterpart, VEL (from WELLE, "wave") rather than KHVALYE, and so on. Normative Yiddish dictionaries do not like such words, omit them, or mark them as "Germanisms" when non-German synonyms are available; but these are facts of the Yiddish language and literature and they carry stylistic differentiation as synonyms do in any language. Even such masters of the Yiddish language as Yehoash or A. Leyeles, who employed some of the richest vocabularies in Yiddish verse, did not shy away from them in their poetry.

Naturally, people of learning (lamDOnim) steeped their Yiddish in a lot of Hebrew; Jews living close to Germans (in Lodz or Silesia) used more German words and synonyms; Jews in the Ukraine used many east Slavic and Russian expressions for names of plants, dishes, and utensils, as well as for official matters. In the Soviet Union after the Revolution, there was a strong trend to minimize the Hebrew ("clerical") vocabulary and to suffuse Yiddish with Russian terminology and expressions.[13] Purists and writers fought time and again

13. The Vilna YIVO linguist, Zelig Kalmanovitch, protesting this Russification of Yiddish in the Soviet Union, claimed that the language is being reduced to phrases like DI DYELO IZ IN DER SHLYAPE, from the Russian idiom DYELO V SHLYAPE (literally: "the thing is in the hat," meaning: "it's in the bag," "not to worry"). This Yiddish sentence uses all nouns in Russian, leaving only articles and prepositions in Yiddish.

against such trends, especially against the most immediate competitor (Slavisms in Russia, Germanisms in intellectual writing, Anglicisms in America). There was always a stylistic feeling, albeit fuzzy at its edges, of what is authentically Yiddish and what is an intrusion, a foreign word, a barbarism.

When modern Yiddish literature emerged in nineteenth-century Russia, its strength was in its emphasis on the fusion language, entailing an abundant use of Slavisms and Hebraisms, to escape the impression of writing German. Then a struggle against an excess of undigested Slavisms was launched by the "Grandfather of Yiddish Literature" himself, Mendele Moykher Sforim (1836–1917). Too many Slavisms in a text were felt to lower the language to the level of uncultured common people. Purity of an integrated Yiddish, as different as possible from its neighbor languages, became the goal of the new Yiddish literature.

Mendele Moykher Sforim was admired as the great master, striking a sensible balance between the components of one, rich, synthetic Yiddish language, which became the prototype of modern Yiddish literary style. His forte, however, was making non-Germanic elements—especially Hebrew, Slavic, and colloquial Yiddish words—conspicuous in every paragraph and sentence, thus stressing the counterpoints rather than the linguistic melting pot. This was "juicy" Yiddish, made to sparkle in the virtuoso hands of his "disciple," Sholem Aleichem. Later, while reworking his novels into Hebrew, Mendele employed the same principle: combating the limitation of literary Hebrew to the lofty "pure" biblical language, as practiced in the Haskalah, he created a fine equilibrium between the various historical and stylistic layers of Hebrew and aspired to merge them into one, "Synthetic Hebrew," which became the revered "Style" (*nusakh*) and the prototype for the revival of both the written and the spoken language. Neither in modern Hebrew nor in Yiddish were the boundaries between the components obliterated altogether. In both languages, the "Synthetic" style was not a homogenous language but the ground for an open interplay of components employed by various writers in a variety of directions.

From a historical perspective, it seems that the fight for purity of the Yiddish language was merely an act of balancing the enormous influx of words from all directions, which came to enlarge the semantic fields of Yiddish and the scope of interests of its speakers as they entered modern urban civilization. Political, cultural, philosophical, literary, scientific, technological, and medical topics flooded the language of newspapers and books. Similar enlargements of vocabulary and semantic domains had occurred in all European vernaculars since the Renaissance, and in Russian since the eighteenth and the beginning of the nineteenth century. Hebrew and Yiddish were latecomers to this process but their achievement was nevertheless impressive. At first, the structure of the Yiddish language as a multicomponent medium made it more amenable than Hebrew to this expansion. This, indeed, was one of the reasons why Yiddish took over the task of enlightenment from nineteenth-century Hebrew and took center stage in Jewish society in the great wave of modernization in the twentieth century: Hebrew, even with the neologisms, looked antiquated, while Yiddish provided a vigorous and flexible vehicle for bringing the new world and its current events and ideologies to its audience.

Books translated from many languages, textbooks for Yiddish schools, books of popular science and history, a wide network of newspapers and cultural, political, literary, and scholarly journals, social and political organizations—all these contributed to an influx of words from German, Russian, and "international" sources or to the coining of Yiddish equivalents. Wide areas not accounted for in the past were absorbed into the Yiddish language, including names of daily objects, plants, animals, food, and terms from science, art, politics, ideology, and philosophy. If there were not enough words for flowers or mushrooms, one could easily coin neologisms or accommodate and "Yiddishize" Slavic or German names. No psychological observation or description of nature in literature was at a loss for words. In principle, the structure of the language permitted unlimited growth, checked only by the limitations of the world of its speakers.

A similar struggle between "purists" and "Europeanizers" went on at the same time and in the same society in Hebrew, which made efforts to revive itself as a modern, living language. The non-European structure of Hebrew made it much more difficult to absorb the new concepts organically into its Semitic vocabulary and grammatical patterns. Much as Yiddish had always accepted Hebrew stock words with their Hebrew spellings, so did Hebrew now absorb international terminology using the Yiddish spelling (abandoned later, with the revival of an independent Hebrew society in Eretz Israel). Furthermore, the authority of the codified classical Hebrew texts and their fixed collocations stood in the way of a free use of individual words in the free combinations of a spoken language. With time, however, the growth of a full-fledged network of social institutions in one territory followed

by the emergence of a modern Hebrew-speaking state in Israel, including an educational system, massive translations of foreign literature, technology, an army, and mass media, more than compensated
for that lag.

Given the openness of Yiddish, there was nothing easier for the
immigrants to America than to use scores of English words in their
Yiddish, especially for the description of concrete items in real life,
working conditions, and social institutions. The sounds and grammar
of such words were not basically different from the rest of the Yiddish
language. Motl's mother, as Sholem Aleichem describes her (in *Motl,
the Cantor's Son*), did not know whether to put the "kitchen" in the
"chicken" or vice versa, but her prototypes in real life learned fast.
Such phrases as MAKHN A LEBN ("to make a living"), GEBN TROBL
("to give trouble"), BADERN ("to bother"), APREYTER ("operator"),
SKUL ("school," as opposed to the Jewish SHUL, "synagogue"), SHAP
("shop," in the sense of "factory"), as well as Yiddishized forms of
sweatshop, Mayor, congress, and so on, were easily absorbed into the
living language.

A poster announcing a mass meeting of the Social Democratic Party
in New York on November 6, 1900, begins: ARBEYTER! VILT IR
VISN YEDE HALBE SHTUNDE DI ELFKSHYON RITOYRNS FUN DER
S.D.P.? ("Workers! Do you want to know every half hour the election
returns of the S.D.P.?") Here, the "election returns" were Yiddishized
with a New York accent: ELEKSHYON RITOYRNS. The use of the
English terms, a natural response of Yiddish, also served a purpose
similar to the German SHTUNDE substituting for the colloquial Yiddish SHO (from the Hebrew SHA'AH); both signaled lofty, serious
political rhetoric. In another sentence in the same document, GENOSE
("comrade") is used for the Yiddish KHAVER; indeed, how could you
use the domestic KHAVER in a revolutionary movement when you have
international GENOSSEN?

A notorious case was VINDE, adopted in America from the English
"window" instead of the German-stock FENTSTER. VINDE became a
symbol of barbarism to the purists but there is no objective reason
why the European Yiddish VINDE for "lift" (which came to Yiddish
from Russian) should be more legitimate than its homonym derived
from the English "window." By the twentieth century, however, Yiddish was established in Europe as a dignified and prestigious language,
and the writers fought against its vulgarization in the American Yiddish "yellow press." In contrast, Abraham Cahan, the editor of the

popular *Forverts (The Daily Forward)*, promoted this influx of Americanisms, absorbed into the unifying Yiddish alphabet, as the language of the masses for whom he worked. In a profound sense, Cahan was not just an opportunist: he understood the open nature of the Yiddish language, as did his readers. The purist writers launched a losing battle against him until both succumbed to complete Americanization, embraced by the sons of their readers.

A telling example is Alexander Harkavy, whose comprehensive *Yiddish-English-Hebrew Dictionary* was recently reprinted from the 1928 expanded edition (YIVO and Schocken, 1988). The early dictionaries of this indefatigable American lexicographer were attacked by such European Yiddish linguists as Prilutski and Weinreich for having included too many Germanizing words (DAYTSHMERISH) and too many English words current in American Yiddish. Unfortunately, Harkavy succumbed to the pressures and purified (relatively speaking) his new edition; this edition, however, contains too many Slavic words for the tastes of the purists. And all Harkavy did was to register diligently words used in printed texts, including newspapers.[14] The purist critics cannot be right because the whole conception of uncontaminated Yiddish—and the sometimes whimsical norms imposed on it—are a very recent development indeed and vary from one writer to another. It is the task of a dictionary to register the state of the language and only as a secondary function may it provide a normative guide.

The problem, of course, is that Yiddish speakers were always multilingual. Furthermore, reaching out for expressions in other languages was a sign of culture. Therefore it is impossible to decide in every case what is a borrowing, an enrichment of Yiddish, and what is a mere quotation. Any sociolinguistic description of Yiddish must bear this in mind.

Throughout history, the openness of Yiddish has created shifting combinations of its components in various cultural and geopolitical spheres. The principle of openness was also a major tool for closing some of the gaps which existed in Yiddish as the language of a society lacking many aspects of full-fledged national life. In the revival of Yiddish as a modern secular language in the last hundred and fifty years, considerable efforts have been made to fill in those gaps. A new layer of Yiddish was constituted by the so-called "Internationalisms,"

14. See Dovid Katz, "Alexander Harkavy and his Trilingual Dictionary," introduction to Alexander Harkavy, *Yiddish-English-Hebrew Dictionary* (New York: YIVO Institute for Jewish Research and Schocken Books, 1988).

that is, words of French, Latin or Greek etymology accepted in most modern languages and coming to Yiddish via German, Russian or English: GEOGRAFYE, POLITIK, PUBLITSISTIK, MILITER, REVO-LYUTSYE, REAKTSYE, EKVIVALENT, MAGNEZYUM, GERANYUM, KHRIZANTEME, REDUKTSYE, INTEGRATSYE, TEOLOGYE, VIS-NSHAFT, ATOM-BOMBE, and so on ("geography," "politics," "journalism," "army," "revolution," "reaction," "equivalent," "magnesium," "geranium," "chrysanthemum," "reduction," "integration," "theology," "science," "atom bomb"). They seemed to be common, international property, hence natural in Yiddish, unlike authentic Russian or German words which sounded "foreign" when used in Yiddish. Like the Hebrew component, this layer, too, deviated from the basic Yiddish stress pattern, thus marking its "foreign" status: words ending in an open syllable are penultimately stressed and are feminine, others are stressed on their first or last syllable, according to the source language.

The openness of the language made it easy to accept such words from the international vocabulary as if they had always been part of the language and to treat them in the forms of the Yiddish grammar: INTEGRATSYE, INTEGRALE YIDISHKEYT, INTEGRIRTE SHULN, INTEGRALN UN DIFERENTSYALN, MIR HOBN ES INTEGRIRT IN UNDZERE LIMUDIM ("integration," "integral Judaism," "integrated schools," "integrals and differentials" [in mathematics], "we have integrated it into our studies").

At the same time, a large body of "intellectual" words came directly from German: it was simple to add new German words to the basically Germanic vocabulary of Yiddish. The name of the YIVO itself, YID-ISHER VISNSHAFTLEKHER INSTITUT, consists of German terms (the same is true for Dutch, for example: LITERATUURWETENSCHAP ["science of literature"] is a mere phonetic transposition of the German LITERATURWISSENSCHAFT, as is the Yiddish LITERATURVISNSHAFT).

This process was recognized by the masters of the language; Sholem Aleichem wrote in 1888: "We believe that it is not superfluous to introduce *foreign* words into Yiddish, but only such words which are indispensable for the literature, e.g., 'poezye,' 'kritik,' 'yubileum,' 'beletristik,' 'ortografye,' 'fanatizm,' 'komizm,' etc. Never mind, we may not be ashamed of it: nicer languages have more than hundreds and thousands of foreign words in their vocabularies."[15]

___

15. In *Di yidishe folks-bibliotek*, reprinted in Joshua A. Fishman, ed., *Never Say Die!:*

The Introspectivist manifesto, a most consciously Yiddishist poetic document, written by a group of poets in New York in 1919, does not shy away from declaring: "Yiddish is now rich enough, independent enough to afford to enrich its vocabulary from the treasures of her sister languages. That is why we are not afraid to borrow words from the sister languages, words to cover newly developed concepts, broadened feelings and thoughts. Such words are also *our* words. We have the same rights to them as does any other language, any other poetry."

The Introspectivist poet A. Leyeles, fascinated by Ouspensky's fourth dimension and by Oriental mysticism, wrote a poem on "Symmetry" (AYP, 130–133) as the rest in mid-movement, the ecstasy of universal unity beyond time and space, division of man and woman, God and Demon. Here is the opening of the poem in transcription, followed by an English translation:

siMEtriye—	Symmetry—
ritm in shtilshtand.	Rhythm arrested.
opru in mitn baVEgung.	Rest in mid-movement.
baVEgung in iber-roym.	Movement in higher space.
siMEtriye—	Symmetry—
geMAtriye fun misTERye.	Anagram of mystery.
misTERye fun rytm	Mystery of rhythm
oyf yener zayt zoym	On the other side of the seam
fun tsayt un roym.	Of time and space.

The concepts and words for "symmetry," "mystery," and "rhythm" are modern internationalisms; GEMATRIYE, however, though matching these terms in sound and meaning as well as in its Greek origin, is an old Talmudic word. "Time and space" reflect the interest in Kantian philosophy and Einsteinian physics among intellectuals in the 1920s; however, TSAYT is an old Yiddish word whereas ROYM in this sense is Yiddishized from the German RAUM. In the rest of the poem we find such words as "sacrament," "lament," "convex," "concave," and "reflex" almost unchanged from their English forms.

The last stanza of the poem reads:

sod fun sod un yiSOD.	Secret of secret and sacred.
freyd fun shed un fun got.	Joy of demon and God.

A Thousand Years of Yiddish in Jewish Life and Letters (The Hague: Mouton, 1981), 660.

blits fun shpiz. mishuGAS.	Flash of spear. Madness.
flantser un zot.	Planter and plot.
zelikeyt. has.	Beatitude. Hatred.
ekstTAZ.	Ecstasy.
eKHOD!	*E-chod*!

SOD and YISOD ("secret, mystery" and "essence, foundation"), both used in Hebrew philosophy, are basic Yiddish words, here endowed with Kabbalistic meaning. The second line uses the simplest Yiddish words, with no distinction between SHED ("demon") coming from Hebrew and GOT ("God") from German. MISHUGAS ("madness") and HAS ("hatred") are basic Yiddish, derived from Hebrew and German, respectively; but FLANTSER (a neologism) and ZELIKEYT seem to be modern adaptations from German and ZOT is a revived archaism for "sowing" or "seed." More important, the internationalism, EKSTAZ ("ecstasy"), is matched—in a stylistic tension of two opposites—with the highest Hebrew attribute of God: EKHOD ("One"). This is the language of fusion, indeed, but with a new awareness of the value of different components and the separate semantic baggage they bring into the text.

In his sonnet, "Evening," describing Madison Square at nightfall, Leyeles (impressed by the Viennese "Secession" in art) underlines the modernity of the experience with a profusion of internationalisms. Here is a transcription of the original (small capital letters indicate the "modern" words):[16]

16. A rhymed translation of the poem:

Evening

Windows flash, flare up above the square.
Lights sparkle—polygonal, anonymous.
Triangles, diamonds—part Secession, part harmonious—
Dance joyfully on windowpanes, straight and queer.

Flickers of black and gold, pointed and sardonic,
Wink to the sky. The sky—in pieces,
Hangs deep and dark, cut up by giant scissors—
Glimmers back its blueness, slant, laconic.

The virile towers—cornerless. They twinkle—
It seems: a crowd assembles, richly sprinkled
With torches for a frivolous carnival.

Debauchery in the square. Electrically-fantastic
Carousing for an hour, boisterous, orgiastic—
A chimera drunk on itself. Unreal ball. (AYP, 107)

shoybn blitsn, shoybn tsindn zikh in SKVER.
s'finklen likhter oyf FANTAStish, POLIGONish.
drayeks, rombn, halb SETSESYE, halb HARMOnish.
tantsn freylekh oyf in fentster—GROD un KVER.

tsu dem himl vinkn shpitsik un SARDOnish
flekn gold un shvarts. un er—farTIFT zikh mer,
hengt tseSHNItn sharf vi fun a rizn-sher,
glantst tsuRIK zayn bloykeyt zaytik un LAKOnish.

di viRIle turems—veyniker GEVINKLT.
bald un s'dakht zikh: s'klaybt a folk zikh, raykh BASHPRINKLT
mit shturKAtsn tsum farSHAYtn KARNIVAL.
a DEBOSH in SKVER. ELEKtrish-LEGENDArish
roysht er op a sho. ORGYAStish un virVArish—
zelbst-farSHIkerte KHIMEre. UMREAL.

Many words in the fourteen lines of the sonnet are used in English
as well: *square, fantastic, polygonal, Secession, harmonious, sardonic, laconic, virile, carnival, debauchery, electrical, legendary, orgiastic, chimera,
unreal.* Most of them could have been adopted from English or from
other languages. They are, however, domesticated with Yiddish sounds
and suffixes and are part of modern Yiddish. Several additional words
are shared by Yiddish and English from their mutual Germanic source:
gold, sprinkled, wink. WIRRWARR is a German word for chaos, confusion, or noise and was used in Yiddish too; but here it is made
strange by transforming it into an adverb by means of the German-
stock suffix -ISH (not used in German for this root), VIRVARISH, and
aligned with other attributes of the modern turmoil (ELEKTRISH, LE-
GENDARISH, POLIGONISH). And all this is so naturally conjoined—
by the unifying flow of the metrical rhythm—with the simplest and
most domestic Yiddish words: SHOYBN, FENTSTER, LIKHTER, HIML,
TANTSN, FREYLEKH, VINKN, FLEKN, SHER, ROYSHT, SHO, FARSHIK-
ERT ("window panes," "windows," "lights," "sky," "dance," "joyful,"
"wink," "stains," "scissors," "noise," "hour," "drunk").

In the forays Yiddish-users made into the domains of neighboring
languages, we may distinguish two different functions, though there
are no clear-cut boundaries between them: (1) the borrowing of words
to enlarge the vocabulary of Yiddish itself; (2) the willful use of foreign expressions as such, to enrich the effectiveness of the message
and to enhance the stylistic tension between the components. The
second function indicates that Yiddish speakers are supposed to be
cultural persons and, by definition, know several other languages and

demonstrate good style by using them. Such expressions are quoted ad hoc, with no intent to include them in the Yiddish language. Their use, nevertheless, is an essential sociolinguistic fact of the "pragmatics," or the real life of Yiddish.

The American Yiddish poet, Yehoash, in his *Fables* (New York, 1912), is a brilliant master of such interplay of components and borrowings, willfully making them clash or selecting the clearly "non-Yiddish" synonym, highlighted by his original rhyme scheme. A good knowledge of Yiddish is a presupposition for sensing the impact of the deviations. I shall cite here merely a few examples. The fable "An assembly of animals" carries a title with lofty Hebrew terms: "An AS-IFE bay di KHAYES" (Hebrew in small capital letters), but the "organizational" language is German-oriented: the Hebrew-derived Yiddish "khayes" becomes "THIEREN" (not normally used in Yiddish but known to the speakers). The opening reads (conspicuously German words in bold):

a grupe **prominente thieren**
bashlosn hobn zikh **organiziren,**
um oyftsuhoybn dem **moral,**
fun khayes **iberal,**
un iber feld un taykh
iz oysgeshikt gevorn glaykh
a tsirkular:

["A group of prominent animals decided to organize in order to raise the morale of animals everywhere, and, over field and stream, a circular was issued:"].

The German words underline the official tone of the bureaucracy (most of the other words, though native in Yiddish, are derived from German too).

In the fable "Der oysgeMENtshlter oRAng-uTANG" ("the humanized orang-utang") [here, interesting words are printed in small capital letters], the professor teaches the monkey "vi men darf GE-BROYkhn [German] gopl-meser/ loyt HILKHES [Hebrew] ETIKET [French] .../ di OBEZYANE [Russian]/ geVOrn iz geVOYNT zoGAR [German]/ tsu roykhern a tayern TSIGAR [international]/ (un davke fun HAVANA) ["how properly to use a knife and fork according to the religion of etiquette. . . . The monkey even got used to smoking an expensive cigar (and no less than from Havana)]. "Hilkhes etiket" is a clash between Jewish religious law and French manners; a monkey in Yiddish is "malpe" and the Russian "obezYAne" is a clear provocation, underscored by the rhyme with the Cuban "Havana."

Later in the poem, Yehoash invents the compound rhyme: NE-FESH—PROTEZHE-FISH ["nefesh," creature, from Hebrew; "protégé" from French; "fish" is Yiddish]. And in another poem, he rhymes Hebrew with American borrowings: the eagle soars "in hoykhn AVER/ vi du volst zayn mit volkns KHAVER-LAVER" ["in the high air, as if you were a comrade-lover of the clouds"]. "Laver" ("lover") is an Americanism and the Hebrew "aver" is not normally used for "air" in Yiddish. The reader is supposed to know the other languages; at the same time, there is a teasing effect about such language-fencing.

The same technique was employed in daily speech and in the popular press. Not only German and American expressions, that is, symptoms of assimilation, were used, but a profusion of Hebrew as well, underlying the linguistic and cultural richness of the author and his audience. An editorial in the *Fraye arbeter shtime* of August 14, 1891 (a socialist-anarchist paper, ostensibly read by blue-collar proletarians in New York), says, inter alia (foreign words are in small capital letters and the initials of their source language in square brackets):

"In BRIDGEPORT [Am] iz geven a MAKHLOYKES LESHEM SHAMAYIM [H]. POLITISHONS [Am] hobn zikh gekrigt . . . VAYISROYTSETSU HABONIM BE-KIRBOY [H] . . . biz es iz geblibn BEHESKEM KULOM [H]: GAM LI GAM LEKHO LOY YIHYE [H], men hot mevatl geven in gantsn dem OFFICE [Am].

["In Bridgeport, there was a quarrel for the sake of ideals. Politicians quarrelled . . . 'and the sons were bickering in her belly' . . . until they all agreed: 'neither for me nor for you,' they cancelled the office altogether."]

And the article ends:

"Nider mit di falshe maskes! Di TSVUYIM [H] in di nestn fun SAMBATYONS VEKHADOYME [H]! Oyf SAMBATYONEN [H] kenen mir nor zogn: LOY LEK-HINOM HOLAKH ZARZIR EYTSEL OYREV ELO MIPNEY SHEHU MINOY! [H]

[Down with the false masks! The chameleons in the nests of Sambations etc.! To the Sambations we can say: not in vain did the raven go to the crow, for he is his own kind!]

All expressions in small capitals are from Hebrew, including the quoted proverb closing the editorial—and this is a Yiddish immigrant workers' newspaper!

In sum, contrary to the preaching and the linguistics of the purists, the openness of Yiddish made all component languages available, within reach of a Yiddish writer and reader, to be used either as a merged element or as a quotation or a "foreign" borrowing. Poets and scholars alike enjoyed this propensity. So did Yiddish speakers, who—almost by definition—were rarely speakers of Yiddish only and did not make much of the fashionable theories of an insulated "national language." Their modern culture was cosmopolitan, even when the thematics and ideology were "Jewish." The fight for a pure, standard language, especially in education, is quite a different matter, and is perfectly legitimate, though it came too late for the survival of Yiddish.

3

Some Sociological Aspects

How Old Is Yiddish?

In the period of rising nationalism in Europe, culminating in the nineteenth century, an ideal of the national language was promoted: one, pure language for one people in one state. In reality, however, there were no single, monolithic German, English, Italian, or Russian languages but rather a range of quite distinct regional and social dialects, superimposed in recent centuries by a standard literary language enhanced by a political bureaucracy, theatre, and literature, and subsequently brought even farther under one umbrella by mass media. Those which crystallized as separate languages (i.e., Dutch vs. German; Ukrainian and Byelorussian vs. Russian) often reflected geopolitical, religious, or historical circumstances more than actual linguistic distance.

It is hard to know to what extent Yiddish, in its first centuries, was more distant from "German" than were other dialects. The concept of purity or separateness of a language did not exist. The very name "Yiddish" came rather late. The earlier name, TAYTSH (meaning: "German" and subsequently "translation") or YIDDISH-TAYTSH ("Jewish-German") reflected its bilingual function: to put a Hebrew text into TAYTSH, or FARTAYtshn, meant "to translate," "to explain," as it still means today.

Due to its open nature, Yiddish could easily be adapted in any discourse to be either closer to German or more steeped in Hebrew: an individual could switch to speaking "German" or writing "Hebrew" or using any mixture in between. Indeed, in translations of the Bible, it was natural to use few Hebrew words and to find German equivalents whenever possible. Likewise, when German epics were adapted for a Jewish audience and transposed into the Yiddish alphabet, the text preserved its original stylistic register and looked much like German. There was, however, a great difference between the style of Yiddish literature before the modern period—mostly "high" style, that is heavily Germanic,—and the spoken or private language used in letters and community documents of the same period where the fusion nature of Yiddish came profusely to the fore and Hebrew elements were conspicuous.

We do not know all the facts of the past: many texts have been lost, the oral speech has evaporated. We can have only competing hypotheses on the exact nature of the language and the extent of its use by Jewish speakers in various countries. It is possible, for example, that Jews in Slavic countries spoke Slavic languages from the early Middle Ages (perhaps in Jewish varieties), much as their brethren in Germany spoke a Germanic language; this Slavic speech was then suppressed by Yiddish brought by immigrants from Germany, but it continued to work as a substratum of the new, Eastern Yiddish. Or, the reverse: Yiddish-speaking Jews came to the East and absorbed expressions from their Slavic environment. In any case, in the sixteenth century, Yiddish seems to have covered most of the territory of Jewish Ashkenazi communities in Europe.

Whether the language was clearly demarcated from "German" (whatever that meant) since its beginning or not, several facts are beyond doubt:

1. The fusion nature of Yiddish can be observed and reconstructed from its earliest documents. The first "literary" text is a rhymed couplet using Hebrew and Germanic words and written in a prayerbook of the thirteenth century.

2. Yiddish was always written in its own (Hebrew-based) alphabet and developed its own spelling system much as German or English did while separating from Latin.

3. It served a separate community with its own body of texts, social, ideological, and religious systems.

4. It developed a separate, oral and written literature which cannot even remotely be considered part of German literature (though some of its medieval texts may be seen so).

5. For about the last thousand years, there has been a continuous use of the same, German-based and Hebrew-related language by the same community, evolving into what in modern times is certainly a separate, often unique vehicle of culture and communication.

Recently, Dovid Katz made a forceful argument, claiming that the Hebrew element in Yiddish was much richer and was not acquired from learning but inherited from older, pre-Yiddish times.[1] Unsuspected support for this hypothesis may come from Primo Levi's recollection of the Hebrew vestiges in his native Piedmont dialect of Jewish Italian, as told in his autobiographical novel, *The Periodic Table* (New York: Schocken Books, 1984). The Hebrew words here fulfill a similar, tribe-related and emotive function as the Hebrew layer in Yiddish and most of the Hebrew words listed by Levi appear in Yiddish as well.

At first sight, Primo Levi's examples seem strange. He did not quite realize that the guttural "ayin" was replaced by a nasal "N," as in some dialects of western Yiddish, hence TONEVA [pejorative for church] is the Hebrew TO'EVA; PONALTA' (feminine: "laborer") is the Hebrew PO'ELET. Also, "D" in this dialect represents the Hebrew soft *tav* ("th") or Yiddish "s." Otherwise, it is closer to the general "Sephardi" pronunciation, which was prevalent even in Ashkenazi Europe before 1300: the strongly emotive SAROD ("troubles") is the Hebrew TSAROT and still lives in Yiddish TSORES; HASIRUD ("nastiness") is the Hebrew KHAZIRUT and lives in Yiddish as KHAZERAY or SHVAYNERAY.

Other words mentioned by Levi and still used in Yiddish, though sometimes with a different connotation, include the following (the first word is Levi's version; the parallel Yiddish form is in square brackets; whenever relevant, Sephardi Hebrew [H] is indicated; and, in parentheses, a translation):

1. See Dovid Katz, "The Semitic Component in Yiddish: An Ancient Linguistic Heritage," *Ha-Sifrut* 3–4 (35–36) (1986): 228–51.

GOYIM [GOYIM]; NARELIM [AREYLIM] (Christians);
TSIPPORA [TSIPOYRE, H: TSIPORA];
RASHEN [ROSHE, H: RASHA'] ("evil person");
PEGARTA' [feminine of PEYGER] ("cadaver");
GOYA' [GOYE]; HAVERTA' [KHAVERTE] ("female friend");
MANO'D [MOES, H: MAOT] ("money");
BAHALOM [KHOLEM, H: BA-KHALOM] ("in your dream");
KINIM [KINIM] ("lice");
SCOLA [SHUL] ("synagogue");
RABBI [REBE, H: RABBI]; RABBENU [H: RABENU];
KHAKHAM [KHOKHEM, H: KHAKHAM] ("wise man");
RU'AKH (to break "wind");
BARAKHA' [BROKHE, H: BERAKHA] ("blessing");
MAMSER [MAMZER] ("bastard");
KASHERUT [KASHRES, H: KASHRUT] ("kosher quality").

Levi had some difficulties of identification that can easily be re-
solved. According to him: "Completely cryptic and indecipherable . . . is the term ODO," alluding to Christ; but it surely derives
from the Hebrew OTO HA-ISH (literally: "that man," *Ecce homo*), as
A-ISSA', referring to the Madonna, derives from HA-ISHA ("that
woman"). Levi tells of an uncle who lived with a GOYA' whom he
described from time to time as 'NA SO-TIA' [HEBREW: SHOTA]
("silly woman"), 'NA HAMORTA' (female "jackass"), or 'NA GRAN
BEEMA' ("a big cow"), epithets used in Yiddish in the same sense
and context: A SHOYTE, A GROYSE BEHEYME [in Hebrew: BEHEMA
means cattle while in Yiddish and in Levi's Piedmontese, it is "a
silly woman, a 'cow' "]. KHAMOR ("ass") is still used in Hebrew in
this sense, mostly in masculine form, while Yiddish favors the Germanic EYZL. Furthermore, Yiddish has the same feminine suffix,
derived from Aramaic, in KHAVERTE (woman friend) BALEBOSTE
(landlady or good housewife) or KLAVTE ("bitch").

Levi finds a "curious linkage" in the collocation MEDA'
MESHO'NA [H: MITA MESHUNA], ("strange, unusual death") used
as a curse, meaning "may he drop dead"; but precisely the same
curse is very much alive as a "juicy" expression in Yiddish: A MISE
MESHUNE ("a strange, unusual death [may befall him]"). I would
even venture to suggest a possible similarity between what Levi sees

as an "inexplicable imprecation": C'AI TAKEISSA 'NA MEDA'
MESHO'NA' FAITA A PARAGUA ["may he have a strange death shaped
like an umbrella"] and the Yiddish ZOL IM KHAPN A MISE ME-
SHUNe! ZOL ER AROPshlingen a shirem un s'zol zikh im
EFENEN IN BOYKH! ["May a strange death take him! May he swal-
low an umbrella and it should open in his belly!"] Clearly, the
whole issue warrants further research. This seems to be a very old
layer of spoken Hebrew words, untouched by Ashkenazi and reaching back before the Jewish crossing of the Alps into German-speaking territory in the tenth century. The Hebrew is still pronounced
closer to the general "Sephardi" dialect, with typical Italian changes,
but the use and meaning of the words is close to their functioning
in Yiddish.

Thus, Yiddish may carry Hebrew expressions that are older than
the language itself. The oldest dated text in Yiddish is a rhymed couplet written inside the ornamented initial letters of a Hebrew word
in the Worms Mahzor (prayerbook) of 1272. It displays the Yiddish
Medieval 4-accent meter and the German-Hebrew fusion nature of
the language. The oldest extant large Yiddish text, the so-called "Cambridge Manuscript," was found in, of all places, Cairo, Egypt (in the
famous Genizah). Dated 1382, it contains poems on biblical topics
(Abraham, Joseph, the death of Aaron) as well as a previously unknown version of a German epic, Ducus Horant, in a Yiddish adap-
tation.
    Even though many Medieval Yiddish texts have been lost, the va-
riety of extant manuscripts of that period shows the span of writings:
adapted German epics; epic poems on biblical topics in German meters; lyrical and historical poems in German and Hebrew verse forms;
dramas; stories; biblical narratives; moral guidebooks; private letters,
and community documents.[2] From the first half of the sixteenth century on, Yiddish books were printed in Germany, Italy, Holland,
Switzerland, and Poland and distributed in the entire domain. With
the flourishing of the Jewish center in the vast Kingdom of Poland
and Lithuania, outside the German-speaking areas, the Yiddish language asserted its independence. It became the medium of oral communication for an elaborate network of Jewish social institutions; no

---

2. For a recent survey of Old Yiddish literature in English, see Khone Shmeruk's
contribution to *Encyclopedia Judaica* and, in Hebrew, his book *Yiddish Literature: Aspects
of its History* (Tel Aviv: The Porter Institute, 1978).

more the language of a small minority, but the accepted, spoken language of an autonomous, legally separate, and densely organized Jewish community, the vehicle of its social and political cohesion.

Yiddish Dialects

With the authority of learning and rigorous, codified behavior emerging from medieval Germany, Yiddish spread in all directions. Eventually, as it branched out across Europe, it developed into two major forms: Western Yiddish, spoken by German Jews until the nineteenth century (some pockets of which still survived in Alsace, Switzerland, Holland, and Southern Germany until the Holocaust); and Eastern Yiddish, which had reshuffled its fusion character to absorb a heavy load of Slavic elements and became the language of modern Yiddish literature, culture and education.

Eastern Yiddish itself developed into a whole range of variants, grouped in three major dialects: Central Yiddish ("Polish"), Northeastern Yiddish ("Lithuanian") and Southeastern ("Ukrainian"). On the whole, these dialects reflect the boundaries between Poland and Lithuania before their merger in the sixteenth century (with the Ukraine, which changed hands from Lithuania to Poland to Russia, as a third area). Thus, the Lithuanian Yiddish FOTER ("father") is in Polish Yiddish FUTER; the Lithuanian FUTER ("fur") is Polish FYTER. The Lithuanian EYN SHEYN MEYDALE ("one pretty girl") is AYN SHAYN MAYDELE in Polish Yiddish. Americans still quoting Yiddish words are often caught in the confusion. (How do you pronounce "New Year": ROSHE-SHONE, ROSHE-SHUNE, ROSH HASHONO, or ROSH HA-SHANA as in Israeli Hebrew?) There are further differences in the selection of words, traditions of learning and cooking, and strongly opposed stereotypes of mentality and behavior ("Litvak," "Polak," "Galitsyaner"), enhanced by the big split in the eighteenth and nineteenth centuries between Hassidism, based primarily in Galicia, the Ukraine, and Poland, and the Lithuanian-centered "Misnagdim" (traditional orthodoxy focusing on learning). Nevertheless, to a very large extent, it is one language with minor variations in vocabulary and clearly different, but mutually translatable, pronunciation systems. Every speaker of one dialect can (if he wants) easily understand speakers of other dialects by merely adjusting the vowel equivalents in his mind.[3]

With the emergence of modern Yiddish literature as a major force in Jewish life at the end of the nineteenth century, and the flourishing of Yiddish schools and publishing in the twentieth century, major efforts were made at standardization of the language into one, super-dialectal, literary language. In one respect, this was done in the tradition of Mendele and Sholem Aleichem in finding a balance between the components of the fusion language and suppressing "foreign" intrusions. In a more immediate sense, it concerned the standardization of spelling and efforts at unifying pronunciation in schools. The new "standard" language of "Literary Yiddish" was modeled on the "literary language" of German and Russian. Its pronunciation and spelling was largely, though not entirely, based on the Lithuanian dialect used by the most prestigious groups in society: by the Lithuanian Yeshivas, by religious and secular teachers who spread southward from Lithuania to the Ukraine or to America and Palestine, by leaders of the labor movement, and by the Vilna Yiddish *intelligentsia*. (Vilna was a major Jewish cultural center, its status reinforced by the prominence of the eighteenth-century figure of the Vilna Gaon, by the great Lithuanian yeshivas, the prestige of *Haskalah* writers, its Talmudic and secular publishing houses, the emergence of the socialist "Bund," modern Yiddish and Hebrew schools and teachers' colleges, and the Yiddish Scientific Institute [YIVO].) In matters of grammar, however, the Litvaks were often overruled. And of course Yiddish literature exhibited rich strains of vocabulary from other regions, notably drawing on Ukrainian and Polish Yiddish.

The Yiddish Alphabet

The fusion of the stock elements in Yiddish became possible while absorbed in one spoken melting pot, without regard for the precise written forms of the original languages. This was enhanced

3. The late Uriel Weinreich of Columbia University launched the huge project of a Yiddish Language and Culture Atlas, continued by Marvin Herzog. The Atlas, though researched at a distance (not in Europe, which it describes, but in America and Israel where the survivors live), reveals a wealth of material on this topic.

by the fact that, from its very beginning, Yiddish used the Hebrew alphabet which unified all its components and isolated them from the literary forms of their stock languages. The Yiddish alphabet recorded Yiddish speech rather than written foreign words which most Jews could not read (except for Hebrew, of course).

There was a major problem, however, since Hebrew uses letters primarily for consonants (as: PRMRLY FR CNSNNTS). Indeed, in Hebrew, most of the vowels are not an essential part of a Hebrew lexeme but merely represent its morphology. For example in KATaV, "he wrote," KoTEV, "I, you, he write(s)," KaTuV, "is written," the consonants, KTV, mean "write," whereas the vowels indicate the person, time or part of speech. For beginning readers or in the holy text of the Bible, the vowels are supplied by diacritical marks (little dots and dashes over or under the letters); otherwise, they are not needed and can be understood from the context.

On the other hand, since Yiddish is a language with a basically Indo-European lexicon, vowels are as essential as consonants; LEBER ("liver") and LIBER ("beloved") have two different roots and lexical meanings. Almost from its beginnings, Yiddish developed a set of Hebrew letters assigned to represent its vowels and diphthongs (based on a partial internal Hebrew tradition, as evidenced by the Dead Sea Scrolls and postbiblical liturgy). Thus Yiddish created its own spelling system, much as European vernaculars had to develop their own spelling systems from the Latin alphabet. Yet, for centuries, Yiddish books continued to use these new vowels only in part and to supplement them with the diacritical dots and dashes of biblical Hebrew, thus wavering between the two systems of vocalization.

Furthermore, until the nineteenth century, Yiddish was printed in a special typeface (called VAYBER-TAYTSH, "women's Yiddish"). Typically, Hebrew books had several distinctly separated canonical typefaces: (1) stylized "square" letters for the biblical text, printed with vocalization; (2) unvocalized square letters for the Mishna and Gemarah; (3) semi-cursive letters (very different in shape), used for Hebrew commentaries and other secondary material accompanying a holy text on the margins of the same page (this typeface is called "RASHI," the name of the most common canonical commentary); and (4) "women's Yiddish." This separation is striking in religious books which often use all four typefaces on one page for biblical text, other Hebrew text, commentary, and Yiddish translation, respectively.

Separated from all other languages by the Hebrew alphabet, and from Hebrew by its different typeface and by the letter signs given to its vowel phonemes, Yiddish gradually developed its own semi-phonological spelling system which unified all the components of the language. For only one component was a separate spelling reserved in Yiddish: for the Holy Tongue. To this day, words or even parts of words of Hebrew and Aramaic origin are spelled in Yiddish as in their stock languages, for example, the word "khaper" ("One out to catch," like the English slang "copper") is spelled phonologically as KHAPER, but the similar word KHAVER ("friend") is spelled ḤVR, without vowels, because of its Hebrew origin. If part of a word is of Hebrew origin and another part (such as a suffix or a member of a compound word) is not, each part is spelled according to its different rules: GANEV ("thief") is spelled GNV, but GANVENEN ("to steal") is spelled GNVENEN, that is, the Hebrew root GNV remains without vowels and the Yiddish Germanic suffix –ENEN with. (Compare the spelling of French words in English, which is closer to its source than the spelling of Germanic words in English is to German.)

In older texts, Hebrew words were set off further from the main Yiddish text in which they appeared: the Hebrew words, members of a "holy tongue," were placed in parentheses (even in the middle of a sentence) and printed in the Hebrew typeface, to separate them from the surrounding typeface of "women's Yiddish." If the latter was embedded in a Hebrew framework on the page, an inverse framing hierarchy resulted:

HEBREW TEXT—*Hebrew commentary*—Yiddish text
Yiddish text—(HEBREW WORD)—Yiddish text

This anomaly of Yiddish spelling, privileging one component of the language in spite of its fusion with the other components, was supported by the bilingual Jewish system: such Hebrew words in Yiddish were "cross-over" words, linking Yiddish to the Hebrew texts. The Introspectivist poets, fighting for the independence of Yiddish and its organic integrity as one language, extended the unified Yiddish spelling to Hebrew words as well; that is, they spelled them phonetically, irrespective of their Hebrew roots. A special dispensation was made by the editors of their journal *Inzikh* as late as December 1940, for Aaron Tsaytlin, a major poet who had just come to the United

States as a refugee from the Holocaust in Poland. The editorial note accompanying his poem published in *Inzikh* accepts Tsaytlin's argument that the words of Hebrew and Aramaic origin in his poem are terms from the *Zohar*, and that without their original spelling, they may lose their "specific Kabbalistic aroma"; hence the deviation from the journal's policy.[4]

The same principle was adopted after the Revolution in the Soviet Union in order to separate Yiddish, "the language of the masses," from the "clerical language," Hebrew, and its religious and historical roots and its Zionist advocates in Palestine. To dissociate themselves from that antihistorical tendency, the Introspectivists eventually had to return, after more than twenty years of using a unified Yiddish spelling system, to the Hebrew spelling for words of Hebrew origin.

In the eighteenth and nineteenth centuries, when a reading knowledge of German became widespread among Jews, German spelling was copied in Yiddish transcriptions, even when it did not represent any actual sounds in Yiddish (or in German itself). Thus, an unpronounced "silent h" was added in words like "MEHR" ("more"), "FEHLER" ("mistake"), and "LEHRER" ("teacher"); "silent *ayins*" (i.e., unpronounced "e") flooded the language: "ZOGEN" (for ZOGN, "to say"), and "LIEGT" (for LIGT, "he lies"); and consonants were doubled as in German ("ALLE" for ALE).

In the twentieth century, with the trend for vindicating Yiddish as an independent language, such Germanizing influences have been abolished. A new spelling system has been introduced, reflecting the phonology of standard literary Yiddish and enabling the various dialects to read the same text in their own fashion. Among the promoters of a modern spelling ("to write a word as you hear it") were the writer Sholem Aleichem, the Marxist Zionist and Yiddish philologist Ber Borokhov, and various linguists and educators. From the several varieties of this spelling reform, the YIVO spelling rules of 1935 are commonly accepted today as the norm. Nevertheless, many publishers and newspapers and, more important, many writers, have often deviated from those rules either because of habit or to express a different stylistic sensibility.

4. A. L[eyele]s, "Again about the spelling of Hebrew words," *Inzikh* 56, December 1940.

A Few Words on the Fate of Yiddish

Yiddish had a considerable body of folklore and a large written literature which flourished in the sixteenth century and again between 1862 and the present. Its international recognition culminated in the awarding of the Nobel Prize for literature to Isaac Bashevis Singer in 1978, and the Israel Prize to A. Sutskever, poet and editor of the prestigious literary quarterly *Di Goldene Keyt*, in 1984. In the last third of the nineteenth century, three "classical" writers of Yiddish literature, Mendele Moykher Sforim, Sholem Aleichem, and I. L. Peretz, lent prestige to a rapidly expanding literary institution. In a short period, dozens of important writers created a literature with European standards, moving swiftly from rationalist Enlightenment through carnivalesque parody to Realism, Naturalism, and psychological Impressionism, and then breaking out of these conventional European modes into the general literary trends of Expressionism and Modernism.

This became possible because of the secularization of the Jewish masses and the trend to join the general world of modern culture and politics in the language they knew. The growing political parties, especially the Diaspora-oriented Folkists and Socialists, but many Zionists as well, supported Yiddish culture and education, seeing it at first as a tool for propaganda and as a way to break out of the traditional religious framework and, later, as a goal in itself. The Orthodox Agudah ("Agudas Isroel") responded by developing their own Yiddish school system for girls. Hundreds of periodicals and newspapers appeared in Yiddish (the earliest was the newspaper *Kurantn* published in Amsterdam in 1686). Libraries sprang up in hundreds of towns. A modern secular school system developed all over Eastern Europe and was echoed in part in both Americas. Massive translation efforts brought to Yiddish readers the works of Tolstoy, Kropotkin, Ibsen, Zola, Jules Verne, Rabindranat Tagore, Lion Feuchtwanger, Shakespeare, Sergey Yesenin, Ezra Pound, and many others.

It was, however, a tragic destiny. As Leo Wiener put it in 1899, "there is probably no other language . . . on which so much opprobrium has been heaped."[5] Traditionally, Yiddish was considered the

---

5. Quoted in Joshua A. Fishman's survey, "The Sociology of Yiddish," in his anthology, *Never Say Die! A Thousand Years of Yiddish in Jewish Life and Letters*.

"servant maid" to the "Lady" Hebrew. With the onset of the Enlightenment among German Jews, Yiddish became the ugly symbol
of everything that kept the Jews from entering civilized western society. Indeed, when viewed from the point of view of a "pure" normative literary German language based in the northern city of Berlin,
Yiddish—based on oral, medieval, southern German dialects and thoroughly "melted"—did look like a contortion, a corrupted medley with
no grammar or aesthetic values. Moses Mendelssohn wrote: "This jargon contributed no little to the immorality of the common Jews" and
he demanded "pure German or pure Hebrew, but no hodgepodge."
(Hebrew was also "purified": the synthetic language into which it had
developed in the Rabbinical tradition, employing components from
various layers of its history of more than three thousand years, was
despised and abandoned by the "Haskalah" writers for the limited but
"classical" and "pure" language of the Bible.)

It was not merely a matter of language: Yiddish became the externalized object of Jewish self-hatred. Pressured by a Gentile society,
Jews internalized many anti-Semitic stereotypes, blaming "Jewish"
character traits, mentality, and behavior for their lot among Christian
nations. Moving out of the Jewish towns in areas of minority nationalities and into the centers of the state languages like Warsaw, Vienna,
Berlin, Moscow, London, Paris, Tel Aviv, or New York, masses of Jews
eagerly embraced the new dominant language and culture. In centralized modern societies, speaking Yiddish would have isolated and
stigmatized them. Furthermore, the language seemed to symbolize the
devious, irrational ways of "Jewish" behavior, the ugly, unaesthetic
image of the caricature Jew, and the backward, lower-class existence
of most of its Eastern European speakers. The movement of many
young, bright, and successful Jews away from Yiddish again left the
language mostly with lower-class readers of limited culture and thus
strengthened the vicious circle. In Israel, too, there was an extreme
emotional hatred of Yiddish—the "potato tongue" of the poor, embodying all the weak traits of the subservient and parasitic "Diaspora
mentality"—reinforced by the guilt feelings of a society created by
young people who had abandoned their parents and the world of their
parents in Eastern Europe to rebuild their own lives, the image of the
Jews, and human society itself.

As Joshua Fishman summarized it: "Just as those Jews themselves
stand accused in the eyes of many outsiders of simultaneous but opposite derelictions (capitalism *and* communism, clannishness *and* as-

similation, materialism *and* vapid intellectualism) so Yiddish stands accused—within the Jewish fold itself—of being a tool of the irreligious *and* of the ultraorthodox, of fostering ghettoization *and* rootless cosmopolitanism, of reflecting quintessential and inescapable Jewishness *and* of representing little more than a hedonistic differentiation from the ways of the gentiles, of being dead or dying, *and* of being a ubiquitous threat to higher values."[6]

A grotesque, not to say tragic, footnote to the self-effacement of Yiddish speakers vis-à-vis German was written in the Holocaust. Forced to speak the language of the Master Race when communicating with Germans, Yiddish speakers "germanized," that is, they selected what they thought to be German words in Yiddish and adapted them to a "German" pronunciation; they were thus reduced to speaking a minimal language divested of the expressive vigor of Yiddish, the stylistic effects and subtleties of meaning of its Hebrew and Slavic elements and subtexts, and its idioms and proverbs which depend on those layers. Germanizing Yiddish in ghettos and death camps was a linguistic dehumanization of people reduced to baby-talk or to a grammatical subhuman stammer vis-à-vis the Master Race, whose orders they subconsciously accepted. One is flabbergasted to see how West German courts in recent trials of Nazi criminals (like the Maidanek trials) again reduced the Jewish witnesses to this minimal, mock-language; the witnesses themselves, when faced with their former tormentors, instinctively succumbed to the "higher" language of the "Masters." Even in Claude Lanzmann's carefully documented film, *Shoah*, based on witness accounts, his witnesses automatically accept German as the "culture language" and some of them are reduced to speaking a minimal vocabulary rather than speaking a full-blown Yiddish (which would then be translated, as was Hebrew). When toward the end of the film, a woman sings a Yiddish song from the camps, she rhymes TRERN—WERDEN, Germanizing the Yiddish VERN, which was obviously the original rhyme for TRERN. All this after the Holocaust!

To be sure, there was a vigorous Yiddishist movement counteracting both assimilation and self-abasement. It was celebrated in the famous "Czernowitz Conference" of Yiddish writers and activists in 1908 which freed Yiddish from the derogatory label "jargon," and pronounced it "a Jewish national language." For the first time in its

6. Ibid., p. 3.

long history, Yiddish literature was seen not as a handmaiden to Hebrew but as an equal, even a preferred cultural force; indeed, as the
very justification for having a separate, autonomous culture. Yiddishism, too, was part of the trend that was profoundly critical of the old
ways of Jewish Diaspora existence (for which it usually blamed religion
and "backwardness" rather than language). A network of schools, libraries, clubs, publishing houses, a Writers Union, and scientific academies were established, especially in post-World War I Poland and
the Soviet Union. Its culmination was the foundation of a Yiddish
Scientific Institute, YIVO, in Vilna, in 1925, a combination of a research center and cultural policy institute.[7] Textbooks were written,
terminologies developed, and elitist theatre and poetry cherished.

In the long-range perspective of Jewish history, however, it is clear
that Yiddish culture served as a bridge between the traditional religious Jewish society and assimilation into western languages. Indeed,
Yiddish literature as an institution existed for seven centuries. But for
each individual writer, it was a matter of one (in rare cases, two)
generations. Most Yiddish writers still grew up with some Hebrew
education in a religious environment and their children were already
steeped in the culture of another language.

It is true that Hitler and Stalin destroyed Yiddish culture in its
European stronghold. The Jewish people lost a third of their numbers
but nonetheless survived; the destruction of Yiddish, however, was
total: Stalin killed the Yiddish writers, Hitler killed the writers and
their readers alike. The Yiddish-speaking masses are no more.

But it is also true that the trend of assimilation was overpowering
everywhere, even before the Holocaust. In 1897, 97.96% of all Jews
inhabiting the Russian Empire claimed Yiddish as their mother
tongue. But this percentage has rapidly diminished everywhere: in
Russia and Poland, in France, Canada and Argentina, as well as in
Israel and the United States.

The lot of Yiddish was never easy. For example, the fight for Yiddish in the public schools failed in New York (compare the attitude
toward Spanish in a later generation). Still, in the 1920s, it was impossible to predict that, in the competition between the two languages,
Hebrew, with its base in a tiny community in Palestine, would survive
and become a full-fledged state language while Yiddish, a "World Lan-

7. After its destruction in the Holocaust, the YIVO Institute for Jewish Research
was re-established in New York.

guage," with its mass newspapers and millions of readers, would disappear. For those who wanted to preserve a Jewish culture in a secular world, this was the choice.

There was, however, no free play of cultural choices but brutal historical facts. The attempt to create a modern, cosmopolitan culture in a separate Jewish language, culturally autonomous and steeped in historical values and associations, was doomed to failure. For the writers sensing the loss of their readership, this was an indescribable tragedy.

4

The Semiotics of Yiddish
Communication

*You may have heard charming, appealing, sentimental
things about Yiddish, but Yiddish is a hard language,
Miss Rose. Yiddish is severe and bears down without
mercy. Yes, it is often delicate, lovely, but it can be
explosive as well. "A face like a slop jar," "a face like a
bucket of swill." (Pig connotations give special force to
Yiddish epithets.) If there is a demiurge who inspires me
to speak wildly, he may have been attracted to me by this
violent unsparing language.*
—Saul Bellow, "Him with His Foot in His Mouth."[1]

This and several similar, often quite contradictory, pro-
nouncements by native speakers of Yiddish seem to attribute to the
language a life of its own, a mentality, a set of values and attitudes,
serving as a source of strength and frustration alike. Clearly, the nature
of Yiddish as a vehicle of communication, as a repository of a whole
semiotics of discourse and "world views" of its speakers is an essential
part in the understanding of the language.

1. Saul Bellow, *Him with His Foot in His Mouth and Other Stories* (New York: Harper
and Row, 1985), 16.

Yiddish speakers have always felt that theirs is quite unlike any other language and provides them with a highly charged means of expression. The difference was conspicuous when compared with the rational, well-ordered, and intellectual but detached or bureaucratic language used in post-Enlightenment western societies. Not growing out of high culture and a refined literary tradition but out of a homogeneous folklore world, steeped as it was in irrational discourse, quintessential formulas of folk wisdom, and highly charged intimate family attitudes, the language was suddenly—in the lifetime of one or two generations—confronted with a pluralistic and specialized modern world and with elitist culture. Speakers, making that leap, either despised their "primitive" language or saved from it precisely the unusual, irrational, folkloristic or symbolic elements, carrying over their full semantic weight into the new, "European" context: the very strangeness of Yiddish expressions and gestures when used in another language served as an emotive, untranslatable "spice" for the initiated as well as a substitute for an authoritative "Bible of quotations" for the new texts.

This leap was acutely felt under the conditions of modern Yiddish literature, written in the big cities of Poland or the Soviet Union or even farther, "on the other side of the ocean," that is, removed—or having escaped—from its two sources of vitality: the old religious world and a living folk ethos. In some sense, this condition may be typical of much of modern literature in general (we may think of Joyce writing at a distance from Dublin), but in other languages writers could rely on a rich written tradition of literature, philosophy, and other discursive writings. Yiddish writers on the move carried their "world" in their language.

It was even more sharply sensed by those who lived and wrote in other languages, when only vestiges of Yiddish were left, in Bellow's words, "fragments—nonsense syllables, exclamations, twisted proverbs and quotations or, in the Yiddish of his long-dead mother, *trepverter*—retorts that came too late, when you were already on your way down the stairs" (*Herzog*).[2]

2. Though the text refers explicitly to Herzog's notes rather than to language, there is the implicit metonymical connection to the language of his "long-dead" mother. (Again a metonymy to mother-tongue.)

Language and Social Psychology

Language as such cannot be either "hard" or "delicate" or "explosive," as Bellow's narrator puts it. In the twentieth century, Yiddish has been used for many kinds of discourse, often quite contradictory to whatever might be its "inherent" or accepted nature. This "oral" and popular language has been successfully harnessed to impressionist prose, historiography, linguistic and statistical research, political propaganda, or "ivory tower" poetry. Nevertheless, in social perception, the language did carry a cluster of characteristic features, developed in its unique history and crystallized in its modern literature. The very fact that native speakers may assign such emotive qualities to the language, rather than seeing it as a neutral vehicle for communication, speaks for itself. Let us say at the outset: the bulk of the language and its grammar may be similar to other languages; what marks it as a different medium are special features interspersed by its users, and these are of interest to the popular and scholarly characterization. Rather than providing a regular grammar of Yiddish or an analysis of representative texts, I shall focus on such "characteristic" features.

By the "semiotics" of Yiddish, I mean a second level of language, built above its vocabulary, morphology, and syntax, that is, the "language" of communication accepted by the speakers of a community: how to behave in human interaction, what to say under what conditions, how to initiate a dialogue, how to go on talking, in what terms to observe the world, and how to express briefly an evaluation or an emotive stance. It comprises a whole network of signals, rules of conversation, encapsulated formulas and labels, allusions to codified and richly connotative life situations.

It seems that, in its popular forms, Yiddish internalized and schematized some essential characteristics of "Talmudic" dialectical argument and questioning, combined with typical communicative patterns evolved in the precarious, marginal, Diaspora existence. These became "second nature" to many Jews—their typical mental and behavioral attitudes, conversational manners, or even psychological dynamics— and were transmitted to the next generation quite autonomous of the language itself or of the amount of culture acquired by any given individual. When Bellow writes at the beginning of *Herzog*: "Late in spring Herzog had been overcome by the need to explain, to have it out, to put in perspective, to clarify, to make amends," he describes Herzog's psychological state, but he could have described the semiotics of one mode of a typical Yiddish conversation in similar words. In *Him with His Foot in His Mouth* (as quoted in the epigraph to this chapter), Bellow seems to understand this connection: the narrator's "demiurge" inspires him to "speak wildly," attracted to him by "this violent unsparing language" (which, paradoxically, he does not speak at all).

A variety of such undefined attitudes and patterns of thinking and speech have often marked the behavior of Jews—their "Jewish" features—but were also felt to be strange or offensive by the users of another, dominant semiotics and were suppressed by adaptable Jews themselves.

Thematic Components

The semiotics formed in a certain sociolinguistic culture contains a flexible cluster of attitudes and communicational signs and gestures, including typical features as well as options for contradictory possibilities. Though susceptible to recent influences, it often has a conservative core reflecting some kind of "mentality" and "beliefs" of a national or ethnic society, as codified in a formative period. This conservative core may reflect previous stages of beliefs and attitudes, no longer held by the speakers but turned into a "language" to speak with. Thus, in European languages, the sun still "sets," though, since Copernicus, we believe that the opposite is true. Many primitive or pagan beliefs are incorporated in proverbs or nursery rhymes of Christian languages and now fulfill primarily communicative, emotive, or aesthetic, rather than referential, functions. Bellow's narrator, claiming that "pig connotations give special force to Yiddish epithets" (in the passage quoted above), probably has no particular attitude toward pigs as nonkosher animals, but he feels the "special force" of pig connotations, which combine the negative pole of the kosher tabu system— the very heart of Jewish identity vis-à-vis a Christian society—with the German negative "swine" language, used against the Jews themselves (in the image of the JUDENSAU, "Jewish Sow"). In *Tevye the*

Milkman,[3] Sholem Aleichem has exposed this discrepancy between the attitudes codified in the language and the speaker's present reality, highlighted by the tacit narrator's ironic point of view. Thus, the inferior status of women assumed in the language is inverted in plot by their superior understanding of reality; the lower status of artisans in the language is both exposed and undercut in Tevye's own words: "A man, says I, is like a carpenter: a carpenter lives and lives and dies, and a man lives and dies."

As we have seen, a whole conceptual world and terminology came to Yiddish from the religious domain and was turned into "language," freed from its specific denotations. Even the word "Torah" itself—the name of the holiest book—came to mean, on the one hand, teaching or theory in general and, on the other hand, any kind of practical knowledge, from cooking to teaching a child how to tie his shoelaces. This was a secularization not in the sense that the speakers abandoned religion but rather that they expanded religious terminology to non-religious domains as well, using the intensity or emotive force of the expression and neutralizing its religious denotation (which, of course, could be revived in a specific context). In the terms of its own speakers, it used the "Sabbath" language to serve the everyday life of the "week-days." Yiddish had no religious obligations, as the "Holy Tongue" did, and thus it could perform such a secularizing function.

Similarly, customs of religious behavior, texts of holidays, and analytical methods of scholarly inquiry permeated Yiddish as part of its semiotic system. You did not have to know Hebrew to use a Hebrew quotation; you did not have to be a "scholar" to exhibit an analytical or "philosophical" attitude or to be inquisitive or critical. All such absorbed attitudes and "folk wisdom" became decontextualized, much as folklore in general (according to Jakobson and Bogatyrev[4]) neutralizes the individuality of a poem's individual author and the particular circumstances of its creation.

Furthermore, in accordance with the open and multidirectional nature of Yiddish as a fusion language, it adopted pieces of beliefs and expressions from other cultures and melted them all into one system. The Vilna marketplace curse, KH'VEL MAKHN FUN DAYNE KISHKES A

3. A new translation by Hillel Halkin, entitled *Tevye the Dairyman*, was published by Schocken, New York, 1987.

4. Roman Jakobson and Peter Bogatyrev, "Folklore and Literature," in *Readings in Russian Poetics*, ed. L. Matejka and K. Pomorska (Cambridge, Mass., 1971), 91–3.

TELEFON ("I shall make your guts into a telephone," i.e., I shall twist them like a telephone cord), exhibits the same fusion of cultural domains as the earlier DI KISHKE HOT NIT KEYN FENTSTER ("The guts [KISHKE] have no windows," i.e., guts have no display windows, you cannot see what you have put into your stomach, which means: you can eat any junk so long as you fill your stomach). The coarse, disgusting KISHKE—which combines the coarseness of its Slavic, "peasant" sound (when transferred to Yiddish), and of cheap, poor people's food ("stuffed kishke"), with Yiddish folklore's obsession with problems of the digestive tract—is conjoined with the elegant innovation, the worldly sounding Internationalism, TELEFON. At the same time, the stylistic effect of the worn-out expression, KISHKE, is made strange and refreshed in the new context, while the modern telephone is degraded to the level of kishkes.[5]

The semiotics of Yiddish communication has a stable core captured in the "mythology" of Yiddish folklore and placed in that particular, imaginary world of the "shtetl" which was projected in fiction by the founders of its modern literature and then reabsorbed into the communal consciousness. (The "shtetl" was a small town, predominantly Jewish or having a Jewish area, surrounded by Christian villages and dominated by a foreign power.) The "shtetl" was not the real background of all Yiddish speakers—some lived in villages and most writers and their readers already lived in larger towns or cities—but it was their proverbial, mythological "space," a collective *locus* of a network of social and ideological relationships wrought in the phraseology of Yiddish folklore and literature. Most modern trends of Jewish life, literature, and consciousness pushed away from the "shtetl," abandoned it, despised it, or at least saw it in an ironic or nostalgic light. But Yiddish classical literature used the iconography of the shtetl, its mythological behavior and language, as a microcosm of Jewish nature: such are the images of Mendele's Kabtsansk and Sholem Aleichem's Kasrilevke. In a sense, this parallels the use of orthodox Jewish figures and religious symbols as "Jewish" iconography in paintings and sculptures by Max Weber, El Lissitzky, Chaim Gross, or Marc Chagall, though the artists themselves were not "Jewish" in their external appearance. This collective imaginary space was supported by a peculiar

5. This may be used in continuation to (and may have been transformed from) such expressions as KH'VEL DIR MAKHN OYS-tsu-DREY-yen; KH'VEL DIR OYSDREYEN DI KISHKES! meaning: "I shall twist you [like a wet floor-mop], I shall wring your guts."

Jewish geography; the Golem of Prague, the merchants and Enlightenment writers of Odessa, the intellectuals of Vilna, the fools of Chelm,
the small seats of famous Yeshivas (Volozhin, Ponevezh) and of Hassidic dynasties (Lubavich, Satmar, Uman') became symbolic places, in
folklore and literature alike.

Yiddish poetry has profusely employed motifs of "Jewish" imagery
as a *store of situational meanings*, as a *language* for expression, even
when the poet was far removed from them ideologically or thematically. Often such motifs may not even carry any overt "Jewish" images.
Thus, Halpern's poem, "What Do We Know, Dear Brothers" (written
when he was associated with the American Communists) employs key
situations from the Bible (the Burning Bush, Moses, Samson, King
David) without mentioning them by name and places them within the
context of a cosmopolitan, "existentialist" perception of his character,
rabbi Zarkhi:

What Do We Know, Dear Brothers

Three rubberbands on a thin tin top
And a pair of glasses looking out to sea.
Maybe it's Zarkhi's longing that weeps—
What do we know, dear brothers.

And maybe it is not Zarkhi that weeps
But a tree that burns and isn't consumed,
Weeping with branches as if they were arms—
What do we know dear brothers.

And maybe it is not a tree that weeps
But the silent lament of an eye and a hand
Of a man dying at the threshold of his land—
What do we know dear brothers.

And maybe it is not a man that dies
But a blind giant a thousand years ago
Weeping over his shorn hair—
What do we know dear brothers.

And maybe it is not a giant that weeps
But the simple silly instrument
Weeping under Zarkhi's aging hand—
What do we know dear brothers.—AYP, 428

With time, however, as "Jewish" concerns became more predominant in Yiddish literature—especially after the Holocaust and the establishment of the State of Israel—what had been a mere "language"

could easily be inverted and turned into *theme*. Yiddish poetry was suffused with motifs from Jewish religion and history serving largely as authentic imagery for the expression of universal human experiences. Now the poets and their readers could invert that relation and read the imagery as thematic evocation.

Sociologically, the "world" of Yiddish as we know it today—its thematic networks codified in language—was an unusual phenomenon. In one tangled web, it combined semiotic elements of the most prestigious group in medieval Jewish society, the "scholars," as they were absorbed in daily communication (what folklorists call "gesunkenes Kulturgut," "sunken cultural treasures"), with elements from the life of the impoverished masses of Eastern Europe in the nineteenth century. The appeal of the latter was reinforced in the romantic idealization of the "people" and their authentic vitality by the post-Herderian, folklore-loving Jewish intellectuals. The Jews in medieval Europe were inherently and nominally (though not actually) a classless society, since they were a "quasi class" unto themselves in the feudal class structure. Within Jewish society, there was no formal caste barrier for social, intellectual, or economic mobility and the poor shared with the rich the same conceptual world. All of them were aristocrats of God, "the Chosen People," any one of them could, in principle, reach the highest levels of learning and prestige.

Thus, Yiddish folklore exhibits a unique combination of attitudes from a socioeconomic lower class with those of an intellectual elite. The Jews were poor but, at the same time, they were, in their own eyes, a fallen aristocracy of the mind, conscious of their history, of their mission, and of ideological attitudes in general. This is why it was relatively easy for a Jew of lowly origin to rise to the highest levels of general society and culture: mentally, he did not have to overcome vertical class barriers (provided he overcame the horizontal religious fence). And this is also why sincere anti-Semitic revulsion toward Jews involved objections to their behavior rather than to their intellect.

Therefore we should not be amazed that the best Yiddish poets of the "Young Generation" in New York were simple workers: Mani Leyb was a shoemaker, Landoy a house painter, Leyvik a paper hanger, Halpern a poverty-stricken jack-of-all-trades. These were not traditional proletarians who turned to writing. They read and discussed the poetry of Pushkin, Blok, Rilke, Hofmannsthal, Baudelaire, Verlaine, and Rimbaud and published translations of their poetry as well as those of Chinese, Japanese, or Indian poets. Shoemaking was merely a necessity; after all, a poet had to make a living, and professorial jobs were not available. Socialist ideology enhanced the poet's pride in being a real shoemaker which, along with tailoring, had been the most despised profession in Jewish folklore. In the minds of these poets, as in the folk consciousness of the East Side Jews in general, being proletarian and poor was a transitory stage, a temporary necessity brought about by the hard course of history, while aristocracy of the mind, ambition to achieve the highest intellectual standards, was inherent in being Jewish or—as they would insist—in being human (whether this goal was actually realized or not is another matter). This is not unlike the theory of the split mind as perceived in Hassidism: while half of one's mind is steeped in the dark of everyday work and worries, the other half should be kept separate, rising high, unifying with God.

Hence the strange combinations we find in the Jewish lower classes (often, in the mothers and fathers of scholars and writers) of semi-illiteracy on the one hand and admiration for learning and for "higher" matters on the other. That is why the same popular Yiddish newspapers that carried melodramatic stories of love, divorce, hardship, and success also published translations from world literature, articles on Spinoza, poems by Leyvik, and novels by Isaac Bashevis Singer. And why a starving Jewish population of London's Whitechapel in the beginning of this century could support a Yiddish journal with the significant title *Germinal: Organ of the World Anarchist Organization*, with contributions by Kropotkin and other ideologues, as well as Y. Ch. Brenner's journal, *Ha-Meorer* ("The Waking Bell"), which launched a new, individualistic stage in Hebrew literature.

At the same time, Yiddish folklore preserved the memories of an earlier age, when there were fewer Jews, many of whom were occupied in trade, in changing and lending money, and in traveling. Trade—symbolizing the mediating function of the Jews as well as their mobility—is almost as much of an ideal in Yiddish folk-consciousness as is learning. Selling shoelaces or apples or peddling in the countryside was considered a "natural" Jewish way of life and could—and often did—lead to a better life; keeping a tiny store was considered more prestigious than any artisan craft. The popular lullaby goes: UNTER YANKELES VIGELE/ SHTEYT A KLOR-VAYS TSIGELE./ DER TATE IS GEFORN HANDLEN./ ER VET BRENGEN YANKELEN/ ROZHINKES MIT MANDLEN. ("Under Yankele's cradle/ stands a pure white kid./ Papa went traveling, Papa went trading./ He will bring for Yankele/ Raisins and almonds.") Travel, trade, communication with strangers, observation of differences between social and religious groups, their habits and languages, and the irony of such juxtapositions are basic to Yiddish folklore.

And so is the uniqueness of the Jew, his suffering in history and his difference from others. Though modern Yiddish literature often resists them, ethnic distinctions are still engraved in the language. A woman is called *a Jewess*, a person is called either *a Jew* or *a Goy* ("Gentile"). Since the image of the "shtetl" implies a Jewish center surrounded by villages with their peasants coming to the Jewish market in town, "*a Goy*" often simply means a peasant. Stereotypically, he may be seen as ignorant, coarse, or drunk; but he may also be endowed with enviable physical and spiritual health. A Christian girl is called "A SHIKSE," which may carry either the negative connotations of "a loose woman" or the positive ones involving the attractions of real, sincere, and physical love. Modern Yiddish literature as a whole tried to invert this relationship which had become fossilized in the language, though it still resorted to terminology reflecting the point of view of an ethnocentric Jewish observer. Such language is used, for example, in Halpern's famous poem, "Zlochov, My Home," a scathing attack on the ethnocentric shtetl and its ugly Jewish behavior (see AYP, 408–11).

Structural Components

Several basic conditions of its history have influenced the nature of Yiddish discourse. One essential fact is that, in a book-oriented society, Yiddish was primarily a language of conversation. Yiddish sentences are replete with gestures of a speech situation. They contain a variety of devices to stress the casual nature of speech, to attract the listener's attention, and to express the speaker's evaluative postures toward the contents of his narrative. Even scholars like Max Weinreich use dialogue markers in their scholarly monographs. Since there was no tradition of Yiddish philosophy or systematic treatises (and very little in Hebrew) and nothing comparable to a Latin syntax to influence Yiddish with written and formal rigor, descriptions in Yiddish tend to be presented not in the form of objective exposition but are imbued with the speaker's attitudes. Positive objects or events are marked with positive evaluative expressions (if a child says something clever, the quote is accompanied by A GeZUNT IN ZAYN KE-PELE, "health to his little head"); negative ones are fenced with reservations ("let it be said of our enemies," "may he have such a black year"); members of contradictory categories (such as Jew and Gentile, man and woman, human and animal) are separated by guarding signals (especially: LeHAVDL, "to be distinguished from").[6] It is a language which strongly conveys the emotive attitudes of the speaker toward the contents of his message (as Bellow and other English-speaking writers have indicated). And it can do so by spicing its discourse with Hebrew, Slavic, or emotively loaded idioms and expressions, or by interposing brief words or interjections with no independent meaning of their own, such as NU, EPES, TAKE, SHOYN, KHAS-VEKHoLIle, MiSHTEYNS GeZOGT (almost untranslatable: "so," "something," "indeed," "already," "God forbid," "in a manner of speaking"), or simply by substituting SHM– for the initial consonants of any noun to deride it, as in BOOK-SHMOOK.

Since Yiddish was primarily a spoken language, the forms of its folklore genres are usually brief. Long forms of discourse were kept for learning, preaching, and argumentation. As we have seen, however, the long forms of most Hebrew texts used in Ashkenaz had no sustained logical or narrative structures of their own and were rather parasitic on primary (or secondary) texts. The major genres of Hebrew writing and formal discourse in Ashkenaz were either commentaries, that is, written or spoken on the margins of some other, established text; or sermons, that is, starting from a quote or the weekly reading of the Bible and shifting, through story, allegory, and parable, to a topical or moral issue and then back to the next quote from the original text.

Typically, such religious and moral discourse—and Yiddish conversation deriving from it—advances not in a straight line, through affirmative statements or the logic of a problem presented in a hierarchical argument, but through many kinds of indirect or "translogical language" (to use Philip Wheelwright's term in *The Burning Fountain*): asking a question; challenging a claim; looking for a counterargument or an alternative possibility; answering with an example, a simile, or an analogical situation; illustrating a point by telling a story, an anecdote, or a parable; quoting a holy text or a proverb; posing a

6. This was richly described in James A. Matissof's *Blessings, Curses, Hopes and Fears: Psycho-Ostensive Expressions in Yiddish* (Philadelphia: ISHI, 1979).

riddle; telling a joke; leaping to metalanguage and metadiscourse and pondering on the language used and on the purpose of the whole conversation; punning on words; digressing into pseudo-etymology; and shifting, by association of language, from any of those to another topic. These are not the metaphors favored in the Western tradition, but their impact is as powerful as that of any translogical language in poetry or myth. The value of metaphor lies in the semantic interaction between two small units of discourse, two disparate frames of reference, and the surprises and effects of that encounter. Here, the encounter between two distant frames of reference is not metaphorical, but the freshness of the surprise and the semantic interaction are as effective. A special kind of indirection, encoded in the structure of Yiddish idioms, presents an extension of a hypothetical situation which might embody the issue at hand. The common expression: "Was your father a windowpane maker?" implies: "Did he make you from glass?" hence: "Do you think I can see through you?" instead of the direct "Why are you standing there and obstructing my view?" Halpern loved this form of *hypothetical* or *analogue situation* as a substitute for poetic metaphor.

All these modes of translogical discourse common in Yiddish communication have three major principles in common: (1) associative digression; (2) resorting to a canonized textual store; and (3) assuming that all frames of reference in the universe of discourse may be analogous to each other.

Yiddish has embraced all these forms of speech. Its folklore is fond of short units—rhymed proverbs, idioms, anecdotes, jokes, "stories," and tales of great men—embedded in longer discourse; they may be ready-made and quoted in conversation or made up ad hoc from material of personal experience or imagination. When Martin Buber excerpted such stories from Hassidic books and popularized the Hassidic world in the West, he lost the double-directed tension between the embedded story and its free-flowing, talkative, and moralizing framework; that is, he sacrificed the impurity of the text to the isolation of an "aesthetic" object, imitating Oriental rather than Jewish genres. In Yiddish storytelling—and in the Hebrew form in which it was recorded—the tale was not an abstract vignette or parable of Oriental wisdom but a story situated in the messy Jewish reality and in the library of texts, all at the same time.

In sum, it is not the systematic essay but the concatenation of an associative chain that characterizes Yiddish discourse and its Hebrew sources. This mode of discourse was captured by James Joyce in the characterization of Bloom and is typical of Bellow's writing (in both cases, this style is motivated by modern psychological theory). In this mode, the small units of language and thematic motifs are not strung on one narrative string and made subordinate to the unfolding of plot or an architectonic structure, but are relatively independent and episodic; they can easily relate to their contextual neighbors in several directions and, more important, they are related to a total universe of discourse outside the particular context. That is, they become emblematic or symbolic. At the same time, such a unit clashes with and relates to its discontinuous neighbors, creating mutual reinforcement, semantic density, stylistic play, and irony in this tangle. Mendele and Sholem Aleichem understood and foregrounded this property of Jewish discourse; they used it as a major tool for characterization, for providing symbolic dimensions to any trivial incident related by their naive characters, and, above all, for the composition of their quasi-"medieval" but actually protomodernist prose.

Poetry is a different matter. Modeling its language on Russian and European examples of "pure" symmetrical and monologue-oriented strophic verse, Yiddish poetry avoided, at first, this rambling, "unstructured" and "undisciplined" dialogue-oriented discourse. However, poets like Jacob Glatshteyn, whose work was closer to the "dramatic monologue" from the beginning, and Moyshe-Leyb Halpern in his later poetry, broke the symbolist poetic conventions of "conciseness" and symmetry and discovered the possibilities inherent in Yiddish communication, in what Glatshteyn called "the wise prosaic smile of Yiddish." They used Yiddish as an unusual tool of *talk-verse*, which may be as fresh, effective, and surprising as the language of metaphorical imagery in Western verse (though perhaps less familiar to its readers). Naturally, the reader has to imagine the character who does the talking, to reconstruct him from his speech, as in the fiction that the Russian Formalists called *skaz*. The talk and the inverse characterization of the talker create a double-directed semantic dependence, further ironized by the narrator or the poet standing above the text. Talk-verse is often a dramatic projection of the poet's voice, as in Glatshteyn's cycle of monologues by Rabbi Nakhman of Bratslav. Moyshe-Leyb Halpern raised this art—almost to a parodic degree—in his long, aggressive, and politically charged monologue to himself (with his year-and-a-half-old listener), "This I Said to My Only Son at Play—and to Nobody Else" (AYP, 490–505).

Associative talking—a national sport in Yiddish—is a long, exuberant, and rambling affair. To its participants, it is a joy too. When Glatshteyn's Rabbi Nakhman of Bratslav turns up in heaven, losing all his words, he complains: "What will you do from now to eternity?/ No tales, no melodies./ Poor soul, you are naked./ You are a mute in heaven." Eventually, he awakens from his dream, is back on earth and says: "May I be damned if I'd like/ To sit on a heavenly rock./ Here, in the sinful world—/ To talk and talk and talk" ("Hear and Be Stunned," AYP, 293–97).

Precisely because it is devoid of clear-cut narrative structure or metaphorical density, the value of such associative talking lies in the many "asides" it can have. Anything may be linked with anything else. From every situation, one can shift to another situation which does not explicitly relate to the problem at hand, but is rich in new experiential detail. In principle, every chain developed in a text may link it with the whole universe of discourse. Thus every trivial anecdote may attain "metaphysical" dimensions. Indeed, the principle of universal analogy, derived from "Talmudic" thinking and domesticated in Yiddish, is typical of Freud's method as well.

Two major devices puncture this discourse: the ironic interplay between the component-languages of Yiddish, employing its double nature of *fusion* and *openness* (as described above) and the abundant use of quotations, proverbs, and idioms. Both quotations and proverbs subsume the case at hand, the individual and concrete situation, under some general law or some distilled wisdom, using the authority of a holy text or of a folk convention. It was a highly codified society and it used codified situations and evaluative "bricks" of experience to describe the world. Anecdotes, quotations, and proverbs also provided a tactic of evasion: in a bind, or in a puzzling situation, instead of answering specifically, there was a ready-made phrase or exemplary "story." Tevye the Milkman, that quoting animal, evades the direct response to any new event or question by referring to an existing "holy" text or proverb. He thus subsumes every experience under some universal "way of the world," turning any trivial detail into a "philosophical" issue about the order of the universe and God's reason.

Sholem Aleichem's Tevye the Milkman

Let us observe one complex example of such Yiddish speech as registered by Sholem Aleichem (1859–1916). His book,

Tevye the Milkman,[7] is constituted as a series of monologues by the main character who tells the narrator how his daughters left home for a tailor, a revolutionary, a Christian boyfriend, a rich man, and so on. The chapters represent the various solutions of centrifugal movement of Jews out of the shtetl world, which Tevye's beloved daughters implemented, breaking their father's heart in the process. As Victor Erlich has pointed out, these are monologues in a dialogue situation: though the listener, Sholem Aleichem himself, never speaks, Tevye fills his monologues with devices to catch his listener's attention or to counter his possible arguments: "How did we get to this point?" "And as to what you say: children nowadays" (Sholem Aleichem, of course, did not say anything); "In short, let us leave alone—how do you say it in your books?—the prince, and deal for a while with the princess" (which actually has nothing to do with Sholem Aleichem's writing, in which there are no princes or princesses).

This monologue in a dialogue situation has embedded within it a second level of dialogues. Events are not presented directly, but through Tevye's rambling, roundabout associative chains telling not about events proper but about other, similar dialogues in the past; often those embedded dialogues are themselves arguments about hypothetical situations in which the speaker imagines a happy outcome for an imminent event, and the dialogues ensuing from it, and then is surprised by an unhappy outcome, or vice versa. Sometimes there are even hypothetical arguments about such hypothetical situations. This is not just a literary structure of a frame story with embedded stories; rather the embedding is intertwined in every sentence and phrase, often by constant interpolations of "says I," "says she," "says I." This double network of dialogues provides ample room for the internal narrator's (Tevye's) meditations, quotations, and metaphysical and meta-discourse remarks, and for the overall narrator's (Sholem Aleichem's) distancing and irony. Unfortunately, this double-layered mediation of talk gets lost in any dramatization of the book which presents the "events" themselves. What remains in that case is the sentimental internal story alone, as in the film *Fiddler on the Roof*, or in some translations that subdue the mediating dialogue and foreground the internal dialogue as a scenic presentation.

---

7. See my Hebrew paper, "Deconstruction of Speech: Sholem Aleichem and the Semiotics of Jewish Folklore," in: Sholem Aleichem, *Tevye the Milkman and Other Monologues* [in Hebrew] (Tel Aviv, 1983).

This ironic interplay and multidirectional prism breaks up the events and situations into small splinters reflected in talk and, reciprocally, reflects rather than describes them. At the same time, the book is a parody of a world based on talking and of a culture steeped in quotations and commentaries of texts rather than in facing realities. When a wave of pogroms sweeps Russia, Tevye refers to it with his typical historiosophical complacency: "when the time came *to talk* about pogroms" (my emphasis).

Let us take a specific example in its complex entanglement. The chapter "Tevye Goes to Eretz Israel" begins with the following associative chain: after years of not having seen him, Tevye meets the writer again, not in Boyberik but on a train, is amazed to see him alive and, in turn, introduces himself: can Sholem Aleichem recognize him?—Tevye is dressed in a festive coat—how come?—He is going to the Holy Land—Why such an ambition?—A long explanation follows. I shall use, as far as possible, a literal translation to convey a sense of the original:

In short, I must tell you, first of all first-of-alls, that I was left, may it not happen to you, a widower, my Golda, may she rest in peace, died. A simple woman she was, with no tricks, no big headlines, but a great saintly woman, may she intercede there for her children, she suffered enough for them, and perhaps because of them she left this world, couldn't bear that they were all scattered, one to Lissy one to Strissy.

In the first sentence Tevye says: "I was left a widower" and explains: "my Golda died"; what follows are either explanations on the mode of the discourse ("I must tell you," "first of all first-of-alls"), or evaluations ("may it not happen to you," "may she rest in peace"). The second sentence is a mere unfolding of the last formula, with Tevye saying good words about the deceased in a traditional manner (that the deceased was a modest person); then superseding his statement with its opposite ("but"); then using the new quality of saintliness to ask her to intercede in heaven for her children (still a formulaic move); then explaining the opposite (that she suffered plenty for them); and thus shifting back to reality and de-automatizing the formulaic style. A statement in five words, "I was left a widower," has thus acquired a chain of embellishments in the irrational folk manner of talking but in the process has introduced a whole tangle of essential motifs.

Thus, in one paragraph, we come from the meeting in a train, to a voyage to the Holy Land, to Golda's death, to her simple and good nature, to a conversational formula used for the deceased (a plea for her intercession for her children), to an aside de-automatizing this formula ("she suffered enough for them"), to her children having left home, to Golda's complaint that her life makes no sense without the children. In response to this, Tevye argues with her in his usual way, quoting some pseudo-holy phrase, thus raising the personal issue to a matter of the order of the universe and then explains it in his own words. The two levels of dialogue—present and past—which intersect with each other are foregrounded by the frequent use of "says I" in one breathless chain:

"Eh, I says to her, Golde dear, there is a verse, says I, *"if as sons or as servants"*— as it goes with children, so it goes without children, I say. We have, says I, a great God, says I, and a good God, and a strong God, says I, and nevertheless, says I, may I have the number of blessings as the number of times The-Master-of-the-Universe, says I, comes up with a piece of work that better, says I, that all my enemies should have such a year".... But she, may she forgive me, is a female, so she says: "You're sinning, Tevye. You must not, says she, sin." "Look at this new thing, says I, did I say something, says I, bad? Would I, says I, go, God forbid, against the ways of the Lord, says I? Because if, says I, He already, says I, created such a beautiful world, says I, that the children are not children, says I, and father-mother are mud, says I, so He probably knows what He has to do." But she does not understand what I say and answers me out of the blue: "I'm dying, says she, Tevye, who will cook your supper?"

As usual, Tevye leaps from the concrete issue of their own children's dispersion to a general "philosophical" statement about children (a poor excuse, though an escape into language), and from "philosophy" to "theology," ruminating about God who thus arranges His world. The sentence about God, broken up after every few words by the second level of dialogue ("says I"), begins with formulaic blessings ("we have ... a great God ... and a good God, and a strong God") and breaks into their opposite, using the slang and curses of artisans. Golda climbs one level higher, to a metadiscourse about the permissibility of referring to God in such a manner. Tevye retells it in the present with a further level of metadiscourse, explaining that her talk is that of a woman and, on an additional level, asking forgiveness for even using the expression "female" in conjunction with male talk ("but she, may she forgive me, is a female"). But, Tevye adds, in the dialogue in the past, she understood nothing and, "out of the blue" (in Yiddish: "out of the attic"), she inserted such a mundane matter as her death. Indeed, true to her feminine role, she brings down the discourse from textual citations and "theology" to concrete detail: "Who will cook your supper?" The super-narrator, Sholem Aleichem, thus inverts the relationship between who is and who is not sticking to the point and, at the same time, through a subtle shift, brings us back from several levels of deviations and metadiscourse to the real issue: Golda's death.

The whole chain of associations is accompanied by several levels of metalingual remarks and evaluative interjections accompanying almost every expression ("may I have the number of blessings as the number of times," "better, says I, that all my enemies should have such a year," etc.). Thus, an incident is presented not through a realistic description but through talk about talk about it, in the course of which the incident itself and the ways of talking are linked to the metaphysical questions of human existence which preoccupy our hero and are conveyed in the manner of Yiddish folklore with quotes, generalizations, blessings, and proverbs—all de-automatized—and with metadiscourse about the ways of talking about such things.

This concatenation may be represented in the following simplified diagram. In the left column, we climb with Tevye, in an associative chain, until the woman interrupts his chatter; in the right column, he goes down the same steps, this time in brief clauses, until we reach the crucial event.

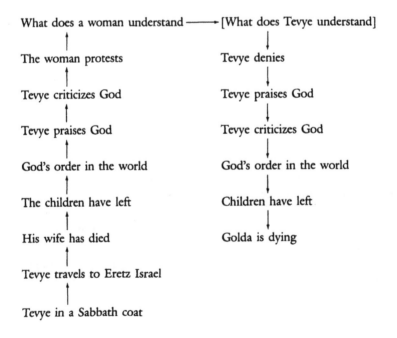

What does a woman understand ⟶ [What does Tevye understand]

↑   ↓

The woman protests   Tevye denies

↑   ↓

Tevye criticizes God   Tevye praises God

↑   ↓

Tevye praises God   Tevye criticizes God

↑   ↓

God's order in the world   God's order in the world

↑   ↓

The children have left   Children have left

↑   ↓

His wife has died   Golda is dying

↑

Tevye travels to Eretz Israel

↑

Tevye in a Sabbath coat

The associative chain is Tevye's irrational mode of discourse. The author himself creates a carefully controlled text in which every element and every order of elements is functional. The second half of this chain mirrors the first half precisely. (As to the unfulfilled symmetry of our diagram, concerning Tevye's travel to the Holy Land, the rest of Sholem Aleichem's chapter will be devoted to explaining that.)

The associative chain of Tevye's rambling chatter thus enables Sholem Aleichem to introduce a whole *kaleidoscope* (to use a key term of the Introspectivist poets) of central motifs omnipresent in the book and his hero's consciousness. Tevye's *kaleidoscopic* visions result from the Yiddish folk ethos in which all things are linked with all things in one, transhistoric destiny, prefigured in the Holy Scriptures, and are compositionally motivated by his "Jewish" way of talking. All these—the kaleidoscope, the folk ethos, and the associative composition—are ironized at the same time. In contrast, as we shall see later, the Introspectivist poets in New York in the 1920s motivated the kaleidoscopic principle by the simultaneity of experience in the stream of consciousness of a modern urban individual.

Halpern's Political Talk-Verse

The New York Yiddish poet Moyshe-Leyb Halpern (1886–1932) uses a similar technique of associative concatenation to present a kaleidoscope of his bitter personal visions, those of an existentialist-anarchist slashing at life in general and at American capitalism in particular, interspersed with coarse curses and surprising *analogue situations*.[8] This technique of shifting to achieve analogue situations instead of metaphors can be seen in such poems as "The Bird Mertsyfint," "He Who Calls Himself Leader," or the two versions of "My Crying-Out-Loud" (See AYP, 451, 447, 467, and 489).

"He Who Calls Himself Leader," one of Halpern's poems of disillusionment with the unions, starts surprisingly:

No one can order his face in advance.
And you should not throw a stone at a dog
Showing its howling muzzle to the night sky.
                    —AYP, 447

8. Ideas on this topic were suggested by Chana Kronfeld in her as yet unpublished analysis of a Halpern poem.

But this particular dog and this particular ugly face belong to a "leader" sitting in a smoke-filled café. A chain of negative situations is evoked, followed by an ode to what leadership should mean, followed again by an evocation of negative situations which are almost casually embedded in subordinated phrases, and only indirectly connected as a negative counterpoint to the description of ideal leadership:

> But even if the man who sits across from me
> Did not remind me, with his talk, of an angry fly
> Buzzing around a pile of shit in the street—
> And even if, while hearing his voice, I could stop thinking
> That it is the evil of the human tongue, which braids words
> Into a rope for a brother in the night—
> Would it be any easier for me
> To imagine him in the white robe of a leader?

Subsequently, the white robe, a metonymy for shining leadership, turns into an evil ghost in the night, only to evoke another image of Eastern European folklore: a child scared by a corpse walking from the cemetery to the synagogue in his white shroud at night. For a moment, there is a distancing from the image: "I've never seen a corpse walking around," only to cancel it again by recalling an encounter with a black woman clad in white in the night:

> I searched in the dark
> For a hand, a human face, an eye,
> And what I saw was a snowman with no head,
> A white figure in a field at night
> To scare away the hungry birds.
> I didn't even hear her breathe.
> Only the smell of her flesh—
> Sulfuric acid on rotting meat—
> Brought me to my senses.

He did not buy the "longing, the holiest in life" that she was trading for pennies. But he could still walk away from her into the night whereas here, in the smoke-filled café, "Here I've got friends—/ And I have no place else to go." Thus, through the white robe, a metonymy for leadership, we are led to two drastic images involving white-clad figures: a black prostitute in a New York night and a ghost in a shroud in the world of shtetl superstitions. Unlike Tevye's concatenations, these have no direct relationship to the basic situation of the poem; they do not stem from any set of folk beliefs but from the narrator's own sick imagination. But they have a much stronger relevance to the topic at hand than do Tevye's digressions, for they fulfill the role of powerful metaphors though they ostensibly move in an austere, direct, nonmetaphorical style. These are analogue situations, connected through the reader's consciousness.

In this poem, however, there is still some kind of closure, a return to the point of departure at the end. But in his later writings Halpern increasingly gave up the technique of coming back to the point, a technique repeatedly used by Sholem Aleichem in what are, after all, structured narratives. In Halpern's text, the narrator and the poet are one; the poet will not structure his protagonist's mental chaos. Through his unbridled breaking out in any unexpected direction, Halpern seems to express the sheer accidental stampede of life.

The culmination of this rambling, hard-to-follow style in his late poetry is the long, unfinished monologue, published posthumously from a manuscript, "This I Said to My Only Son at Play—And to Nobody Else" (AYP, 491). Toward the end of the first part of this poem, the speaker, Moyshe-Leyb, in a long, wildly associative tirade, warns his son against war, shifting from invective against the powers of this world and its false Messiahs to the child's play and back. Instead of epithets or metaphors, analogue situations are flashed out, comparing the high and the low, the drastic and the sentimental. Especially effective are the similes which bring something enormous down to the level of domestic detail. In one passage, everything prepares for war:

Forests supply whips and gallows-wood
And flagpoles for a warship that lies at foreign shores
Like an inkstain on a loveletter.

What a peaceful metaphor for gunboat diplomacy! And here is the figure of Christ, hovering, bound to poles, with nails in his hands and "not even a bottle-stopper on his pierced body," his blood not mentioned but reflected in the red sky:

And not merely the cloud above
In the gleam of a city fire—
The bedbug on our bodies, too, is red in the light—
Like the sun at dawn, like measle-sunset on baby-skin!

The miseries of daily life seem to be as devastating—and as familiar—as the grand images of history and class warfare.

The concatenation is endless, leading from one thing to its opposite by comparison, and then to a continuation of the new situation until a new link is sprung on us. Of course, all the links compose one ideological universe, one anti-war pathos and one existential anguish, but there is scarcely any structural backbone or any hard-edged subdivisions between the situations-images chasing each other. Hence, any example that we introduce here must cut something out of its context. We shall start in medias res: On the last page of the first part of the poem, the poet's year-and-a-half-old son is warned against the President's call for war:

And if the President—who is everyone's father, only God knows how—
Should call, let him go first, to see
That sky-plum and hungry-face are blue
In the enemy's country, too!

[. . .] And he can hire himself to a shoemaker.
Ruling is not a craft. It is old-fashioned like a squeak in new shoes.

From here, we shift to the obsolete crowns, which merely keep the sun from bringing light onto our heads, and to the "top hat"—that symbol of the bourgeois in Halpern's poems and George Grosz's paintings—to the following chain:

Yet a top hat will not let through one drop of air—
Thus says medicine,
Which protects even a fly so the spider won't get sick.
Because we need spiderweb for science, as Ceasar's patriot
Needed pork on Jehovah's altar.

Simplified, the chain goes like this: *President* → *crown* → *top-hat* → *theories of fresh air* → *the use of medicine to protect the spiders* → *capitalist science* → *Roman desecration of the conquered Temple in Jerusalem* → *anti-Semitism as a weapon of diverting popular protest.* He continues:

And blood spilt in vain can be diverted to the Hebrews.
All he has to do is wash his hands like Pilate
And at your table eat (if it's the Sabbath) *gefilte fish*,
Which is sweet like guests as long as they are fresh.

The symbolic "washing his hands" like Pilate becomes transformed into the innocent Jewish ritual of washing the hands before eating, which leads in turn to the Jewish dish which Goyim are supposed to love, "gefilte fish." From here—with no thematic justification, out of sheer whim or malice—he inverts the Yiddish proverb, "a guest is welcome like fresh fish, after three days he stinks."

We have thus gone from the President's call for war to his eating fish. But this may be dangerous: he may choke on a bone; and again, in a typical inversion, the chain leads to a positive event: the little Negro, the friend of Moyshe-Leyb's son, will rejoice at the President's death. But the little Negro—like Moyshe-Leyb's son, for whom war is mere play with bottles on the stairs—does not understand a thing; suddenly, Halpern transforms the little Negro's dance with an unexpected stab at the reader:

But he must watch out not to choke on a bone,
This may bring so much joy—that your friend, the little Negro,
Will go dancing. That's how he rejoiced
When they burned his father alive—
Two years ago, as he walked by a bakery, the smell of bread
Struck his nose—and he said "Good-Morning" to a white broad.

A simple, direct description for which we have not been prepared by anything before, leaves us breathless at the end of the poem.

Questions

A whole array of semiotic moves may be said to characterize "typical" Jewish behavior, though none is exclusive to the Jews. Let us examine one such "Jewish" mode, namely starting and advancing a conversation by asking a question and answering with a counter-question.

One reason for asking questions is the need to make contact with strangers on the road, to get acquainted quickly—acclimatized, as it were—to look for allies or for business possibilities. Sholem Aleichem, who was a master at catching and distilling the essence of Yiddish talk, imitated a train conversation between strangers:

—It looks like you're travelling to Kolomea?
—How do you know I'm going to Kolomea?
—I heard you talking to the conductor. Are you really from Kolomea or only traveling to Kolomea?
—Really from Kolomea. Why do you ask?

—Nothing. Just asking. A nice city, Kolomea?
—What do you mean, a nice city? A city like all cities in Galicia. A pretty town, a very pretty town!
—I mean, are there any nice people, rich ones?
(etc., etc.)

—"It's a Lie: a Dialogue in Galicia"

The proverbial riddle asks: "Why does a Jew answer a question with a question?" And the answer, appropriately, is: "Why not?" In reality, however, the answer is even less straightforward: "Why do you ask?" or "Who says he does?" or "Who answered you with a question?" or "Wasn't I the first one to ask?"

Questions have a variety of purposes: to understand the world; to search out information; to avoid revealing too much by passing the ball of affirmative description to the interlocutor; to know one's interlocutor as quickly as possible; to question his motivations for asking that particular thing; to question his general assumptions; to question his assumptions about one's own motivations; beyond that, to inquire about other possible alternatives to the given situation; to question the nature of the words used, that is, to leap from object-language to metalanguage; and even further, to question the reasons and forms of using them, that is, to shift to metadiscourse.

One other obvious source for such a mode of conversation is the Talmudic argument. The structure of the Talmud is not that of an essay or a systematic treatise but a juxtaposition of oral arguments, pro and con, concerning sentences from the Mishnah. The text advances by raising all possible questions and solutions to a problem or interpretation of a legal sentence, calling up quotations from the Bible, reinterpreting those, and arguing out the alternatives. In the learning process, too, the same questioning method is used for the Talmudic text itself, by evoking later writings as well as the holy texts and the student's own ingenuity. Asking questions and questioning the answers is encouraged. The Talmudic term KUSHIYA (or KASHE, frequently used in Yiddish) means a "question" (such as the "four questions" a child asks at the Passover Seder) but, more profoundly, it means: "a difficulty in an argument," "a contradiction." A modern Hebrew dictionary defines it: "a difficult question, a contradiction, an objection to an opinion or to a law with the purpose of proving that they are wrong" (A. Even-Shoshan, *Ha-Milon he-Hadash*, 1988). That is, asking a question is equivalent to questioning, raising a difficult or problematic point in an argument. Indeed, the expression SHTELT

ZIKH A KASHE (literally: "[if so,] a question poses itself:" i.e., "that raises a question" or "One may ask, why . . .") followed by a question is a conventional opening for an explanation, in Talmudic learning as in Yiddish discourse.

Asking questions, raising alternative possibilities to a situation, or questioning the interlocutor's assumptions that such an alternative was comtemplated, was a usual mode of Jewish conversation from early childhood. The very first word in the first sentence of the Bible that a child learned, BEREYSHIS, *"In-the-beginning (God created the heaven and the earth"*), is accompanied by Rashi's commentary challenging God's structure of the text: "He should not have started the Torah other than with 'this month is for you,' which is the first good deed that the Israelites were ordered to do; then what is the reason that He started with 'In-the-beginning'?" As if to begin with "in-the-beginning" was neither logical nor natural!

Via Yiddish, this mode traveled to Jewish behavior in other languages. It is enough to leaf through Henry Roth's *Call It Sleep* (1935), describing a Jewish childhood in New York, to see the hundreds of question marks that cover the text. They serve both the child's curiosity about the world and his mother's "positive" guidance. They also underline the clash between the immigrant mother and the American child. For example:

"You don't seem to be hungry?" she inquired. "You've hardly touched the oatmeal. Would you like more milk?"
"No. I'm not hungry."
"An egg?"
He shook his head.
"I shouldn't have kept you up so late. You look weary. Do you remember the strange dream you had last night?"
"Yes."
"How did such a strange dream come to you?" she mused.
—p. 69

Here, even the affirmative sentences imply questions about possible alternatives: "I shouldn't have kept you up so late."

In comparison, in Joyce's "Eveline," when a Dublin girl is about to leave her home and is pondering: "Was that wise? She tried to weigh each side of the question," there are no question marks in the text, just the evocation of situations to be judged by the reader himself.[9]

9. Asking questions is hardly a universal value, as can be seen, for example, from

Whether the source lies in religious learning, in the precarious Jewish existence—the question marks it raises, or the need for evasive behavior—in the relativism of a marginal group, in the skepticism of a people exposed to bitter experiences throughout the ages, in foreign influences, or in some combination of all of these, a set of attitudes has crystallized and become typically "Jewish," incorporated into typical Yiddish speech. It seems that these attitudes, transferred to secular situations and to other languages, became the basis for what could be seen either negatively as the Jewish "inquisitive" or "argumentative" behavior, or positively as a questioning, "scientific" attitude, challenging any authority.

An example of the latter kind can be found in the story about Nobel Prize-winning physicist Isador Rabi: when he returned from school as a small child, his mother would ask him: "Did you ask any good question in school today?" This is not just encouragement to learn actively and successfully, but a question which prods the child to ask questions.

The negative side of this discourse pattern in the eyes of European behavioral norms was observed in Jewish literature itself. Mendele Moykher Sforim (1835–1917) introduces himself, the persona of the narrator, at the opening of his novel, *The Little Man (Dos kleyne mentshele)*:

What's your name? The first question one Jew asks another, a total stranger, whenever he meets him and stretches out his hand to greet him. It would never occur to anyone that you could respond, for example: "What's it your business, buddy, what my name is? Are we going to marry off our children? My name is the one they gave me and leave me alone. On the contrary, the question, "What's your name," is quite natural. It lies in the nature of things, just like feeling a guy's new coat and asking how much a yard; like asking for a cigarette when a guy opens his tobacco pouch; like sticking your fingers in somebody's snuffbox and helping yourself to a pinch of snuff; like poking your finger into a guy's tub, dipping a greasy handkerchief in it and rubbing your body; like walking up to two people talking to each other, cocking your ear and listening to their conversation; or like throwing a question at someone out of the blue about his business and jumping on him with advice though he doesn't need it at all and can get along without it. Things of that kind and similar things are quite usual. This is the way the world has been since

---

the words of Mr. Betteredge in Wilkie Collins's novel, *The Moonstone*: " 'How do you come to know about the jugglers, sir?' I asked, putting one question on top of another, which was bad manners, I own. But you don't expect much from poor human nature— so don't expect much from me" (Penguin, p. 61).

time immemorial and raising your voice against it would just sound strange, wild and crazy, an unnatural act. Not only in this world but even over there, in the next world, Jews believe that, as soon as you set foot in it, the greeting angel's first question is: "What's your name, buddy?" The angel that wrestled with our father Jacob, even he didn't change the order of the world, asked him right away what's your name. Not to mention a man of flesh and blood. I know very well that as soon as I enter Yiddish literature with my stories, the first question of the crowd will be: "What's your name, uncle?"

My name is *Mendele*! [. . .]

But I can't get away with this. After the first question, Jews really start pouring all sorts of questions on you, like: Where does a Jew come from? Does he have a wife? Does he have children? What is he selling? And where is he going? And more and more such questions, as it is the custom in all the Diaspora of the Jews to ask if you want to appear in public as an experienced man and not a benchwarmer and that it is only human to answer just like you answer "A good year!" to a greeting of "Good Shabbos!" or "Happy Holiday!" I don't want to quarrel with the whole world and I'm ready to answer these questions too, as short and as fast as possible.

I myself was born in Tsvyatshitsh, a small town in the region of Teterivke . . .

Mendele understands that this is as ingrained a mode of communication among Jews as saying "Good Shabbos!" Franz Kafka, in his "Letter to his Father," imitated this mode of pushing by asking:

An admonition from you generally took this form: "Can't you do it in such-and-such a way? That's too hard for you, I suppose, You haven't the time, of course?" and so on. And each such question would be accompanied by malicious laughter and a malicious face.

But Kafka's own writings are filled with the protagonist questioning every move he makes, usually after the fact. And in "Investigations of a Dog," which is but a veiled allegory on the Jewish condition, he brings questioning itself into the center of his investigation and into the center of Dogs' existence. And he does this, again, very often through questions. As the typical Yiddish speaker, he asks questions about asking questions and shifts the questioning to the central existential problem: who am I? Who are we? What is the meaning of our asking questions? Here are a few excerpts from the story:

And all really because of my questions, my impatience, my thirst for knowledge.—*The Basic Kafka*, p. 289

. . . but you are yourself a dog, you have also the dog knowledge; well, bring it out, not merely in the form of a question, but as an answer. If you utter it, who will think of opposing you?—p. 290

To be precise, is it in the hope that they might answer me that I have questioned my fellow dogs, at least since my adult years? Have I any such foolish hope? Can I contemplate the foundations of our existence, divine their profundity, watch the labor of their construction, that dark labor, and expect all this to be forsaken, neglected, undone, simply because I ask a question?
—p. 291

Every dog has like me the impulse to question, and I have like every dog the impulse not to answer. Everyone has the impulse to question. How otherwise could my questions have affected my hearers in the slightest—and they were often affected, to my ecstatic delight, an exaggerated delight, I must confess—and how otherwise could I have been prevented from achieving much more than I have done?—p. 293

Moreover, who but is eager to ask questions when he is young, and how, when so many questions are going about, are you to pick out the right questions? One question sounds like another; it is the intention that counts, but that is often hidden even from the questioner. And besides, it is a peculiarity of dogs to be always asking questions, they ask them confusedly all together; it is as if in doing that they were trying to obliterate every trace of the genuine questions.—p. 297

This penchant for questioning was recognized in psychoanalytic circles as well. Peter Gay quotes Isidor Sadger's talk at the Wednesday Psychological Society in Vienna in 1907:

... the disposition of Jews to obsessive neuroses is perhaps connected with the addiction to brooding—*Gruebelsucht*—characteristic of them for thousands of years.
—Peter Gay, *A Godless Jew*, p. 135

It seems to me that GRUEBELSUCHT here, as pronounced by a Galician Jew, is used not in its German dictionary sense ("brooding") but in its Yiddish meaning, where ZIKH GRIBLEN is almost a technical term for "Talmudic inquisitiveness," the exaggerated tendency to delve deeply, dig and upturn any piece of ground, uncover hidden motivations and alternatives.

To be sure, questioning is merely one of a whole array of semiotic attitudes internalized in Yiddish discourse and in the behavioral patterns of Jews from both the tradition of learning and the predicament and mythology of their historical existence.

PART TWO

Literature in History: Ideology and Poetics

5

The Modern Jewish Revolution

And the migration of my parents has not subsided in me.
My blood goes on sloshing between my ribs
Long after the vessel has come to rest.
And the migration of my parents has not subsided in me.
—Yehuda Amichai, "And the Migration of my
Parents"[1]

Yiddish literature as we know it today is one branch, one expression, of the modern Jewish revolution which evolved after the pogroms in Russia of 1881–82, and which changed the face of Jewish culture and consciousness and the very modes of Jewish existence.

Prelude: The Jewish Enlightenment

To be sure, the processes set in motion by this revolutionary situation can be traced to an earlier time as well. Although the results of industrialization and urbanization affected the traditional Jewish communities later than other medieval societies in Europe, in-

1. Translated from the Hebrew by Barbara and Benjamin Harshav, *Orim*, III, 1, p. 28.

dividuals broke out of the orthodox framework as early as Benedict Spinoza in seventeenth-century Amsterdam. We must remember that, in spite of the slogans of equality raised by the French Revolution, equal rights were not actually accorded to the Jews as individual citizens in England and Germany until the second half of the nineteenth century, and in the Russian Empire, where the largest concentration of world Jewry resided, not until the Revolution of 1917.

Nevertheless, even before full liberalization, a movement of Enlightenment ("HASKALAH," in Hebrew: "education"; from SEKHEL, "ratio") developed among the Jews of Germany and Eastern Europe, centering around the towering figure of a provincial Jew half-legally residing in Berlin, the Hebrew writer and German philosopher Moses Mendelssohn (1728–1786). This movement coincided with the crystallization of modern German bourgeois culture (Mendelssohn was one of its founding philosophers); it was encouraged by the processes of centralization in the Austro-Hungarian Empire, and was later influenced by the social ideologies of the Russian intelligentsia in the second half of the nineteenth century.

The naive beliefs of the Jewish Enlightenment—that equality would be achieved through internal reform of Jewish life and the modernization of the individual—included the drive to join European culture by learning proper German or Russian, becoming intimate with the literature of those languages, studying science, and acquiring Western aesthetic norms in literature as in daily behavior. "Beauty" and "learning" seemed to be keys to acceptability in the world. Hebrew poetry in the lofty biblical language could serve as a vehicle for both. But, seen from a social perspective, Hebrew was only a transitional tool, its *Haskalah* literature a mere side-effect, an internal reflection of a more general tendency of "enlightenment" and cultural assimilation increasingly implemented in the small Jewish communities of Western Europe and in the centers of power of Eastern Europe. As many saw it, the real road to equality led through entering the dominant Christian society. Individual Jews assimilated or converted to Christianity and entered the Gentile economic, political, and cultural structures. Individual Jews built Russian railroads and German banks and increasingly became prominent in European societies. Some were divided between the two worlds; thus, Aba Konstantin Shapiro (1839–1900) converted to Christianity, became a high-society photographer in Petersburg, and then wrote heart-rending Hebrew poems on love, the role of the poet, Jewish historical figures, and the destiny of the Jews.

The *Haskalah* movement initiated a new trend in Hebrew literature in Central and Eastern Europe (about 1780–1880), employing European literary genres, especially in verse, and in some respects continuing the tradition of secular Hebrew poetry developed in Italy since the Renaissance. Simultaneously, the beginnings of a modern Yiddish literature emerged. When modern Hebrew and Yiddish literature came of age, around 1890, they grew out of the literature of the *Haskalah*, though they transformed it entirely.

The Enlightenment itself, however, touched only the surface of Jewish society in Eastern Europe. Politically, its literature was by and large naive, simplistic, and rhetorical, and did not confront any deep human concerns. The rapidly multiplying and impoverished masses of Jews were kept as in a prison in the densely populated small towns of the "Pale of Settlement" in the western parts of Russia. Jews were expelled from the villages; schools and universities were barred by a severe *numerus clausus*; entering the Russian proletariat was practically impossible. When the same territories had still belonged to the great Kingdom of Poland and Lithuania, Jews had, on the whole, fulfilled a mediating role between the landed aristocracy centering in Crown Poland and the peasant population of the Ukraine. When, however, the Polish head of this triangle was cut off and the number of Jews grew immensely, they lost their economic function and the basis of their existence. The beginnings of industrialization in Russia—from which the Jewish masses were excluded—dealt a further blow to this alien and superfluous population.

In a sense, modern anti-Semitism fed on an unresolved aspect of the disintegration of the medieval Polish empire. Galician Jews pushing into Vienna (where Hitler formed his early impressions), "Ostjuden" percolating into Berlin, Jews from the "Pale" infiltrating Russian capitals—everywhere evoking hatred for their lack of a "decent" profession, or for competing with the professions of others, and for their strange manners and accents—were all manifestations of an attempt to an obsolete socioeconomic and ethnic position.

Defeat and Victory of the Enlightenment

In March, 1881, the Russian Tsar Alexander II was assassinated, a wave of Jewish pogroms was unleashed in the south of Russia, and the Enlightenment was shattered. The *Haskalah* writers were shocked by these events, unforeseen by their naive beliefs in liberalism and progress.

Indeed, as all textbooks proclaim, the *Haskalah* as a literary trend was over. But its triumphs were just beginning to materialize in actual life. The principles of the *Haskalah* were put into effect not just by the few, the rich or the educated, but by millions of Jews. These can be summarized in three slogans: *learning, aestheticization,* and *self-realization* as avenues to finding a place in the world. These principles were internalized in the mentality and attitudes of each individual, rich or poor, educated or semiliterate, and have worked as a powerful internal force in the relocation and social mobility of the Jews in the last hundred years.

Learning included learning new languages, "secular" (i.e., Christian) culture, and rational science on the one hand, and on the other, building up a modern secular culture within Jewish society, in Hebrew and in Yiddish as well as in another, dominant language (at first Russian and German, then English and French).

Aestheticization meant changing external appearance and behavior; shaving one's beard and dropping the medieval garb (still worn in orthodox Jewish communities today); suppressing noisy behavior, "excessive" gesticulation, or the disharmony of individually paced prayer in the collective of a synagogue; as well as valuing the "beautiful" in literature and art.

Self-realization meant not relying any longer on traditional communal structures, but "doing it" or "making it" by yourself: learning a trade ("productivization" of the Jews); realizing in your personal life the ideals of Zionism through *hagshama* (i.e., "personal implementation of an ideal" through *aliya,* or as a pioneer in a Kibbutz in Palestine) or of Communism (fighting and working for the Russian Revolution); becoming a city proletarian (in Warsaw, Lodz or New York) as part of a large population that had never before worked at physical labor; operating a grocery store or supermarket in black Harlem, or entering the new and risky areas of film-making or science.

Though, in principle, the trend had begun earlier, we can see the year 1881–82 as a major *watershed in the history of Jewish culture and consciousness,* unmatched, in its results, by anything since the expulsion of the Jews from Spain in 1492, or even since their exile from the Land of Israel two thousand years ago.

As is well known, the shocks were repeated: in the expulsion of the Jews from Moscow in 1891 and from all Russian villages in 1892, in the waves of pogroms preceding and following the first Russian Revolution of 1905 (the pogrom in Kishinev of 1903 assumed mythological proportions), and in the terrible wave of extermination that swept the Ukraine during its struggle for independence from Bolshevik Russia in the crucial year of 1919. The processes launched in 1881–82 were reinforced by these new events, but the basic course can be traced from that year.

There was nothing really new in pogroms against Jews in the Ukraine: Yiddish folklore preserved memories of the massive extermination of the Jews during the national Ukrainian peasant uprising of Khmelnitsky in 1648–49 and of Gonta's pogroms in the late eighteenth century. And there was a "surprising" pogrom in 1871 in the young, very Jewish city of Odessa. The new aspect was rather in the shattered illusions of those who formulated consciousness—the Jewish intelligentsia, who had grasped onto the great culture of Russia and were now frustrated by the hidden hand of the government in unleashing the pogroms. The shock waves were so immense that they undermined all certainties of the Jewish community in Eastern Europe. With secularization in the air, there was also a new sense of daring and dignity which resulted in a whole people moving or contemplating moving from its physical place and social situation.

External forces, both negative and positive, contributed to the historical dislocation of the Jews in the last hundred years: on the one hand, there were persecutions in Russia and, eventually, the Holocaust of European Jewry. On the other, there were possibilities for immigration, equal rights brought by the Russian Revolution and Western liberalism, and the need for new intellectual power in newly opened and fast-developing areas. But the creative achievements of this period and the new position of Jews in the world are due to *the responses from within* to these overpowering conditions. The spiritual forces mobilized by each individual and by collective institutions actively shaped modern Jewish history and determined the place of Jews (or the descendants of Jews) in Gentile society. Immense energies went into these responses: they were personal and collective, centripetal and centrifugal, and crystallized in a whole array of attempts at alternative answers in the realms of culture, ideology, individual consciousness, and action.[2]

2. See my Hebrew paper, "Eretz Israel and the Modern Jewish Revolution," in:

Responses from Within: Literature, Ideology, Migration, Assimilation

What were the responses to history launched by this new realization?

One response was to create an internal cultural alternative both to the obsolete religious culture and to the absolute dependence on beauty and ideas found in foreign literatures. The generation that grew up after 1882 in Russia created and nourished a modern literature in Hebrew and in Yiddish, aspiring to match the standards of the best of European nineteenth-century writing. Though both Hebrew and Yiddish literature had antecedents in previous centuries and experienced a new beginning in the nineteenth-century *Haskalah*, their stature as modern European literatures emerged only in the late 1880s and 1890s and in the first half of the twentieth century. Both Hebrew and Yiddish literature as we know them today are unimaginable without this revolution. All their recovered past history, too, was made possible and reflected through this achieved base.

In this period, too, a new strain of "Jewish" literature developed in non-Jewish languages—from Joseph Roth, Franz Kafka, Bruno Szulc and Else Lasker-Schiller to Saul Bellow and Philip Roth. These works by Jewish authors may be read from two perspectives: either as part of the literature of the language in which they were written, merely using "Jewish" material and sensibilities (much as Faulkner used Southern materials), or as part of a multilingual "Jewish" literature, representing Jewish experiences and attitudes. Integrated into the literature of another language, such works did not remain isolated in a Jewish "ghetto," as was Yiddish literature.

Along with the literature, trends of thought and scholarship emerged in Hebrew, Yiddish, and Russian. On the one hand, they were influenced by Russian intellectual criticism and, on the other hand, they responded to the "science of Judaism" that flourished in nineteenth-century Germany. This trend culminated in the great Jewish Encyclopedia ("Evreyskaya Entsiklopediya") published in the Russian language just before the Revolution.

Nurith Gertz, ed., *Perspectives on Culture and Society in Eretz Israel* (Tel Aviv: Open University, 1988), 7–31.

In spite of many obstacles and with the realization of the failure of liberalism, masses of young boys and girls plunged into Russian secondary education, the highly academic "gymnasium" (mostly as "externs," for only a very few Jews were allowed into the schools themselves). If modern Yiddish and Hebrew literature adopted the norms of European classical writing, it is largely due to this education acquired by its writers and readers alike and the models of high literature they acquired. Many of them went on to universities, wherever they were admitted, mostly in Western Europe.

And if the regime was against them, they would not bow to pressure but would rather strive to change the regime or move out of the country. A gamut of ideologies was passionately argued, especially by the second and third generations that grew up after the great shock, examining the foundations of human society and of Jewish existence in history and offering all imaginable solutions, closely related to the ideologies voiced in Russia and Europe.

Most Jewish political parties were organized in the late 1890s and in the first decade of the twentieth century, clustered around programs oriented toward the future. In addition, many Jews wanted to "change the world" and played an important role in the foundation of Russian political parties. Among the ideologies and parties emerging at that time were Socialists—internally Jewish like the "Bund" or Russian like the Mensheviks, Bolsheviks, and Socialist-Revolutionaries; Anarchists; Zionists, and Labor Zionists (left and right Marxists and anti-Marxists); Territorialists; Folkists, Seimists (proponents of an autonomous Jewish parliament); and Religious Zionists. Later came the radical Zionist right (the "Revisionists"), headed by a Russian poet and journalist, Vladimir Jabotinsky, at one end of the spectrum, and the "Jewish Section" ("Evsektsiya") of the Soviet Communist party, at the other. Even the reaction of religious orthodoxy to these trends took the form of a modern political party ("Agudas Isroel"). Moreover, a whole network of social organizations spread among the people: societies for the promotion of learning, for professional training ("ORT"), for popular health; Jewish school systems, trade unions, publishing houses, public libraries, and so on.

Symbolically, five events occurred within the Jewish world in one year, 1897:

1. The World Zionist Organization was founded in Basel (though an earlier Zionist movement and migration to Palestine, even including quasi-communist ideals, had been launched from Russia in 1881–82).

2. The illegal Jewish Social-Democratic mass party, the "Bund," was founded in Vilna. (In the following year, its leaders helped to organize the Russian Social-Democratic Party which led eventually to the Russian Revolution.)

3. The literary critic and historian, Simon Dubnov, began publishing, in Russian, his *Letters on the Old and New Judaism*, promoting the idea of cultural autonomy as the mode of Jewish Diaspora existence.

4. The "spiritual Zionist" Achad Ha-Am founded in Russia the Hebrew cultural periodical *Ha-Shiloah*, which became the standard-bearer of modern Hebrew literature.

5. The (then Socialist) daily Yiddish newspaper, *Forverts* (*The Daily Forward*), was founded in New York and helped in the absorption of masses of Jews in the New World, enhanced their self-knowledge and self-esteem, and promoted Yiddish literature along with American *engagement*.

As we can see, it took a generation from the earthquake to the formulation of political responses. Young people, who experienced the pogroms in their early childhood, were in their twenties when the political responses took shape. What happened in the interim period? In the 1880s and 1890s, a new Hebrew and Yiddish literature of European stature emerged in Russia. It unfolded a critical but humane fictional panorama of Jewish existence, thus providing a powerful image for the self-understanding, self-criticism, and self-confidence of a new generation, which then joined the political and cultural institutions evolving in 1897 and later.

To be sure, beginning in 1881, millions of Jews responded to the events instinctively. Even before any ideological answers were translated into political terms, hundreds of thousands left their ancient East European homelands and migrated overseas to the United States and, in smaller numbers, to many other countries, including those in Western Europe and Palestine. There had been poverty and fear of persecution before as well but, with the shock waves as a powerful force of social psychology, many enterprising men and families moved with no intention of returning (a trend helped by the introduction of the steamship and the open door immigration policy of the United States). Additional masses moved, whenever possible, from the small towns to regional centers and to what were then considered big cities, within the Pale and outside it, and participated in the general trends of urbanization and modernization. By World War I, a third of the

Jewish population of the "Pale" had left for overseas. At least another third left by the 1930s for the big cities in Central and Eastern Europe and the previously forbidden heartland of Soviet Russia. And many of the young who still remained in the small towns changed their culture and outlook. This was an unprecedented move of a people away from its base. The writers left too: Mendele to Switzerland; Tsunzer, Shomer, Imber, and Sholem Aleichem to America; Brenner to London and Palestine; Agnon, Bialik, Chernikhovsky, Shimonovich and Grinberg to Palestine, Germany, and again to Eretz Israel; Steinberg, Ben-Zion, Hameiri, and Fichman to Tel Aviv; Bergelson, Markish, and Kvitko to Germany and back to Moscow; others to the big cities in Poland and Russia.

Thousands of Jews, especially in Western Europe—where assimilation to the dominant language was firmly established in the nineteenth century—and later in the United States and Russia as well, entered the general culture, the arts, medicine, science, commerce, media, and so on, and often made unique contributions in those fields. Some of them assimilated thoroughly into the dominant culture, some converted to Christianity or otherwise denied or despised their Jewishness; others did not.

It is hard to imagine the psychological struggles taking place in the hearts of individuals who are convinced they have to suppress gestures, questions, even mentality inherited from their parents and to eliminate the first, emotion-laden language of their childhood from their lives. Indeed, this was often a process repeated and divided among several generations: those born ostensibly integrated into the general culture often relived the same dilemmas or suppressed them. We can still encounter in literature that terrible break and the courage of facing it head-on, or the alienation of children from their foreign-born parents who thought they had assimilated into the new language but were still immigrants in the eyes of their own children. The external result of integration, however, may be very successful, as can be observed in contemporary Western societies.

On the face of it, Yiddish writers remained faithful to the language of their parents but they too were utterly alienated by moving to the strange world of the "Goyim," to their amazing literary forms, themes, and ideas—especially so when moving to a world separated from their past by an ocean, to America.

Internal Criticism of the Jewish Existence

Naturally, the specific circumstances in each place and each personal biography may vary greatly. But the various kinds of responses—in literature, education, ideology, migration, and assimilation—had basic foundations in common. Fundamental to it all was a double-directed criticism of the traditional framework of Jewish existence: of its limiting external conditions and of its habitual internal weaknesses.

As for the first, many Jews were in the vanguard of the struggle for equal rights in every society and, alternatively, for the establishment of a State of their own. It was the spiritual and cultural revival—in literature, ideology, and education—which influenced action rather than vice-versa. After the humiliating pogrom in Kishinev in 1903, the poet Ch. N. Bialik wrote a scathing poem in Hebrew (translated by I. L. Peretz and then by Bialik himself into Yiddish) chastising the victims for accepting the shame and the slaughter. The poem had a major influence on the ideology of self-defense, an attitude radically opposed to the religious tradition of accepting fate and dying passively, as martyrs, "al kidush ha-shem." Groups of "Self-Defense" were organized by Bundists and Zionists which, though illegally armed, diverted or curbed several pogroms and initiated a movement of Jewish "self-defense," soon to be transplanted to Eretz Israel (the Israeli army inherited this term, HAGANAH, in its name, "Israel Defense Forces"). Enormous efforts were also invested in changing the social structure of the Jews through the teaching of practical professions, through developing Jewish agriculture in Argentina, Palestine, New Jersey, or in the Soviet Union after the Revolution, and through struggling to enter fields forbidden or closed to them.

The analysis of the predicament of the Jews as dependent on their typical social structure was suggested in the beginning of the twentieth century by the Socialist Zionist, Nakhman Syrkin, and the Marxist Zionist, Ber Borokhov. Borokhov's views can be summarized in the influential image of an inverted pyramid. Normal nations, according to this image, have a class structure resembling a pyramid: a broad base of peasants supports a wide layer of workers and, only at the top, are there narrower strata of middlemen, merchants, intellectuals, and aristocrats. The Jewish pyramid, however, is upside down: it has a narrow base in the working classes and wide tiers of middlemen and intellectuals. As a triangle standing on its sharp point, any wind can blow it over. This image, of course, matched the Marxist view of the proletariat as the class of the future and the Tolstoyan and similar political views of a healthy nation based on its "productive" classes and attached to the soil (originally, this was the ideology of a society dominated by the norms of a landed aristocracy, which totally over-looked the economic importance of trade and knowledge).

This kind of insight, which undermined certainty about the very foundations of Jewish social and economic existence, had a profound impact on the perceptions and solutions sought in all political direc-tions, and greatly influenced the tendencies for inner revision and change. Most individuals, nevertheless, followed their own impulses, which often went counter to those ideological directions and followed general historical trends toward urbanization rather than agriculture, America rather than Palestine, capitalism rather than communism. As a result, the descendants of the Jews—who for one generation went through a proletarian stage—again occupy, statistically speaking, an unusual, slanted position in society, quite like that described by Bo-rokhov, though one would hope that this is not as dangerous in today's Western world as that Zionist Marxist imagined.

The internal criticism was no less bitter. Ever since the *Haskalah* movement, Jews have internalized many negative stereotypes about themselves. To be sure, some of those could be supported by actual observation of facts, whether caused by external pressures or not, whether really "negative" or only viewed as such through "moralist" and "Western" lenses. Much of the self-criticism can be seen as a trans-lation of the modern change of norms—West against East, pseudo-aristocratic bourgeois culture against medieval and lower-class behav-ior—into age-old, grotesque, though sometimes historically founded, anti-Semitic stereotypes. Jewish literature itself has provided unfor-gettable satirical images of such critical, even plainly "anti-Semitic" views, and thus molded the public self-image of its readers. These stereotypes were reformulated by Jews into various forms of ideolog-ical self-criticism and a massive departure from traditional ways through "secularization," ranging from the attempt at rejuvenation in Zionism or internationalist communism to so-called Jewish self-hatred and Jewish anti-Semitism. The changes from medieval and lower-class norms of behavior to upper-class "polite" manners, modern sensibil-ities, and admiration for the arts were telescoped in Jewish society in the lifetime of one generation. What in Europe were class differences was conflated in Jewish society in the biographies of those same individuals. Such transformations encompassed a large part of the nation. This resulted, naturally, in extreme psychological tension and emotional criticism.

The Centrifugal Trend: Not Here, Not Like Now, Not As We Are

The great impulse behind this centrifugal movement— away from the confines of the traditional religious small-town community and its vestiges in mentality and discourse—can be described in two clusters of negative and positive tendencies typical to this stage in Jewish history (though often matching similar trends in other cultures and reinforced by them).

A common denominator of the various alternative trends can be seen in the negation of all or some of the basic coordinates of existence as located in the old community (which was elevated to mythological proportions in the literary image of the East European small town, the "shtetl"). The three basic deictics of language—HERE, NOW, I—from which orientation in the world begins, were put into question. Deictics are crucial linguistic tools: though they carry no lexical meanings in their own right, they relate the semantic material of a text to the speech situation, its place, time, and speaker. It was as if all these new forms of physical and cultural dislocation said, in various ways, in different combinations, and to different degrees: We want to be NOT HERE, NOT LIKE NOW, NOT AS WE WERE.

The "NOT HERE" was expressed in a mass migration movement out of the Pale of Settlement, from Russia to Western Europe and overseas, from small towns to larger towns and cities and, after the Revolution, from the Pale to the East, to Russia proper; in admiration of and attraction to the centers of culture and learning in Russia, Germany, Switzerland, Belgium, and France; or in dreams of a national future in Zion or in some other Jewish territory (as formulated by the Yiddishist "Territorialists").

The "NOT NOW" resulted in ideologies oriented toward the future (socialism and communism) or toward the future as a revived heroic past (Zionism).[3] Even those, like the Bundists and the Folkists, who embraced the fact that the Jews live "here," in the Diaspora, did not mean it in the sense of the traditional orthodox "shtetl" civilization but intended to restructure the "here" entirely, by building a new, secular, urban, "healthy" Jewish culture, with secular Yiddish schools, libraries, a literature, and social and political institutions, as well as by struggling actively for a future of socialism or ethnic equality and autonomy in the larger society.[4]

Of the three deictics, negation of the "I" is the most difficult for a person to accept. The young and celebrated Viennese philosopher Otto Weininger did so, out of a radical, racist anti-Semitism, and committed suicide. Joseph Roth invented for himself a Polish aristocrat who raped his mother. Others solved this dilemma by putting the negation in the plural and, if possible, in the past—"NOT AS WE WERE"—and by translating it in two directions: the suppression of negative "Jewish" traits in themselves and the externalization of the negation, locating it in other Jews or in other ("negative") trends or aspects of Jewishness. While fighting others, they fought the fear of having inherited negative "Jewish" traits within themselves, or of being blamed for them.

This negation assumed a variety of forms, depending on the time and place or on the political or cultural direction chosen. The terrifying predicament of Jewish existence and the immense external pressures fomented tremendous guilt feelings ("It is our fault," "Something in us is rotten" or the admonitions of mothers: "Don't shout like a Jew," "Don't gesticulate with your Jewish hands") which were hard to bear. These were readily externalized and fed the vicious squabbles and hatreds between Jewish parties, ethnic groups, or languages.

---

3. Cf., the Hebrew poet Bialik's vision of a ruin or a spark remaining from a holy fire of a temple in the past, to be revived, perhaps, in the future (or else lost forever).

4. It may be argued that the quest for a "not here, not now" was a typical trait of Romanticism, especially when it is located in an idealized past. In a broad sense, the various trends of the Jewish revolution did feed on a general European Romantic mood reinforced by a Jewish messianic, though secularized, longing for a utopian future society of peace and equality. In Romanticism, however, this was merely a spiritual departure from a firm base, from established coordinates of a territorial society living HERE AND NOW; whereas in the Jewish upheaval, the base itself was undermined. In this respect, it has affinities with the spirit of America, without having a continent at its disposal.

There is a structural similarity between the various ways of externalizing the self-negation, though their targets changed from case to case. German Jews (who had already lived for a generation or two in Berlin or had spoken "pure" German for the last two or three generations) saw the real danger in the disgusting and pushy newcomers from the east ("Ostjuden") who would expose the negative Jewish traits to the eyes of the Gentiles and bring hatred upon them all. A similar pattern was repeated in the relation of Jews of German origin in America to their immigrant East European kinfolk—Yiddish folklore in New York recorded it as "Uptown" versus "Downtown," as recently as the beginning of the twentieth century. Of course, such sentiments were also counteracted by major efforts of aid and sympathy, expressed, for example, in the "Educational Alliance" built by Uptown Jews to educate their Lower East Side brethren, which has produced such artists as Chaim Gross, Jacob Epstein, Raphael Soyer, and others.

A similar mixture of loathing and hatred was common among the new, "Hebrew" society in Palestine toward the "Jews" of the Diaspora who were considered crooked, devious ("Diaspora mentality"), subservient ("sheep going to the slaughter"), parasites living on sheer air (*luft-mentshn*), or wheeling and dealing speculators who perhaps deserved whatever they got ("We told you so!"). The Hebrew language, as the language of proud rejuvenation and independence, was opposed to the despicable Yiddish which symbolized the ugly characteristics of the Diaspora. Furthermore, the "Sephardic" pronunciation adopted in Israeli Hebrew, with its strong, "masculine" stress on the last syllable of each word, was the symbol of virility and determination as opposed to the whining "oy" and "ay" of Ashkenazi Hebrew: RABOTAY, KHAVERIM, LIVNOT, seemed more resolute than RABO-O-OY-SAY KHAVEYRIM, LIVNOYS. With many, the negative image of that Diaspora derived from childhood memories of the persecuted and impoverished shtetl of their parents, and was magnified by the negative fictional images of Jewish literature. There was no realization that the same self-criticism had, in the meantime, led to radical changes—urbanization, aesthetization, a sense of dignity—and to movement out of the shtetl within the Diaspora itself.

Similar distancing developed among the urbanized, "big-city" Jews in Poland and Russia, Berlin and Paris, toward their primitive and melodramatic small-town cousins with their singsong intonations; among Jews who participated in the Russian Revolution and its power structures toward their "petit-bourgeois," semi-"clerical," and "anti-social" parents in the small towns; and among Americanized Jews, already there for five or ten years, vis-à-vis their uncivilized, "green-horn" relatives. "Jewish anti-Semitism" usually found a target outside its own body. This is true not only for the German Foreign Minister, Walter Rathenau (1867–1922), the son of a wealthy and assimilated Berlin industrialist, but also for the young Soviet communist Yiddish poet, Izi Kharik, who admits in a nostalgic poem of 1930 that, during a visit to his old home shtetl, his people called him an "anti-Semite."

Within Yiddish literature, the negative target was often the backward or fossilized and confining religious society, or small-town primitivism, with its lack of culture and worldliness and its irrational ghetto mentality. In turn, Yiddish language and literature were themselves targets of similar prejudices from the outside, by Jews trying to assimilate to Hebrew or to foreign languages.

Naturally, there were also trends that opposed this schizophrenia and sentimentalized the shtetl, Yiddish folklore, and East European religious traditions. This tide grew after the Holocaust, which evoked guilt feelings, fears, and Jewish self-assertion. And there were many combinations and much ambivalence in between. Whether positive or negative, or a mixture of both, such responses reflected the situation in which very real or merely lurking external pressures were translated into irrationally exaggerated internal tensions which seemed to magnify the chasm between Jew and Jew. From our perspective, the unbridgeable alternatives on both sides of the chasm were but different roads of one, multidirectional trend.

The External Context

The centrifugal movement launched by these enormous historical forces released mental and intellectual energies pent up for generations. It was enhanced by external forces (like persecution) and was made possible by changing world circumstances. The opening of new fields in science and communications, the need for intellectuals and technocrats loyal to the regime after the Russian Revolution, the booming American universities in the 1960s—these are but a few examples of meeting points between external opportunities and the internal drive of "Jews" (or persons of Jewish origin) to integrate and make a mark in general society.

The same is true of Modernism: the extremities of innovation and the disregard for tradition which are typical of the avant-garde were achieved more easily by outsiders coming into a society from the periphery. Having no ties to its conventions and social order, the outsiders promoted a new set of norms for the "inside," creating a new "center." Such was the case of Marinetti, who was born in Egypt, achieved recognition in his first stop, Paris, as a French poet, and then came to Italy to dictate the new literary order of Futurism with its radical hatred of libraries, museums, and Latin syntax. The same holds for Picasso, who first won recognition in Malaga and Barcelona and then conquered Paris; for Chagall, who stopped over in Petersburg before becoming a legend in Paris; for Gertrude Stein, a German Jewess from Oakland, California, who received an education at Harvard and became the American Gertrude Stein in Paris; or for T. S. Eliot from Missouri, who became a poet at Harvard and changed the face of American poetry in London. Jews were part of a typical sociological pattern but it was a pattern that fit their historical situation, fed on their internal talents, and made them conspicuous in the general trend.

The intelligence, imagination, inventiveness, and creativity that many persons of Jewish origin have exhibited in the last hundred years (and, to a lesser extent, in the preceding century) were not activated in earlier times on such a large scale. All this happened when Jews entered the rational, intellectual, and organizational framework of post-Enlightenment European culture and science. Within that framework, where merit was bestowed on the achievements of the individual (not without prejudices, of course), they were able to release their abilities and the analytical habits of their minds to the fullest extent.

This is also true of the achievements within the newly founded *intrinsic* Jewish institutions: Hebrew and Yiddish literature, Jewish ideologies, the State of Israel, American Jewish social institutions— all of these became possible in their full stature when modeled on European-American patterns (even when specific or uniquely Jewish connotations were added). The State of Israel is first of all a "State" in the modern European sense of the word, with all the attributes of a state, both positive and negative, and only as such is it, in some respects, a specifically Jewish state. The same can also be said for Modern Hebrew and Yiddish literature.

The Positive Impulse

The imprint made by people of Jewish origin on many areas of the modern world—as well as the internal Jewish culture created at the same time—would not be possible without the positive forces which complemented the negative impulse. As the wide variety of such positive manifestations and the complex cluster of intersecting motivations make it impossible to discuss them fully here, I shall merely indicate a few points.

The freedom of the individual from a set of traditional coordinates and norms in his own background made it easy for him to question accepted theories and knowledge in the general world. He was a self-made man (or the son or daughter of one) and could rethink everything from the beginning. At the same time, in his own eyes he did not come up from a lower caste but from outside the dominant culture, and he had the internal confidence of an "aristocrat of the mind." For many, the force of throwing off the weight of a tradition worked, by inertia, against external traditions as well. This was reinforced by the "Jewish" habits of constant questioning, raising the possibility of alternative answers, employing metalanguage to examine the meanings and validity of words.

A set of other qualities and mental habits—such as alertness, adaptability (what Woody Allen in *Zelig* called "the Chameleon Phenomenon"), irony (developed by people with a pluricultural perspective or those whose language thrived on the margin of several languages), and swift shifting from one attitude to another—was complemented by a deep-seated penchant for theorizing and abstracting. The latter was due to many factors, among them the habit of Yiddish speakers to subsume every individual case under a general principle, moral value, or proverb; as well as the fact that Jews were newcomers to the languages they mastered and learned them not in the dialects of local and concrete speech but in the idealized form of intellectual and literary discourse.

Cut off from the conventions of an overwhelming, normative society and left to his own self-realization, the individual immersed himself in his new world and saw in it the purpose of his actions, a new existential base to hold on to. The negative impulse described above can be seen as a moving historical force, but each individual and each trend found a positive, constructive avenue as well for a new "HERE AND NOW," new existential coordinates for his orientation in the world. He held onto it as a firm base for himself or for society, either in some "Jewish" form or in the general world. Within the frame of reference of this new "here and now" came the effort at creating a new "I," especially if he were a young person on the move to a new place, language, and profession unheard-of by his parents. The words of a Zionist song proclaiming ANU BANU ARTSA LIVNOT U-L-HIBANOT BA—"we came to the Land [of Israel] to build and to rebuild ourselves by it"—are valid for all other modes of this centrifugal revolution. It is no accident that the vast majority of Jewish immigrants to the United States intended to stay there for good, unlike many other European immigrant groups who planned to go back "home."

Yiddish poets in New York, Berlin, or Moscow were not blind to the decline of their language or to the ominous dwindling of their cultural base, but they immersed themselves in tending their own island, in the precision of writing Yiddish verse as if it were the only worthy goal. The same could be said for a handful of pioneers, for example, building a kibbutz in the swamps of the Jezreel Valley in 1920, living in tents, surrounded by swamps, with only 50,000 Jews in all of Palestine and not properly knowing either the new language of Hebrew (which they insisted on speaking exclusively) or the arts of agriculture and warfare they forced themselves to practice; they did this as if building this kibbutz were the only worthwhile goal in life, as if this would save the world, create a "New Hebrew" person and a new human being.

It is important to realize that when a Yiddish poet wrote poetry, it was not an activity in a normal national state with a fully stratified society. He did not have Yiddish schools, universities, philosophers, sociologists, research institutes, police stations, bus drivers, and such all around him. Literature was "everything," it was a substitute for religion and for statehood, it was a State in itself, "Yiddishland"; to abandon it was to abandon the whole culture. Hence the enormous importance of literature in the eyes of its adherents (reinforced by the romantic view of the poet as prophet of a society, acquired from German philosophy via Russian literature) and the desperation of its isolation. To be sure, literature fulfilled that role in conjunction with the Yiddish press and some social organizations linked to the same cluster. But the close relationships of Yiddish writers with the popular press, on which their existence depended, were love-hate relationships: succumbing altogether to newspaper discourse would mean giving up an "elitist" dream of a separate culture; abandoning the press altogether would mean losing a means of livelihood and undermining any road to an audience.

Outlook: The Jewish Revolution and the Period of Modernism

It is intriguing to ponder the parallels and connections between the trends of Jewish history in this past century (1880–1980) and the trends of Modernism in European art and literature which essentially covered the same period. In spite of the obvious difference in the nature of the problem, there was a parallel fermentation and mood. There is, at least, a common historical and ideological background for the antitraditional alternatives and the rapidly changing reformulated traditions.

There were many convergences between these two cultural revolutions. It was natural for "liberated" Jews not only to be attracted to rethinking basic theories and scientific concepts and to be in the forefront of radical scientific changes but to create in the modes of Modernist art as well, as their role in the "School of Paris" and in the "School of New York" shows. And, internally too, it was natural for Yiddish and Hebrew poets, revising an ancient cultural tradition, to be attracted to one or another form of Modernism. But, more profoundly, it is the parallel historical movement that is intriguing. In retrospect, it was, in both domains, a century of radical upheaval of value systems *expressed in modes of communication and orientation in the world*. The focus on language as a medium is central to both trends.

Bialik's first poems, which launched a new era in Hebrew literature, appeared, paradoxically, concurrently with the Russian poet Bryusov's first issues of *Russian Symbolists* in 1892–93, signaling the beginning of the avant-garde period in Russian literature and art. Bialik's was not a Modernist poetry at all, but in a historical perspective we can see its innovative force, residing in the very use of Hebrew for the creation of melodic and personal verse—in the image of Russian poetry—and for the creation of poetic fictions unified by the poet's lyrical biography and autonomous of direct references to the holy texts. Only in retrospect can we see its revolutionary value in Jewish society: it symbolized a self-consciously new literature in a language of canonized texts and commentaries and created the possibility of a secular, "European-type" alternative to an ancient culture. Yiddish poets and such masters of style as Mendele and Sholem Aleichem effected a similar revolution through their virtuoso attention to the aesthetic qualities of the language of art in a colloquial and undisciplined medium.

The period ended, on the one hand, with a sense of achievement. Modernism became classical and the Museum of Modern Art is not contemporary anymore. In the Jewish domain we may list the established State of Israel, the solidified Jewish communities in the West, the Nobel prizes in literature awarded for Yiddish fiction to Isaac Bashevis Singer and for Hebrew to J. S. Agnon, both of whom summarized the vision of the lost Jewish continent in Europe. On the other hand, in both domains, there is a sense of bewilderment, of exhausted possibilities; a partial return to older values, in which the same modes are revived in eclectic combinations; an aggressive conservatism; or a quiet retreat from the whole field. Just as we live in a *post* Modernist period, when Modernism can be more easily studied than embraced— though its achievements are part and parcel of our museum culture— so we live in a *post* revolutionary period of Jewish culture and consciousness. As for Yiddish literature—the great product of this revolutionary period—the very *language* of its innovation is almost a closed book.

6

The Historical Perspective of Modern Yiddish Literature

The Optimist Opening

The new Yiddish literature emerged at the end of the nineteenth century and became canonized as early as the beginning of the twentieth century, when the newly pronounced three "Classics of Yiddish literature," Mendele Moykher Sforim (1835–1917), Sholem Aleichem (1859–1916), and I. L. Peretz (1852–1915), saw their collected works published in multivolume editions.

After World War I, a true mass movement of Yiddish readers and writers carried the day. Great centers of Yiddish literature emerged on the new map: in Poland, the Soviet Union, and the United States, with minor centers in Rumania, Lithuania, Argentina, Eretz Israel, France, England, Canada, South Africa, and elsewhere. Yiddish newspapers, schools, libraries, unions, and theatres spread everywhere. With the participation of artists like Marc Chagall and El Lissitzky, Modernist Yiddish journals were published in Warsaw, Berlin, Paris, Moscow, New York, and other cities.

The early 1920s were the best years for Yiddish poetry, just as they were the heyday of European and American Modernism. Yiddish had no tradition of a high-style literary language or of Latinate verse. The Yiddish language was colloquial, "juicy," expressive, and powerful.

The smooth, metrical and symmetrical forms of verse in the neo-Romantic manner developed in Yiddish poetry at the beginning of the twentieth century, especially by the "Young Generation" ("Di Yunge"), from 1907 on in New York, elevated Yiddish words to the general poetic mold, but had little room for their capricious ironies. The influences of Expressionism in Germany and Futurism and Revolutionary poetry in Russia made the new trends after World War I amenable to giving free reign to the spoken language in poetry—including ironies, puns, harsh sounds, wild associations, and conversational gestures—as well as to opening the doors of poetry to slang, dialects, Hebrew allusions, and the international vocabulary of urban civilization. Yiddish poetry came of age and became part of the international movement. It learned the lessons of Yiddish fiction, worked on the unique aspects of its language, and faced the imaginary world of Jewish historical existence head-on.

Embattled though it was in the face of other social alternatives—Hebrew, assimilation to other languages, socialist "relevance," and sheer materialism—inwardly Yiddish literature enjoyed an atmosphere of optimism and confidence in the value of its work and in the talents engaged in it. Here was an age-old civilization, the oldest continuous culture (but for the Chinese), permeated with a sense of its historicity and wisdom, carrying high moral values, and—as some saw it—burying its energies in ancient learning of irrelevant issues, under the aegis of a rigid religious code of behavior written in two languages incomprehensible to the masses (Hebrew and Aramaic). Yiddish would speak directly to the people in their own rich and living language, express their experiences in the present as full-fledged, free human beings, communicate to them the events, works, and ideas of the great modern world, and call up their vitality and folk wisdom, the only guarantors of a rejuvenation from within.

In a Yiddish literary journal, *Shtrom* ("Stream" or "Torrent"), published in Moscow in 1922, a former Soviet commissar of art, writing on the question of whether Jews, who had never created graphic art, could achieve it now, concluded:

I myself know very well what this little nation can achieve.

Unfortunately, I am too shy to utter the words. It's really something, what this little nation has done.

When it wanted—it showed the world Christ and Christianity.

When it wanted—it gave Marx and Socialism.

Can you imagine that it will not show the world some art?

It will!

Kill me, if not.

The conversational tone of this essay is typical, sentimental, ironic Yiddish speech. The mood is of unlimited Jewish national self-confidence. The bravado is revolutionary style. The author was Marc Chagall. Such optimism about the possibilities of the new creative impulse among Jews was widespread and gave Yiddish literature and culture its boom years of the early 1920s (notwithstanding some gloomy thematics, such as the pogroms of 1919, that often appeared in it).

This exuberant atmosphere, the hard realities and world-embracing ambitions of young Yiddish poets in New York, are nostalgically recounted in Leyeles's long poem, "A Dream Under Skyscrapers" (1947). He takes stock of a generation, writing in virtuoso rhymed Byronian octaves which cannot easily be translated without losing the effect of their metrical patterns and the play with Yiddish sound and language-fusion. Let us quote four separate stanzas in transcription and in English prose paraphrase:

in di hoykhe un geKEStlte geBAYdes
fun der vunderbarer, tumldiker shtot New-YORK
zitst geENGT a yungvarg, i mit zorg, i on shum zorg.
un di volknkratsers zenen vakhe eydes,
vi mit der yeRUshe fun di tates, zeydes
vert geSHTELT a nayer binyen—do, inMITN torg.
s'iz a verter-binyen, s'boyen yunge boyer,
un zey leygn tsigl mit a freyd un troyer.
. . . .
s'voltn di khaLOYmes fun dem dor geSTAyet
oyftsuboyen Pisem, Ramses un a zayl fun gold,
rundaRUM hot raykhkeyt zikh geKOYlert un geROLT.
nor dos umruyike yungvarg hot farTAyet
oysgeshmidt a nayem ol, a naye frayhayt,
un geSHRIbn, un fun himl s'telerl gevolt,
un geMOStn zikh mit ale hekhste likhter,
un a tsekh geSHTELT fun shtoltse, naye dikhter.
. . . .
bay di taykhn fun New-YORK bin ikh geZEsn
un der nayer, frayer, breyter luft mayn troym farTROYT.
kh'hob a kholem raykh farKHOlemt, kh'hob a troym geBOYT

unter shvere volknkratsers durkh mesLEsn,
unter shteyn—nisht palmes, lipes tsi tsiPREsn.
nisht tsu visn oft dem khilek tsvishn morgn-royt
un dem ovnt-gold, hob ikh geHIT di likhter
fun a yid an akshn, fun a yidish-dikhter.

. . . .

un bay undz? Es hot a nayer stil un zhaner
oykh a bloz geTON oyf undzer gas, oyf undzer veg.
nisht umZIST geSHVUmen tsu dem nayem vaytn breg,
nisht umZIST geLEyent s'lid ameriKAner,
un geZAPT in zikh dem nusakh dem WhitMAner
durkh di umruyike nekht nokh shvere arbets-teg.
s'land aMErike iz heym geVEN, nisht gast-hoyz.
lib geVEN dos land on yikhes un on kastes.

[In the soaring checkered buildings
Of the magnificent, tumultuous metropolis New York,
Young people sit cramped-in, careworn, careless,
And the skyscrapers are alert witnesses
To a new edifice being erected—here, in the marketplace,
With the heritage of fathers and grandfathers,
A tower-of-words is built; the builders are young,
They lay the bricks in joy and in sorrow.

. . . .

The dreams of that generation were enough
To erect Pithom, Ramses and a Pillar of Gold.
All around, wealth has unfurled and unrolled.
But the restless youth have secretly
Forged a new burden, a new freedom,
And created, and wanted pie in the sky,
And measured themselves with the brightest lights,
And founded a guild of proud, new poets.

. . . .

By the rivers of New York I sat down
And confined my dream to the new, free, wide-open air.
I dreamt a rich dream, I built a vision
Through days and nights, under heavy skyscrapers,
Under stone—not palms, poplars or cypresses.
Often, unaware of the change from evening-gold
To morning-red, I watched over the lights
Of a stubborn Jew, a Yiddish poet.

. . . .

And in our own domain? A new style and genre
Blew in our street too, on our road.
Not in vain did we swim to the new, distant shore,
Not in vain have we read the American poem

And inhaled, absorbed the Whitman tone
Through restless nights after hard workdays.
The land America was home, not a guest-house,
We loved the land with no pedigrees, no castes.]

What was the historical background of this forward-looking trend and
what were its relations to the past?

The Peculiar Nature of Jewish Literary History

The idea that young poets learn the long history of their
literature and then add their own, new layer is unrealistic in any culture. Rather, they create first, perhaps departing from the preceding
generation or from the work of some selected dominant poets; then
some of them may go back to the past, reread the poetry, and reconstruct a new "tradition."

In modern Yiddish poetry, the lack of tradition was far more radical, since hardly any poet learned Yiddish literature in school. Most
Yiddish schools were founded in Eastern Europe after World War I,
i.e., *after* the major writers and poets appeared, using their authority
for validation. Naturally, they imbibed a vivid Yiddish language spoken in their homes and environment. But only in rare cases did they
receive any knowledge of Yiddish literature from their parents. Most
Yiddish poets had a basic Hebrew religious education; some continued
in general schools in other languages; eventually, all of them made up
their private university by reading books in a number of languages,
including Yiddish. Quite often, the first poetry they read was not in
Yiddish. Many Yiddish poets even began by writing poetry in other
languages—Leyvik in Hebrew; M. L. Halpern in German; Dovid
Edelshtat and A. Leyeles in Russian; Malka Heifets-Tussman in
English—before they turned to Yiddish verse. The socialization of
these young writers, coming from different provinces, with different
dialects and language backgrounds, to the metropolises of Warsaw,
Moscow, Berlin, or New York, was in their common culture, literary
Yiddish.

Modern Yiddish poetry grew out of one bilingual Jewish literature,
long dominated by Hebrew. The peculiar existential situation of the

Hebrew and Yiddish writer who lived in the interstices of several languages and cultures—literary and nonliterary—contributed to the unusual nature of its history. We must keep in mind that the institution of literature itself was not always an unambiguous part of the Hebrew religious tradition (though there were many formal poetic and narrative texts in it). Poetry was written in Hebrew and later in Yiddish too, throughout the ages, but most of the models for literary genres and poetic language were adapted from other cultures.

Until some seventy years ago, a Hebrew poet did not even speak the language he wrote. He was usually polylingual. Typically, in the beginning of the twentieth century, he spoke Yiddish, read Russian, perhaps studied in Germany or Switzerland, and wrote Hebrew verse. In principle, a Hebrew poet of any age did not evolve within one line of development but at an intersection of at least two or three lines: (1) the tradition of Hebrew poetry in his own place; (2) the literary tradition of the language he spoke and the country in which he lived, and, in many cases, also (3) the tradition of Hebrew poetry in another geographical center, quite different from his own. To these was often added (4) the model of another prominent culture as well as (5) of Yiddish. A similar intersection of contexts worked for the Yiddish poet as well, further complicated by the migration of the whole literature from country to country.

For this reason even the poetics of Hebrew poetry, in spite of its inbred conservatism, underwent radical transformations. Rather than having a smooth and steady development, Hebrew and Yiddish anthologies exhibit zigzags and sharp shifts.[1] The impetus for these changes was often the leap of a new generation from one of those intersecting lines of evolution to another.

A Yiddish poet could switch from writing Russian poetry to Yiddish, as did S. Frug in Russia or Dovid Edelshtat in America in the 1880s, or from Hebrew to Yiddish and vice versa, as we see in Bialik and most Hebrew poets of the early twentieth century, notably Uri Zvi Grinberg. In each of these literatures, there were different poetic norms at any given time, a different conception of what poetry was.

---

1. "In the cramped and brief existence of Yiddish literature, the historical line of poetry is discontinuous, like an erratic zigzag" (Irving Howe, *A Treasury of Yiddish Poetry*, p. 2). A similar observation can be made while reading Ch. Shirman's famous anthology of Hebrew poetry in Italy, including poets from the ninth to the twentieth century.

Furthermore, Yiddish poetry itself, in any given generation, had an autonomous existence in each cultural center—in the United States, Warsaw, Vilna, or the Soviet Union—and the differences between them were like the difference between American and British poetry. Since poets tend to continue their personal style, immigrating or shifting from one of these countries, languages, or orientations to another often led to at least a partial transfer of norms and to changes in the receiving literatures.

S. Frug (1860–1916), a respected Russian poet in St. Petersburg in the 1880s who wrote sad lyrical poetry and sentimental verse in Russian on Jewish national themes, accepted Russian meters as a matter of course and brought them along, unwittingly, when he turned to write Yiddish verse. He thus caused a revolutionary change in the history of Yiddish and Hebrew versification. The young Chaim Nakhman Bialik, studying the Aramaic Talmud in the famous Lithuanian yeshiva of Volozhin, read Frug "under the table," swallowed it lock, stock and barrel—including the sentimental national content, the individual voice, and the scanning meters—and made them his own. Hence a new, Russian-type Hebrew poetry was launched. Similarly, when Dovid Edelshtat, writing in New York, shifted from Russian to Yiddish, he unwittingly transmitted the Russian metrical norms to his new language.

A generation later, in Eretz Israel in the 1920s, when Hebrew Modernist poets revolted against the poetry of Bialik and his followers, their work did not evolve from Bialik's poetics but simply leaped into Hebrew from two other evolutionary lines: one was carried by Shlonsky and Rakhel, who grew up with Russian poetry and created Hebrew verse in the poetic modes of that literature, including Futurist, Symbolist and Acmeist elements. The other is represented by Uri Zvi Grinberg, who saw the horrors of World War I as a soldier in the trenches and wrote Yiddish poetry in Warsaw and Berlin in the 1920s under the impact of German and Yiddish Expressionism, which included marked influences from Russian Futurism and from Walt Whitman. When Grinberg suddenly left Europe for Eretz Israel in 1924 and resumed writing in Hebrew, he brought Whitmanesque rhythms, Futurist metaphors, Expressionist rhetoric, and the syntax of a spoken language saturated with political, journalistic, and "International" diction from Yiddish to Hebrew poetry, which did not permit these elements before. Both directions—the "Russian" and the Expressionist—changed the face of Hebrew poetry, though they did not grow out of its dominant fold, the poetics of Bialik.[2] At the same time, Moyshe-Leyb Halpern brought German poetic rhetoric from Hofmannsthal's Vienna to the Russian-oriented verse of the Yiddish "Young Generation" in New York before and after World War I.

By the time Yiddish assumed center· stage in Jewish culture and society, at the beginning of the twentieth century, the potential sources of influence were unusually complex. The modern Jewish intellectual confronted several languages and cultures, all of which were thrown into great turmoil and ferment precisely at this juncture. He toured an imaginary museum of periods and styles which, to the eager outsider, appeared in a panoramic display rather than in historical sequence. As I have indicated elsewhere, "for reasons of cultural history, Yiddish literature had not shared the development of its neighbors for hundreds of years; consequently, when the East European Jewish intelligentsia, in one grand leap, landed in the general twentieth century, Yiddish poetry undertook not only to catch up with Europe's deepened appreciation of the classics and the modernistic trends of recent generations, but also to take an active part in the discussion of the most timely cultural problems and in the artistic movements of the environment."[3]

In the 1880s, Hebrew and Yiddish poets were still extremely naive and primitive, following Russian poetry at its lowest point: the rhetorical-sentimental, socially engaged but cliché-ridden Russian verse of the late 1870s and 1880s. However, from the 1890s on, young Hebrew poets discovered the great tradition of Russian classical poetry of the 1820s and 1830s, the "Romantic" and "Realist" poetry of Pushkin and Lermontov. From this position, it was only natural to get an inkling of Goethe and Heine. All at once, the achievements of European poetry from the Renaissance on, in which neither Hebrew nor Yiddish had fully participated, opened up before their eyes. In terms

2. One might argue that reliance on foreign examples occurs in the shifts of tradition in other languages too. This is certainly true, but the change is usually an internal one at first and only then resorts to foreign authorities. T. S. Eliot, for example, grew up in the English language and began writing in the manner and meters of Edwardian verse, as his early poems show, and only then found kindred spirits in French Symbolist poetry. The same is true for V. Bryusov and other Russian Symbolists who really learned French Symbolist poetry only after declaring themselves "Symbolists."

3. B. Hrushovski, "On Free Rhythms in Modern Yiddish Poetry," in Uriel Weinreich, ed., *The Field of Yiddish* (New York, 1954), 219–66; reprinted in Benjamin Harshav, *Turning Points*, Porter Institute, 1990.

of comparative literature, it was a leap "backward," an *inverse evolution*. It occurred under the influence of the new learning provided the young Jewish intelligentsia first by the Russian high school program— at a time when Pushkin was declared a "national poet" and a "Classic"—and then by a wide range of reading in the accepted "Culture," especially in Russian and German, and, increasingly, in Yiddish translations and mediations.

At the same time, however, in the 1890s, Russian poetry itself went through a radical rebirth, with the emergence of Decadence and Symbolism. Yiddish poets at the beginning of the twentieth century, barely having discovered European Romantic and Classical poetry, inhaled the neo-Romantic air of Russian Symbolist and German Impressionist poetry and emulated its vague suggestive moods and mellifluous verse forms. Again, only a few years later, the next literary generation plunged into general European Expressionism and other post-Symbolist trends. Compared to Russian poetry, it was as if Jewish poetry, in the lifetime of one generation, leaped back and forth in history from 1880 to 1830 to 1905 to 1920 to 1912; connecting, in between, with German poetry of 1750 (the genre of the Idyll, masterfully revived by Chernikhovsky), and then with Heine of 1850 and Berlin of 1920.

Naturally, in the creative writing itself, the reception of influences was highly selective. Individual knowledge is rarely as profound as the cultural potential would allow and the development of a poetic language is a much more internalized and homogenizing process than what can be provided by a poet's wide reading. The hodgepodge of styles and thematics perceived in reading could not be absorbed in writing without risking a confused medley. Each poet or group of poets carefully developed their own rather closed and limited poetics and thematics, responding to the historical context of the literature and linking their own life experiences. Only then, from this individually wrought poetic language, molded differently in different genres, did a natural continuation unfold and an autonomous, internal tradition build up.

In sum, the historical development of Hebrew and Yiddish poetry alike was not necessarily one of persistent linear evolution following the evolution of other literatures. It often proceeded by leaps and bounds, picking up threads from one neighboring line or another or from the cultural museum. A young poet, sometimes sitting in the same New York café as poets five years his senior, did not necessarily continue from the point his colleagues had reached, but from a point his peers in another country or in another language had arrived at some time before. The change from Impressionism to Expressionism in Yiddish and in Hebrew poetry after World War I in Europe was connected with a shift from a Russian- to a German-dominated orientation; the change from the poetics of the Young Generation ("Di Yunge") in New York to Introspectivism, which occurred at about the same time, was combined with a shift from an orientation toward the lyric-ironical Heine and the meters of Russian Symbolism to Anglo-American free verse.

The Poets' Relation to Literary History

We have no tradition. We have found very little that could serve as tradition for us. The tradition begins perhaps with us, strange as it may sound.
—*Inzikh*, March, 1923

How did the young Yiddish poets of the twenties, aware of a horizontal multicultural perspective, relate to the vertical axis of the history of their own literature? The simple answer is: Hardly at all. But there are less simple answers as well.

Medieval Yiddish literature, as written until the eighteenth century in Germany and Italy, had some impressive achievements, notably in narrative and historical verse. But it had very little impact on modern poetry; it was hardly known and the texts were not readily available. This is not surprising, given the low prestige of Yiddish vis-à-vis Hebrew on the one hand and the lack of historical awareness among Jews, living simultaneously in an intense Present and in a transhistorical Jewish Destiny, on the other hand.

Rather the reverse happened: the newly achieved standards and self-confidence of Yiddish culture in the twentieth century created a base on which historical scholarship could develop and establish a respectable pedigree in the past. At first, the nineteenth century was discovered (e.g., in Leo Wiener's book in English, *History of Yiddish Literature in the Nineteenth Century*, 1899). Then, especially in the 1920s and 1930s in Poland and the Soviet Union, histories of the older

Yiddish literature were written and several poets tried their hand at writing poems in Old Yiddish. Typically, Max Erik, then a young scholar, claimed in an Expressionist journal in 1922 that old Yiddish literature and contemporary poetry were two, altogether different, incommensurable cultures; but he then went on to write a history of that old literature. Another example is N. B. Minkov, one of the founders of Introspectivist poetry in New York, who turned to criticism in his later years, uncovered a tradition in his three-volume history of the *Pioneers of Yiddish Poetry in America* (1956), and wrote books about the sixteenth-century Italian Yiddish poet, *Eliyohu Bokher* (1950) and the early eighteenth-century Yiddish prose memoirs of a German Jewish woman, *Glikl Hamel* (1952). In fact, some of the basic old Yiddish texts were published only after World War II, bringing the first extant writings of Yiddish almost to its last readers.

For Yiddish writers in the twentieth century, the living Jewish literature of their experience actually started with the prose of "the Grandfather of Yiddish literature" (the nickname itself is indicative!), Mendele Moykher Sforim (1836–1917). Yiddish poetry of high, poetic quality emerged only in the twentieth century and attained admirable standards after World War I as part of the general European-American poetic wave. Young Yiddish poets were justified in feeling that a poetic tradition was beginning now, as the epigraph to this chapter indicates.

Of course, they, too, shared in a Jewish cultural tradition looming above history, primarily the Bible and the texts for holidays, both as a classical base and as a historical burden. Some of these Hebrew texts were intimately known to Yiddish writers since early childhood but were not easily absorbable in another language (Yiddish) and in the poetics of another age (Modernism).

A different matter was Yiddish folklore. Parallel to the history of old Yiddish literature, an oral literature in Yiddish had accompanied European Jews for centuries. The folklore texts gathered at the end of the nineteenth and in the twentieth century and the songs, still sung during the Holocaust and after, show the same fusion of influences that was basic to the language. Elements of songs from the German Baroque, from old Hebrew liturgy, and of recent Slavic vintage lived there side by side with folklorized poems originally composed by Yiddish poets. The language of Yiddish folk poetry was the modern spoken Yiddish; it was vivid, direct, sentimental. It offered the Yiddish poet ready-made poetic lines, a flexibly constrained free verse, as well as the authority of an "authentic" tone of voice, legitimizing naive and coarse language.

Yiddish poets tried to write poetry either by fitting spoken Yiddish words into the written patterns of Russian or German verse or by continuing the genres of folk song and jester versification. Only when the first goal was achieved, when an ease of writing flexible metrical verse in Yiddish became second nature to the poets, could a deeper understanding of poetry evolve and, with it, a deeper probing into the possibilities of the Yiddish language as they were laid bare in wise folk humor and in modern Yiddish fiction.

These are paradoxes that haunted modern Yiddish poetry: we are so old and we are just beginning; we are young and independent of Hebrew and dependent on its cultural stock; we can feel the richness and the folk vitality of our language and face its poverty at the same time. The poet becomes a discoverer, a pioneering master of a new language and creator of new poetic norms; and, in the process, he uncovers the hidden resources in the ore of his past.

Yiddish and Hebrew Literature— an Intertwined History

The problems of poetic art are very different from those of other genres. Hence, when observed internally, poetry has its separate history. A new poetics develops against the background of the poetics of earlier poets. But, from a social perspective, the history of poetry is linked with the history of other genres. Thus in some periods, poetry becomes dominant; in others, fiction takes the upper hand and, in still others, literature recedes in favor of philosophy or social ideas. In modern Yiddish literature, there is an added dimension: the alternation between an emphasis on Yiddish and an emphasis on Hebrew literature, within the same society.

In his Introduction to the *Treasury of Yiddish Poetry*, Irving Howe observed that "In fiction, Yiddish literature finds its fulfillment almost at the very beginning," whereas "The development of Yiddish poetry is very different. It comes to its maturity a bit later than does Yiddish prose." Indeed, that was the feeling of the Modernist Yiddish poets themselves, who had little use for the Yiddish poetry written before

1919. At the same time, in the 1950s and 1960s, Shimon Halkin, Professor of Hebrew literature in Jerusalem, pondered the reasons why good Hebrew fiction was late in coming, as compared to the persistently strong showing of Hebrew poetry in the nineteenth century. In both cases it is a mere optical illusion perceived when dividing what was then one bilingual literature into its two participating languages (which were, indeed, well separated by the time these observers wrote, in New York and Jerusalem of the 1960s). The answer to both critics is the same: the renaissance of Jewish literature at the turn of the century in Eastern Europe brought forth unique works of both poetry *and* fiction, which laid the foundations for a mature literature in both languages; the best poetry, however, was written in Hebrew and the innovating fiction was in Yiddish.[4] As we shall see, the reasons for this functional division are not merely accidental. To a large extent, Hebrew and Yiddish were one literature, with the same writers and the same readers often shifting from one language to the other, though each language had its own, entirely separate, books, journals, and publications.

In the medieval period, Hebrew and Yiddish were two bodies of texts coexisting in one community but largely separated in their genres, functions, and audiences. In the nineteenth century, under the aegis of the Hebrew *Haskalah*, some remarkable works were also written in the despised language, Yiddish, often by the same Hebrew writers. This trend grew, especially after the emergence of Yiddish periodicals in the 1860s. After 1881, the hierarchy was inverted: the dominant literature became Yiddish (with a special role reserved for poetry in Hebrew and essays in Hebrew and Russian).

In the 1880s and 1890s, three great and original masters of Yiddish fiction emerged: Mendele Moykher Sforim, Sholem Aleichem, and I. L. Peretz. At the beginning of the twentieth century, they were declared "Classics"; their collected writings were published in several editions and their works were widely read and revered. Before 1880, all three were Hebrew writers of the *Haskalah*; but only now, with a new, radical shift to the Yiddish language and in re-forming their world view and conceptions, was their work transformed into a really significant and unique literature, bringing out the full brilliance of

---

4. The range of the genres was completed in each literature with the process of their gradual separation from each other, the turning of Hebrew into a spoken language, and of Yiddish into a cultivated literature.

Yiddish and the world embodied in it. Instead of being intellectual, satirical observers from the outside, these former *Haskalah* writers turned to illuminating the same prototypical Jewish world from within, and in Yiddish. The place of the "national poet," a poet-prophet symbolizing the stature of a culture, like Goethe or Pushkin, was reserved for the Hebrew poet, Ch. N. Bialik (1873–1934).

Then, the second literature tried to emulate the achievements of its counterpart. Toward the end of the century, Mendele began to rework his great Yiddish novels into Hebrew—the old jester called his bilingual creativity "breathing with both nostrils"—thus laying the foundations for a new, dense Hebrew prose which developed side by side with Yiddish literature. And, on the other side of this bifurcation, one of the Yiddish disciples of Hebrew poetry, Yehoash, who became a major Yiddish poet in America in the beginning of the twentieth century, translated the whole Bible in one of the greatest master strokes of modern Yiddish, incorporating medieval Yiddish archaisms and modernisms in one organic web, thus granting new prestige to the Yiddish language.

The interaction of the two languages was amazing considering the cardinal difference between them: one was basically Germanic and European in its syntax, the other Semitic; one was colloquial and folk-loristic, the other lofty and classical. In Mendele's novel *Fishke the Lame*, a beggar sits down on the ground on a hot afternoon. When he translated the novel into Hebrew, the author had no simple Hebrew words for "a hot afternoon" and used a biblical phrase, "in the heat of the day." This immediately recalled the patriarch Abraham resting under a tree and invited an ironizing comparison between the two.

With time, the two literatures drifted apart, their rupture aided by the split between the political parties, by the "war of languages" (between Hebrew and Yiddish), as well as by the massive victory of Yiddish as the language of politics, culture, and newspapers in the Diaspora. Jewish literature after World War I—and in the United States, even before—was predominately Yiddish, with only a few Hebrew writers living outside the new center of Hebrew literature in Eretz Israel. However, the writers themselves on both sides of the artificial fence were still steeped in the bilingual culture. Their work cannot be understood from a monolingual perspective: Agnon's Hebrew still reverberates with a Yiddish subtext in the speech of his characters and narrators, and Hebrew subtexts enrich the pages of Yiddish poetry.

Creating a modern, European-type literature and working out a
style, a fictional world, characters, and genres for it—in a culture that
had no major fiction to speak of and no clearly stratified class society
to support authentic bourgeois novels—posed overwhelming problems and required different solutions in each language. In fiction, the
problem was twofold: first, to adopt European forms of narrative,
characterization, dialogue, description, and so on, and then to invent
an imaginary world made of home-grown materials, carried on the
shoulders and through the points of view of its characters, and presented in a language fitting its peculiar traits. The challenge of creating
great fiction does not lie in the masterful execution of a well-known
genre or a conventional narrative scheme, but rather in the formation
of a new, coherent *"Social Space,"* an interdependent cluster of time,
space, characters, ideas, and style which motivate each other and also
represent some conception of a society and a language—realistic, grotesque, or fantastic as it may be. The *texture* of fiction is made of
dialogues, interior monologues, external descriptions, and so on, and
those depend on the characters from whose positions they are presented and who, in turn, are linked in a social network, including class
relations, ideology, and the like.[5] Such a *Social Space* was constructed
in several different modes in the new Jewish literature.

The search for an original fictional world that would be both removed from naturalistic descriptions and sufficiently representative of
the problems of the time, including a self-critical perception of Jewish
existence in history, was not easy for a Jewish writer. The new secular
or assimilated Jews were not different enough from the Russian or
European characters they wanted to imitate in real life, and could
provide food for only derivative novels. Hence, the tendency to
ground the fictional world in the specifically Jewish small town, raised
to symbolic proportions. But how do you write a plausible narrative
about a world that has no private experiences to speak of and whose
characters are not even in the habit of killing people or carrying on
involved love affairs? And in a culture without a language for philosophy or for the description of subtle psychological states? Rather than
invent an artificial plot, the writer had to resort to character types who

5. The concept of *Social Space* introduced here is intended to enlarge Bakhtin's
concept of the *chronotopos*, cohesion of time and space determining a novel, to include
the other components in one unified cluster.

had a full and real world of their own and let them observe this world from within, in their own language, and communicate about it with each other. This world was basically uneventful on the level of the individual—and "European" literature was to be a literature about individuals. But it was a world rich in talking and free-associating and relating any small event to a universe of collective wisdom and texts.

Only Yiddish was suited for this task of creating plausible fictional worlds out of conversation. Even the author's own representative in the text, the narrator—whose task it was not only to introduce the scenes to the reader but, first of all, *to listen* to his characters' dialogical monologues—even he assumed the persona of a semi-intellectual, semi-folksy storyteller, as the names of these narrator-authors suggest: "Mendele the Bookseller" (Mendele Moykher Sforim) and "How-Do-You-Do" (Sholem Aleichem).[6]

Like James Joyce re-creating a detailed fictional world of Dublin from an ironic distance, the Yiddish writers, Mendele and Sholem Aleichem, created classics of Jewish literature by evoking—from the distance of intellectuals living in big cities—a stylized fictional world of the small town in the Pale, elevated to the symbolic stature of the essential Jewish existence, an ideal, self-critical "lower Jerusalem."

This world was presented to the reader in the language of its own characters, Yiddish, and structured around the most profound traits of that language: its wavering, ironic, multilingual perspective and its rambling, exuberant, irrationally associative dialogue. The ambivalent qualities of Yiddish were a perfect vehicle for conveying simultaneously the rich and authentic naive world view of "simple people" and the deeper metaphysical and panhistorical insights of a "fallen aristocracy." That is why the really great work of Jewish novelists was not in their imitations of the much-admired Russian Realist novel, but was achieved when they reached back to the pre-Realist stage of European literature (Gogol and Cervantes), or to the parallel line of

6. A similar problem was faced by Russian literature which, in the eighteenth century, had imitated the genres of Western Europe. Only after developing its own imaginary world and national style, with Pushkin and Gogol, did it become a significant literature with its own, unique contribution. In a different form, this was the dilemma of American literature, which began by continuing English literary genres and came of age when it dared to depart from them and find its specific fictional worlds and their matching structures, with the Transcendentalists, Melville, Whitman and Mark Twain. Both in American and in Russian literature, the "normal" European novel was not acceptable, but new structures of fiction had to be worked out to embody the unique Social Space re-created in them.

satire, grotesque, and *skaz* (monologues characterizing their own speakers), and developed an almost surrealist concatenation of argument as the backbone of their fiction. For these forms, rather than for the bourgeois social novel, unique and authentic internal material could be found; material based on the qualities of the conversational language and the associative style, filled with a mosaic of embedded stories, typical of the Jewish sermon tradition.

In this respect, modern Jewish fiction picked up the threads preceding European Realism and brought them straight into the styles of the twentieth century, with their subordinate and incoherent plot structures, their ironic and ambivalent visions, and their emphasis on the problematic nature of language. A few years later, around 1905, Uri Nissan Gnessin (1879–1913) employed this associative kind of composition in his psychological stories of alienated individuals, replacing the Yiddish dialogue with internal monologue in Hebrew— a private language referring to the protagonist's consciousness which reflects events not immediately available to the reader until he reconstructs them. As Leah Goldberg has suggested, his work was a precursor of the European Stream of Consciousness. In Gnessin's prose, the cosmopolitan characters, moving in internal monologues and scenes recollected in memory, are lost in time, space, and language. His young men and women, apparently speaking and reading Russian with their peers in the city, and cut off from their Yiddish-speaking parents, who are aging in some small town, are transposed into a transparent, finicky, classical Hebrew which breathes the long periodic sentences of Russian Impressionism. These were the intensely introverted and alienated predecessors of Kafka's protagonists. Only much later did Jewish literature go back and recover the skipped stages of Realism.

Since its very inception, the imaginary Jewish world of classical Yiddish fiction was a re-creation of a disintegrating past. It caught the élan of a national character—grotesque, exaggerated but seemingly indestructible—which later became the foundation of Jewish imagination, ideology, and literature. This was not realism at all. (In fact, when the same writers published their own memoirs, their childhood world looked idyllic and peaceful, in comparison to their fictional creations.)[7] When Mendele's *Fishke the Lame* first appeared in a short

---

7. See Mendele Moykher Sforim's autobiographical "Of Bygone Days" in: Ruth R. Wisse, *A Shtetl and Other Yiddish Novellas*, New York, 1973.

version, it was subtitled, "A Story of Jewish Beggars"; when transformed, in the expanded and canonized version, it became a symbolic image of the Jewish predicament in general ("All of Israel—one begging sack"). And so did the figures of Mendele's Benjamin the Third and Sholem Aleichem's Menakhem-Mendl and Tevye the Milkman. The stature they acquired in the Jewish social imagination was akin to that of Hamlet and Faust.

I. L. Peretz added new dimensions to this foundation by reviving romanticized Hassidic and folklore stories, again as a way of retroactively constructing a past for a new literary community. Hence, when Yiddish fiction and drama in America continued to locate its stories in that world, it was not just for lack of familiarity with the new circumstances, but basically because that was the acquired, private territory of Yiddish literature with its own typology of characters, father-son and religious-secular tensions, and differentiated language. Depictions of the "shtetl" were rarely realism but rather the creation of a mythopoeic world, a "Yiddishland," where the beliefs, prejudices, proverbs, primitive jokes, and naive "wisdom" of its characters—those poor knights of a fallen aristocracy—were still untouched by the all-flattening Enlightenment and could still be believable. In spite of their outlandish garb, they could plausibly represent essential humanity (much as Joyce placed problems of modern ambivalence in the world of his naive characters in the *Dubliners*). Futhermore, though Yiddish literature often alluded to the Bible, to biblical imagery, characters, and situations, it constructed its past in Eastern Europe.

Thus, at the end of the 1880s, Yiddish fiction established its new foundations. The new realistic sense of the historical moment demanded prose. A few years later, when the response became less political, more idealized, and turned inward, the time was ripe for the crystallization of a new poetry. Both Hebrew and Yiddish poetry of the preceding *Haskalah* period (in the nineteenth century) were almost oblivious to the great German and Russian poetry around them. Hebrew poets in the nineteenth century continued to write didactic and rhetorical Enlightenment poems in syllabic meters (inherited from Italian Hebrew verse) and Yiddish poems were free-accentual, sloppily imitating a folksy style. The accentual-syllabic versification which gave so much precision and rhythmical flexibility to English, German, and Russian poetry and which directly affected the senses of the reader—both with its musicality and the rhythmical departures from it—was accepted by Yiddish and Hebrew poetry only toward the beginning of the 1890s. This was achieved via Peretz, Frug and Bialik and through the Yiddish "proletarian poets" in England and the United States—Dovid Edelshtat, Morris Vinchevsky, Morris Rosenfeld—in the 1880s and 1890s. They found it natural to write their verse in the meters of Russian poetry, the language of their ideological inspiration.

The real challenge, however, of the newly learned Russian literature required a poetry emerging from the image of the poet as prophet. This image had shaped Russian poetry since Pushkin—who, in turn, was influenced by the ideas of the German Romantic philosopher, Schelling, promoted at that time in Russia, as well as by English Romantic poetry. The unifying force of a body of poetry, in this conception, was the figure of the poet as a Romantic introvert endowed with individual sensibilities, feeding on his own life experiences, perceiving nature in metaphysical contemplation, evoking memory in language, and speaking through the language of symbolic imagery. Biblical Hebrew was a better vehicle for this task than colloquial Yiddish. In his famous poem, "The Prophet," Pushkin himself alluded to the Bible. Bialik, influenced by this poem, could do better with the original, rephrasing it in its own language, in a new poetic framework. Perhaps, if the emergence of a new poetry had occurred in a period of Expressionism, Yiddish would have been better suited to the vacancy (as indeed it was in the 1920s); but in the 1890s Hebrew was the poetic language. (And besides, Yiddish poets were busy promoting socialism and writing rhymed rhetorical poems for their proletarian readers.)

From the 1890s on, accepting the classical nineteenth-century Russian and German poetics of individually experienced lyrical poetry, Bialik, Chernikhovsky, and their disciples launched a trend of sophisticated, language-sensitive, personal poetry in Hebrew. It combined the poetic traits of biblical Hebrew with the metaphorical mode of nature descriptions of European Romanticism, and confined them to the classical molds of precise metrical and strophic forms. It also favored the long poem and the lyrical narrative which the Russian poets had adapted in dialogue with English Romanticism. Its main strength lay in the interplay between the direct poetic fiction created in a poem (with the image of the poet in the present at its center) and allusions to the canonical texts inherent in the language.

The problems of creating poetry in Yiddish, however, were formidable. The epic narrative of the medieval *Shmuel Bukh* and the well-made octaves of Elye Bokher in sixteenth-century Venice were forgotten; the *Haskalah* did not produce any Yiddish lyrical tradition (the fine poet, Shloyme Etinger, remained unpublished until the 1930s); the folksong was discredited by its travesties in the primitive and didactic Yiddish poems of folk singers and wedding jesters and the hardly more subtle verses of Yiddish popular theater (from Goldfaden to New York's Second Avenue). The poets themselves often doubted whether "the cholent-language," as Frug dubbed it, was not too coarse for the refined feelings of poetry.

At the beginning of the twentieth century—especially after the failure of the Russian Revolution of 1905 and the turning inward of Russian intellectuals—Yiddish poets adopted the models of Russian and German lyrical poetry. But the individualist poetry of their Romantic or Symbolist masters provided models for poetic monologues rather than dialogues; poetic language was condensed in a pure and high style; it was not talkative and jocular but sophisticated, aristocratic, and refined. After some training, one could fit Yiddish words into those lyrical, metrical molds, but there would be nothing uniquely Yiddish about it, hence nothing interestingly new. Still, the excitement of writing "beautiful," metrical, and mellifluous verse and subjective poems reflecting the feelings of the individual swept Hebrew and Yiddish poetry before World War I. This poetry came to the fore after the demise of the ideological stage of 1897–1905, with Zionism's Uganda crisis and Herzl's death on the one hand, and the failure of the Russian Revolution of 1905, with the ensuing cynicism or mystical individualism of the Russian intelligentsia on the other.

Naturally, this exaltation of the lyric was enhanced by a general aestheticist, art for art's sake trend. In Jewish society, it had the added value of a general yearning for culture and refinement. For the first time in history one could hear in Yiddish the symmetries and counterpoints of scanned lines known to European poetries for centuries. The fine, well-metered poems of Leyb Naydus in Lithuania were filled with French words, pianos, Chopin nocturnes, and nostalgia. Some of it permeated the poetry of the "Young Generation" in America, though New York was a harsher place to sing so softly. It can be seen in Leyeles's early poetry with its mysterious women veiled in such un-Jewish, unreal, and mellifluous names as YuOla, YoLANda, ElaDEa, SeLIma, KaraHILD (as well as in his own poetic name,

LEYELES, and his alter ego, FABIUS LIND) or in his poem "Tao," with its colonnades, stone gladiolas, gliding gondolas, vases, topazes, chrysoprase, and Aurora Borealis.[8] Yiddish could be made to sound so beautiful, so un-Jewish!

Only in the twentieth century did a full range of genres attain prominence in both languages. Though the masses turned more and more to reading Yiddish—the language that mediated culture, politics and education for them—and the hopes for a national revival in Israel did not seem very realistic for the millions, these were great days for Hebrew poetry, impressed by the melancholy, escapism, and individualism of the Russian intelligentsia after the failure of the first Russian Revolution of 1905. There was almost no audience in Hebrew but the poets of "individual sadness" needed no audience; it was the saddest language to write in. A similar mood and similar Symbolist and neo-Romantic influences were carried overseas by the young people escaping from Russia after the failure of that Revolution; among them were the poets who proudly promoted the ivory tower of individualist poetry in Yiddish, the founders of the "Young Generation" ("di Yunge") in New York: Mani Leyb, Y. Rolnik, and others.

Yiddish poetry around the world participated in this trend but it was at its best when it could evoke parts of the Jewish fictional world through the shards of language. The intonations and gestures of the prototypical speakers were imprinted in the Yiddish phrases, and their context had to be reconstructed, evoked in language, along with the social universe which molded them, much as Hebrew poetry evoked the echo-space of the Bible. This process could come only very late, when the ideal of "pure poetry" was abandoned and poetic language was opened to all possibilities and intonations of the spoken idiom, when fiction could be "lyrical" and poetry "prosaic," and when Jewish poets were not afraid to cover the subtle poetic instrument with coarse, ironic and "Jewish" markers. Jacob Glatshteyn always understood this problem and felt uneasy with poetry that was too refined for "the wise prosaic smile of the clever tongue."[9] Time and again, he reached out in various ways to mine the "prosaic" resources of Yiddish, even going so far as to lose his grip on the rhythms of verse. He embedded his most personal feelings in the primitive ramblings of a gregarious mystic, Rabbi Nakhman of Bratslav. And, in their own ways, Halpern,

8. See Leyeles's early poems in AYP.
9. See "Chronicle of a Movement," No. 27 (AYP, 802–3).

Teller, and Leyeles did the same. Readers who judge Yiddish poetry by the ways it attempts to achieve what English poetry does will miss the unique aspects of an ironic, allusive, evaluative, conversational, and talkative medium, even when it is confined to the bare bones of poetic selection.

7

Yiddish Poetry in America

American Literature in Yiddish

There was once a lively, buoyant American literature in Yiddish, perhaps the most coherent and full-fledged literary institution in the United States outside of English. Except for its exclusive language, it was not a parochial phenomenon. It spanned a wide gamut of themes and ideologies—from utopian socialism to American *engagement*, from cosmopolitan universalism to Jewish nationalism—and encompassed as variegated a range of styles and genres—from naturalist fiction to avant-garde experiments, from popular melodrama and stirring novels in newspaper installments to virtuoso sonnet garlands and hermetic free verse. The first book to include Yiddish and Hebrew poems appeared in the United States in 1877, and several poets and writers are active in Yiddish to this day, however little known they may be outside of the dwindling Yiddish publications. The most prolific period of American Yiddish poetry can be marked by the dates 1890–1971, that is, from the establishment of the socialist-anarchist newspaper, *Fraye arbeter shtime*, to the death of the major poet, Jacob Glatshteyn.

While English poetry was dominated by the exquisite elitism of T. S. Eliot and Ezra Pound and steeped in cultural allusions to the European past of Dante, Shakespeare, and the Provençal bards, Yiddish poets—shoemakers, housepainters or "poor newspaper writers" as they were—often confronted American realities directly: the wonders of construction and city architecture, the subway, the harbors, labor unions, the underworld, the plight of the blacks, the trial of Sacco and Vanzetti, alienation of the individual in the jungle of the metropolis, social injustice, and immigrant longing. At the same time, they were also fascinated by contemporary ideas. Modernism, Freud, the Russian Revolution, Buddhism, the Tao, Nietzsche, Baudelaire, Villon, Isaiah and Homer, Whitman and Rabbi Nakhman of Bratslav mark the range of intertextuality of American Yiddish poetry.

Young Yiddish poets in New York talked "about eternity, death and grammar" (as Glatshteyn put it in his poem "On my Two-Hundredth Birthday," written at the age of twenty-five)—and talking was at the heart of the culture. They created a chorus of voices, inscribing with emotional and intellectual intensity their responses to the human condition,—to nature and the modern city, alienation and love, the "Golden Land" and the "Old Home" overseas—in existential or melodic lyrical poems or in long and descriptive verse narratives.

Seen in retrospect, Yiddish poetry written in America has two faces. On the one hand, it is a prominent expression of modern Jewish culture. It gave voice to yet another permutation of Jewish history: the migration of a whole people to a new world, the changes in their social fabric and value system, the traumas and internal richness of Jewish existence, the ties and tensions between collective pressures and individual freedom. It also laid bare the treasures and the contradictions of the Yiddish language and the Jewish tradition. Yiddish poetry transformed the language of a popular, age-saturated, oral culture into the aristocratic and cosmopolitan forms of post-Symbolist poetry or the coarse and cutting metaphorical outbursts of Expressionist verse. And, in its decline—perhaps like no other literature—it gave voice to the tragic vision of the Holocaust in Europe, enmeshed in the tragedy of the poet's own disappearing language.

On the other hand, Yiddish poetry was no mere vehicle for the expression of "Jewish" experience. This was a time of mass movement of people of Jewish origin into general Western culture, the business world, art, and academia. Yiddish poets were part of it. They responded to the modern world as human beings and as Americans, embracing the forms of Western culture while working in their own language. As the Introspectivist manifesto of 1919 put it, "poetry is, to a very high degree, the art of language . . . and Yiddish poetry is the art of the Yiddish language and is merely a part of the general

European-American culture."[1] Thus, much of Yiddish poetry written in the United States was consciously and effectively a cosmopolitan, even primarily an *American* literature, expressing the emotions and thoughts of the individual in the modern metropolis. It was attuned to all facets of modern life and history, though written in the Yiddish idiom and using "Jewish" experiences (among others) as a language to express the human condition. These poets were creating a modern literature that would be "merely a branch, a particular stream in the whole contemporary poetry of the world" (as the Introspectivist manifesto stated), just as the founders of modern Israel wanted to build "a nation like all nations." From an American perspective, Yiddish poetry must be seen as an unjustly neglected branch of American literature, a kaleidoscope of American experience and art entombed in yellowing, crumbling books, in the muteness of its own dead language.

The Social Setting

Yiddish writers in America often felt that they were refugees from a great literature; that the Jews in America were too pulverized, too busy making a living or assimilating for a vital reading community to be established; and that the real, deeply rooted base of Yiddish was in the Jewish masses of Eastern Europe. Actually, a new, quite different literature developed in Yiddish in the United States, independent of its counterpart in Europe. In Dubnovian terms, the historical center of Jewish life and culture wandered from Poland and Russia to the United States, where it remolded the old forms—among them, Yiddish literature—and at the same time developed new forms, more organic to the environment and institutionalized in the English language, or integrated into the general American framework.

In its heyday, Yiddish poetry not only explored the full range of the Yiddish language and enriched it in many ways but also benefited from the extraordinary cultural junction in which the generations of its writers and readers found themselves. Along with the historical layers and multilingual components of the Yiddish language itself, Yiddish poetry reverberated with the themes and images of the Hebrew-Aramaic religious, mythological, and cultural tradition, the reminis-

1. AYP, p. 774 ff.

cences and figures of Jewish history. It also drew on the stories, allusions, and intonations of Slavic folklore and literature, as well as on some highlights of German literature and on the imaginary museum of modern (including Oriental) culture, mediated through those languages.

It may be said, schematically, that modern Yiddish literature was written in the genres, forms, and conventions of Russian (and through it, European) literature, in a basically Germanic language that was impressed by layers of Hebrew texts and mythology and by "Jewish" images, typology, and intonations of speech. This complex and unique poetic language was open to the themes, motifs, ideas, and aesthetic trends of modern Europe. In this conglomerate, Yiddish came to America, responded to its stimuli, and absorbed some influences of its literature, life, and ideological atmosphere. A reader or critic would have to travel the same road, at least intellectually, to perceive the full impact of the competing voices in a Yiddish text.

For example, the poet A. Leyeles (born Aron Glantz, 1889–1966) who grew up in the big-city atmosphere of Lodz, a Jewish-and-German Polish city under Russian rule, received a Jewish-Hebrew education, then lived for five years in London, and spent most of his creative life in New York. Besides Yiddish and Hebrew, he knew Russian, German, Polish, English, and some French and was well read in those literatures. Leyeles was a master of Provençal and Italian poetic forms (probably under the influence of Russian Symbolism as well as of German and Yiddish Impressionism); he wrote sonnets, villanelles, rondeaux, ottava rima, triolets, terzinas, and invented his own exacting strophic patterns; at the same time, he created a variety of American-influenced but original and rhythmically intense free verse forms. Leyeles translated a book of *Aesthetics* by Broder Christiansen (who influenced the Russian Formalists) from German into Yiddish, as well as poems by Poe, Keats, Whitman, Verlaine, Amy Lowell, Goethe, Lermontov, Pushkin, and Stephen Spender. Leyeles's poems echo themes from Buddhism, psychoanalysis, American architecture, the Russian Revolution, the Bible, Baudelaire, and the Holocaust. Under his real name, A. Glantz, he published hundreds of newspaper articles, reviews, and essays on cultural and political topics.[2]

2. In his later years, Leyeles added his famous poetic name to his civil name and became known in life as Glantz-Leyeles. But this does not justify the reverse: calling the poet "Aron Glantz-Leyeles," as some translations do, is like calling the author of

This does not mean that every Yiddish poet was a multilingual walking library, but that Yiddish poetry as a whole stood at this unusual intersection, attuning its antennae to "Culture" and open to winds from all sides. The contemporary American reader or translator can hardly match the immediacy and fusion of moods and modes that met at that junction.

Yiddish literature in America was based to a large extent in the daily and periodical press, which included literally hundreds of publications unhampered by the censorship that plagued Yiddish publications in Russia. The first daily newspaper appeared in July, 1881.[3] In certain periods, the combined circulation of Yiddish dailies was very high (762,190 in 1914). The Yiddish press felt that promoting culture and knowledge was one of its chief responsibilities. It became a major vehicle for Yiddish literature and criticism, published the works of the best authors, and eventually gave many writers who were willing to practice journalism a livelihood and a forum in which to express their opinions on culture, politics, society, Jewish history, and world events. At first, "selling oneself" to a newspaper was considered degrading for a real artist and some "held out" longer than others. "If there is a profession in the world which rubs off words like coins changing hands, it is the anonymous journalism which provides bread and butter for Glatshteyn's table" (*Inzikh*, July, 1934), wrote his friend and fellow poet A. Leyeles, who himself earned his daily bread as a journalist and editor in the daily *Der Tog*. But journalism also fulfilled a real need of the Yiddish writer, who was constantly reminded of the problematic aspects of existence and of the intentional choices that had to be made in any effort against the current in this turbulent and politicized century. "Every genuine poet," Glatshteyn wrote on another occasion, "should have a lot of opportunity to write journalism so that he can write it out of his system, steam it out of himself, so that when he comes to write a spoken poem, he is already shouted out" (*In tokh genumen* [*Sum and Substance*], p. 131).

Thus the "anarchist" newspaper, *Fraye arbeter shtime* ("The Free Workers' Voice"), first published in 1890 and edited from 1899 on by S. Yanofsky, published some of the best Yiddish writers, promoted

---

"Tom Sawyer": Samuel Clemens-Twain. As a mature poet he never signed his poetry with "Aron" or "Glantz" but simply: "A. Leyeles."

3. In Russia, a Yiddish newspaper was founded in St. Petersburg in October, 1881, but it was a weekly. The earlier weekly, *Kol mevaser*, which practically launched modern Yiddish literature, appeared between 1862 and 1873.

new talent, and published essays on theoretical issues. The newspaper *Forverts* (*The Daily Forward*), founded in 1897, though originally socialist and actually rather sensational and popular, did a lot to support major writers or to bring them over from Europe. All papers published poems as well as literary criticism. In addition, there were dozens of monthlies, cultural journals, little reviews, and periodical collections devoted to literature, to social and political matters, or specifically to poetry. The prestigious monthly *Di tsukunft*, published from 1897 to this day, originally had a subtitle: "Journal for Socialism, Science and Politics" but shifted course later, under the long-standing editorship of A. Valt (the poet, A. Lyesin), to become a major worldwide organ of Yiddish literature. Dozens of Yiddish publishers were active and hundreds of books appeared. Literature was at the heart of this abnormally unbalanced culture, where the Yiddish language could not serve any broader political purpose and where the system of daily life and the bureaucratic and educational networks were increasingly conducted in English. Poets, however, kept complaining; they felt the urgency of the idealized mission of the poet-as-prophet (as perceived in post-Romantic Russian and Hebrew literature) and forgot that it was not easy to publish Modernist poetry in English, either.

Yiddish culture in America was active for over a century. It sustained the lives of several newspapers, publishing houses, schools, and institutions; but there was little continuity of human resources and a mere vestigial internal development of new generations. Most of the young and the intelligent kept leaving the Yiddish-speaking enclave and thus drained its intellectual resources. The continuity of this culture was supported rather by wave after wave of new immigrants. Most Yiddish writers in America, no matter when they crossed the ocean, came from religious homes in Eastern Europe. They left the old world of Jewish existence in Eastern Europe and its overpowering traditional religious framework. Theirs was a radical revolt—part of a sweeping trend among the youth in the "old country"—against those two ancient and conventional social frames. It was accompanied by the emotional upset of leaving one's parents' home, often at an early age. For example, the sculptor Chaim Gross and the poet Moyshe-Leyb Halpern left their parents at the age of twelve and went into the big world (Vienna and Budapest), to make it on their own even before they moved to America. Halpern reached America when he was twenty-two and had already published some poems in German in Vienna. Jacob Glatshteyn arrived in New York at the age of eighteen.

A. Leyeles came at the age of twenty but had left his parents' home in Lodz for London when he was sixteen. Leyvik came from Siberia at age twenty-five but had been arrested and taken from home as a young revolutionary at eighteen. Many of their readers had shared this experience. When they came to America and rebuilt their lives with the profound motivation of becoming "American," some of them joined the already existing institutions of secular Yiddish culture.

Thus most Yiddish American poets came to the United States as young men in their late teens or early twenties. They had not yet formed their poetic personalities, not yet integrated into the Yiddish literature of their old homes, and hence were able to feel the exhilaration of creating a new literature in a new country and their own lives with it. They were old enough to have imbibed the atmosphere of a full-bodied Yiddish language and culture in Europe and too old to embrace English as a creative language in the new country.

An analysis of the ages of immigration of all the poets included in the two comprehensive anthologies of American Yiddish poetry published in Yiddish shows that these examples are representative. Of the 31 poets included in M. Basin's immense anthology, *Amerikaner yidishe poezye* ("American Yiddish Poetry," 1940), about two thirds were 18–23 years old when they reached America. The average was 20.5. (However, some stopped over for several years in London or elsewhere, i.e., left their homes at an earlier age.) M. Shtarkman's anthology, *Hemshekh* ("Continuation," 1946), included 50 poets, with a larger proportion of the younger generation. Here the average age of immigration was 16. Two-thirds of the poets came at ages 14–19.[4] The younger immigrants grew up in the early 1920s, in an atmosphere of great hopes for Yiddish literature around the world, when writing in Yiddish was still both interesting and possible.

An exceptional case is that of J. L. Teller, who came to America at the age of eight. He was an "iluy" ("genius") in Hebrew and Talmudic studies and had an excellent English education (culminating in a Ph.D. in psychology from Columbia University). As a young man, he was obviously influenced by contemporary American poetry, notably by "Objectivist" verse; he also wrote books of history and journalism in English, but in poetry, he opted neither for English nor Hebrew but for his mother's tongue, Yiddish—still an option in 1930. His friend

---

4. Three others were born in America, four came as children, and only six came to the United States when they were older than twenty.

Gabriel Preil, who began as a Yiddish Introspectivist poet, did shift to Hebrew and became one of the most interesting Hebrew poets in New York.

In contrast, few immigrants of an older age joined the ranks of the American Yiddish poets. Though written in Yiddish, this was a new poetry of a new country. To be able to understand the situation and contribute to it, you had to build a new life here. Furthermore, those young writers who established themselves in the still vital Yiddish literature of Europe became part of the literary establishment there. Only a few recognized poets reached American shores as refugees: Kadye Molodovsky in 1935, Aron Zeitlin in 1940, Chaim Grade and others after the Holocaust.

A comparative analysis of the biographies of American graphic artists of Jewish origin who came from the same Eastern European background shows that most of them arrived at a somewhat earlier age: Ben Shahn was eight years old, Max Weber ten, Louis Lozowick fourteen, Raphael Soyer thirteen, Mark Rothko ten. They were young enough to enter American culture proper, receive an American education, and create art, but were not rooted enough in the language to be able to write poetry. The few immigrants who did write in English, like Anzia Yezierska, Abraham Cahan, or Judd L. Teller, did so in prose rather than poetry. Their writing still reflected a Yiddish-speaking society. It took another generation for creative Jews like Saul Bellow or Philip Roth—the children of immigrants—to have an impact on English literature.

Yiddish poetry in America is nevertheless a truly American literature. Leyeles's *Rondeaux* or *Fabius Lind*, Glatshteyn's *Free Verse* or *Credos*, J. L. Teller's *Miniatures*, Berish Vaynshteyn's *Broken Pieces*, Zishe Vaynper's *Grand Canyon*, or M. L. Halpern's two posthumous volumes of *Poems* published in 1934 are as American as anything written in English in that period. It was the consciousness of being American that gave the poets a sense of freedom of thought and ideas. Here, their perceptions of literature were formed and their poetic language crystallized. America was the real and imaginary space from which the material of their poetry was drawn, where they made their acute observations with the fresh eyes of involved and critical participants, and where the overwhelming power of the melting pot metropolis found them unprotected and sent them off to political protest or to "escapist," individualistic lyrical fictions. Even their recollection of the "Old Home"—negative and derisive at first and nostalgic later—was made from an irreversible position on American ground. To call M. L. Halpern a poet from Galicia makes no more sense than calling T. S. Eliot a "poet from Missouri" or Ben-Gurion a "Polish politician." But, while their peers, the graphic artists, became part of the accepted history of American art and their contemporaries who wrote in English (like Charles Reznikoff) are part of American poetry, the Yiddish poets—who could certainly match them in form and theme—remained quarantined within their alien language.

The Major Trends

The trends of Yiddish poetry created in America were never extensions of Yiddish literature in the old country; they evolved from the concrete dynamics of the independent American Yiddish literary center. Though its poets often felt like the young branch of a lush tree, like refugees washed up on a strange shore, Yiddish poetry actually developed concurrently with the Yiddish literary renaissance in Europe and even preceded the latter in its major achievements.

Many American Yiddish poets still read European languages and often drew on various sources from the Jewish and non-Jewish culture of Europe to which they had grown attached in their youth. These influences, as well as the autonomous development of an American Yiddish poetry and poetics, combined with the pressures of their separate readership, made their writing different from the English poetry next door. But no generation of American Yiddish poets was part of any worldwide Yiddish poetic trend either. Life in the United States, which included not only harsh working conditions but also a more peaceful atmosphere than that in Europe—and a sense of freedom—contributed to this difference, as did the impact of American poetry and social ideas. The terrifying events of the twentieth century shook Yiddish-American poets to the quick, but those events did not occur in the streets of their own cities and spoke, instead, to their more general historical sense of humanity and Jewish destiny.

We can observe five major groups of Yiddish poets that emerged in the United States:

(1) The "Proletarian" or "Sweatshop" poets of the end of the nineteenth century—Morris Rosenfeld, Dovid Edelshtat, Yoysef Bov-

shover, Morris Vinchevsky, and others—were inspired primarily by socialism and anarchism, but at the same time expressed panhistorical despair about Jewish destiny in the Diaspora and dreamed of Zion. Even the extremely popular radical revolutionary poet, Dovid Edelshtat (1866–1892), wrote: "Brothers, we carry a triple chain—/As Jews, as slaves, as thinkers" (from "The Jewish Proletarian," a well-known song). They were known for their personal involvement in the life of the sweatshop proletariat, their concern with social and political issues, and their direct revolutionary rhetoric, and were popular with Jewish workers. They also considered themselves inspired "poets," however, and wrote poetry on "lofty" subjects like love, nature, or the art of poetry, vacillating between their interests in "Jewish" and in "cosmopolitan" themes. They were masters of the art of versification and were the first to establish the rule of accentual-syllabic meters in Yiddish poetry. Furthermore, they affirmed the dominance of poetry in Yiddish literature which, in its European center, at that time, focused on representational prose. Distant from the Jewish shtetl and the European shtetl fiction, they promoted the here and now, the pathos of poetic diction, rhymed song-like verse and effective political rhetoric.

An account of the Yiddish poets in America, published in a Russian Yiddish newspaper in 1905, demonstrates their plight:

[Many of them had to suffer] the most bitter poverty which has shackled the poetic imagination in chains and destroyed the beautiful, rich aspirations one after another. We mean, of course, the writers who did not agree to accept compromises with their concept of art, who did not want to sell out their inspiration for a mass of pottage, did not want to serve with their pen purposes which have nothing to do with literature. In the end, they were forced into factories, into sweatshops, into the streets and marketplaces to peddle newspapers, apples and suspenders. Look what happened to our best poets: one died in the flower of his youth of tuberculosis [Edelshtat], a second one is confined to a madhouse [Bovshover], a third, sick with consumption, has a tailor's shop in Colorado [Yehoash], two or three write news items and articles in the daily papers, and others have neither time nor courage to create poems in the prosaic, oppressive atmosphere of American hustle-bustle.[5]

(2) "The Young Generation" (also known by their Yiddish name, "Di Yunge") emerged with their first journal in 1907.[6] It included such

5. ℳ. Alexandrov, quoted by Sh. Nigger in *General Encyclopedia* [in Yiddish], vol. *Yidn G'* (New York, 1942) p. 123.

6. The life of the major poet of this group, Mani Leyb, was described in a well-documented book: Ruth R. Wisse, *A Little Love in Big Manhattan*, Harvard University Press, 1988.

poets as Mani Leyb, Y. Rolnik, Zisho Landoy, M. Dillon, Anna Mar-
golin, as well as M. L. Halpern and H. Leyvik. They were interested
to a large extent in art for art's sake, in exquisite Impressionist poetry
of mood and atmosphere, in mellifluous, masterfully formed verse,
written in a smooth, "poetic" diction. They would not harness their
verse to any political purposes, nor become the "rhyme department
of the labor movement," as Zisho Landoy expressed it. Instead, they
centered on the experiences of the individual. They translated from
world poetry into Yiddish and, in general, introduced a cosmopolitan
spirit into American Yiddish literature. In some respects, their poetry
was akin to English Edwardian verse or to the general European neo-
Romantic trend, but it was also influenced by the playful irony of
Heine's lyrics. The Young Generation was a purely American product.
Though influenced by a general European mood, its poets had little
in common with contemporary Yiddish writers in Europe, where
prose still carried the day. Interestingly enough, it was individualist,
Impressionist prose that their contemporaries in Europe (Bergelson,
Gnessin, der Nister) were writing in Yiddish and Hebrew. The
"Young" poets' counterpart were a few Hebrew poets in Europe and
Eretz Israel who were exposed to similar Russian- and German-
mediated influences, though the two groups hardly knew of each other
at the time. The Young Generation established in Yiddish poetry the
mastery of verse forms, a cultured tradition of poetry translations, and
children's poetry of high literary quality.

(3) The individual writers that can be grouped together as "cultural
poets" never constituted a social group or a recognized literary trend
but were nevertheless an important force, counterbalancing the political rhetoric of the "sweatshop" poets and the short lyrics of transient
moods fostered by the "Young Generation." Indeed, they lived and
published along with the poets of the first two groups. We may include
here such great masters of Yiddish verse as Yehoash, A. Lyesin, Men-
akhem Boreysho, I. I. Shvartz and, in part, H. Leyvik. They re-created
in Yiddish poetry themes and characters from the Bible, from all periods of Jewish history, from Hebrew poetry in Spain and the Kabbalah, as well as topics from Oriental and European literature and
philosophy and, especially, images from recent Jewish history, ideological movements, and migration. They developed the genres of epic
poetry, poetic drama, the narrative ballad, the fable, and the declam-
atory poem. Most of them were steeped in Hebrew literature and the

Hebrew textual tradition. They tried to capture in formal Yiddish verse the density and the mythopoeic and dramatic qualities of a fictional but historically representative "world," as pluralistically interpreted as possible, in a period that favored the short lyric and the emotive and figurative response. The cultural poets are almost unknown to the English reader, for it is very hard to translate their large bodies of narrative texts, written in metrical and rhymed verse and in an epic poetic diction that is not fashionable in English today. The *world* of their poetry, however, carries substantial chunks of Jewish experience and has much to offer to a contemporary reader (e.g., Boreysho's *der Geyer* ["The Wanderer"], a philosophical epic on the ideological trends and the crisis of Jewish thought at the turn of the century).

(4) The "Introspectivists," a literary trend launched in 1919, began a theoretical and practical revolt against the dominance and "poetical-ness" of the Young Generation. Beside the founders, Jacob Glatshteyn, N. B. Minkov, and A. Leyeles, it included Y. A. Vaysman, Ruven Ludwig, B. Alquit, Celia Dropkin, and others. For the Introspectivists, a poem presented a kaleidoscope of broken pieces from the social world, as perceived in the psyche of a sophisticated urban individual and as expressed in a unique rhythmical "fugue." Theirs was a post-Symbolist poetics, stressing free verse, open thematics and language, and an end to the poetic ivory tower. But they, too, were radically different from their Yiddish contemporaries in Warsaw, Berlin, Kiev, Moscow, or Tel Aviv who loudly screamed the slogans of Expression-ism, Revolution and Zionism. The Introspectivists developed a rather Anglo-American poetics of irony, dramatized and objectified poetic situations, and intellectual understatement; they formed a much more mature, antisentimental, and honestly harsh view of the real world. They were the focal point of the best poetry written in Yiddish.

(5) The leftist poets of the 1920s and 1930s clustered around the "Proletpen" and more or less openly communist journals like the daily *Frayhayt* and the monthly *Hamer*. Among them were Moyshe Nadir, Zishe Vaynper, M. L. Halpern, and H. Leyvik. Most of them were fuzzy sympathizers rather than party members, and many broke with the "line" whenever a moral or national issue arose. It was chic at the time to have your heart on the left. Communist ideals had a great fascination for many justice-seeking Jewish writers and readers in the face of the harsh aspects of American capitalism. Communism was

also a dignified way of shedding the burden of Jewish particularism—
or so they thought. In addition, it was nourished by the nostalgia for
the Russia of the books, its literature, "open soul," melancholy songs,
and revolutionary spirit. The memory of the liberation of the Jews
from unbearable czarist oppression and pogroms (which many re-
membered with horror from their own childhood) was still fresh, as
was the impression of the truly equal rights granted them by the early
Soviet regime, and of the visible role many Jews were able to play in
the new Soviet culture, science, and government. Moreover, Jewish
communists in the United States had a real audience and readership
devoted to the cause, to Yiddish international culture, and to a collective spirit that lured many a lonely poet.

The writers of the left did create some interesting poetry of naturalist description of urban realities and poetry of social protest, ranging from the obligatory topic of the Sacco-Vanzetti case to a book-
length poem on *Little Rock*. But the pressures of Soviet-inspired pol-
icies, with their demands for flattening the language of poetry and
making it a propaganda tool or a rhetorical jingle of Socialist Realism
that could be "understood by the masses," coupled with their anti-
Zionist attitudes (especially their pro-Arab stance during the Arab uprising and anti-Jewish outbursts of 1929 in Palestine), estranged most
of the important poets from their fold.

Many creative poets did not belong to any of these groups. Furthermore, certain basic trends and historical events had an impact on writers of various leanings and there was a great deal of mutual influence
among them. In many ways, describing literature in such groupings
reflects the clusters of typical literary alternatives rather than airtight
compartments and absolute differences among poets. For instance,
Moyshe-Leyb Halpern and H. Leyvik began their poetic development
with the Young Generation. But the young Introspectivist Jacob
Glatshteyn, while dismissing the Young Generation altogether, as early
as 1920 sensed the different poetic value of these two poets (See "A
Quick Run Through Yiddish Poetry," *In zikh*, 1920). Indeed, Halpern
exhibited strong Expressionist features in the 1920s; Leyvik—who
began with the Young Generation—and Leyeles, the Introspectivist,
shared in the 1920s a certain tendency to an aura of mysticism in their
verse as well as a lifelong friendship. From the mid-1920s, the achievements of all these trends and the general impact of English Modernist
poetry became common property. Poets of various backgrounds used
them according to their personal development, as was the case with

Modernism in other literatures. In the next chapter we shall analyze in detail the cluster of problems faced by one of these groups, the Introspectivists.

After World War II, an influx of refugees from Europe brought a number of important poets to America and, for a short time, increased the number of Yiddish readers. The Holocaust in Europe, disenchantment with Stalinism, recognition of the great light coming from the State of Israel, and the dissolution of any firm body of Yiddish readership made all the writers share in a common destiny.

Few Yiddish writers were added after the 1950s, however. With the passing of the poets of the generations that had emerged in the 1920s and 1930s, Yiddish literature in America dwindled to a tiny band. The famous *Daily Forward*, which had epitomized Jewish immigrant life in America and the struggles of the Jewish world for eighty-five years, and which had often lowered Yiddish culture to the level of the street, but had also published some of its best writers, including Nobel prize winner Isaac Bashevis Singer, stopped daily publication in 1983, but is still operating as a weekly.

8

Introspectivism: A Modernist Poetics

The Introspectivist movement can serve as an outstanding example of the critical ambience in American Yiddish literature and of the basic tensions that permeated it.[1] The problems that preoccupied the Introspectivist theoreticians—the relations between art and life, language and form, the individual and social reality, the "Jewish" and the "universal"—were central to other trends and generations in American Yiddish poetry as well, beginning with such "sweatshop" poets as Dovid Edelshtat and Morris Rosenfeld. But the Introspectivists formulated a consciously Modernist poetics, supported by their own creative work and related to Modernist poetics in the international context.

After seventy years of international literary theory and criticism, the theorizing of the Yiddish poets around 1920 may seem somewhat naive, but theirs was a more mature and complex view of poetic art than the one formulated in the early manifestoes of Anglo-American Imagism. Theorizing by poets in manifestoes, programmatic articles, or critical essays uses a very different language and serves a different function from academic theory or criticism, and should not be judged

1. See the English translation of the Introspectivist manifesto and excerpts from Introspectivist literary theory and criticism collected in "Chronicle of a Movement" in AYP. The following quotations refer to the "Chronicle." AYP contains also a large selection of poetry by the Introspectivists A. Leyeles, Jacob Glatshteyn, and J. L. Teller.

by those standards, but rather as a direct expression of artistic ideology and polemics in a specific cultural context. The writings of the Yiddish theoreticians are often misleadingly didactic and chatty, trying to explain difficult issues of literary theory to an audience of autodidacts and newspaper readers. But when we distill their ideas we discover a mature and complex view of art.

The Yiddish Introspectivists absorbed the ideas on art that were developed in recent Modernist movements. In their arguments one can find traces of Italian and Russian Futurism, German and Yiddish Expressionism, English Imagism and Vorticism, as well as ideas raised by Nietzsche, Croce, Freud, and T. S. Eliot. Sometimes it is hard to tell to what extent such echoes derive directly from primary texts and to what extent they are part of a cultural aura available to intellectual readers after World War I. The important point is the attempt to integrate such elements into a single, coherent, "classical" Modernism, rather than to voice the slogans of one extreme position.

In 1918, A. Leyeles published his first book of poems, *Labyrinth*, each page of which was appropriately adorned with a frame of swastikas, the ancient Indian symbol. Though still steeped in neo-Romantic moods and forms, his was a radical individualism and a sophisticated, intellectual stance. As such, it was hardly acceptable either to his contemporaries, the poets of the "Young Generation," or to the politicized (i.e., leftist) environment of Yiddish cultural life in New York after World War I. Sometime in 1918, two young students, Jacob Glatshteyn and N. B. Minkov, came to Leyeles with their Yiddish poems and "actively raised the idea of a new [poetic] trend." All three were intellectuals, well read both in general and in Jewish culture; they met and talked continuously, developing the ideology and poetics of a new, Modernist trend in Yiddish poetry (see A. Leyeles, "Twenty Years of 'Inzikh,'" *Inzikh*, April, 1940). At the time, they published their poems in H. Gudelman's journal, *Poezye* ("Poetry," like the name of its English-language counterpart and Marinetti's *Poesia*), along with members of the Young Generation and several European Yiddish poets.

In 1919, the three poets formulated the principles of their new trend and published them as an introduction to an anthology, *In zikh* ("In Oneself"), including their own poems as well as those of several like-minded young poets. This introduction, entitled "Introspectivism," became the so-called manifesto of their movement. It is written as a declaration of principles, although in a discursive and didactic tone, addressed to the general Yiddish reader. The anthology appeared in January, 1920, and the first issue of the journal *In zikh* appeared shortly thereafter. In time, the title of the journal was contracted into one word, *Inzikh*, and became the Yiddish name of their trend, "Inzikhism," and of its poets, "Inzikhists."

In zikh was a typical little review, devoted primarily to poetry and also publishing poetic theory, criticism, and polemics as well as political and cultural essays written by the poets. It appeared, with several interruptions, from January, 1920, until December, 1940. In all, one hundred poets and writers participated in *Inzikh*, among them some of the young European Yiddish Modernists like the Yiddish poetess, Dvora Fogel (the friend of Bruno Schulz) and Abraham Sutskever.[2] Though suffering from the lack of an intelligent readership and from vicious attacks by newspaper critics, moralizers, and leftist party hacks, *Inzikh* became the standard-bearer of Yiddish Modernism in America.

At the end of the 1930s, the plight of the Jews in Europe diverted the critical focus from the theory of poetic language to the problem of art in an age of destruction. The poets, however, never abandoned their concern with art and language, as is clear from Glatshteyn's essays of 1945–47, collected in *Sum and Substance*.[3] The shift of emphasis was also accompanied by a shift from Leyeles's dominance in the early years as a theoretician of poetry and free verse to Jacob Glatshteyn's prominence as the major Yiddish literary critic and poet after the Holocaust.

In zikh, the first journal of its kind, was soon followed by Yiddish Modernist journals published in Warsaw, Lodz, Berlin, Moscow, and Paris and devoted primarily to poetry, poetic theory, and graphic art. Such journals as *Shtrom* ("The Torrent"), *Khalyastre* ("The Gang"), and *Albatross* promoted a new, Modernist poetry in Yiddish, a poetry influenced mainly by Expressionism and Futurism and the impact of the Russian Revolution with its messianic mood, futuristic utopia, and atrocities. The American Inzikhists shared neither the horrors experienced by the European Yiddish poets in World War I nor the pogroms of 1919. Nor did they share the Expressionist poetics of "Scream"

2. J. Birnboym, "The Journal *In zikh*," in *Pinkes far der forshung fun der yidisher literatur un prese* (New York, 1972), 28–49.
3. This is Glatshteyn's own translation of the book's title. The Yiddish name, *In tokh genumen*, was the title of Glatshteyn's column in the Labor Zionist cultural weekly, *Yidisher kemfer* ("The Jewish Fighter"); a closer translation of this title would be "The Heart of the Matter."

about "Horror" and the "Twilight of Humanity" or the politicized views of communist- or Zionist-inspired literature. They were, however, aware of these European waves.

The name "Introspectivism" seems to be a direct challenge to the slogan of Expressionism that swept Europe. The opposition of "Expressionism" versus "Impressionism" was used to describe the radical shift from an art registering external mood and atmosphere, the subtleties of air, light, and psychological nuance, to the coarse and pathetic expression of the rhythm and spirit of modern, urban civilization with its technology, wars, masses, corruption, radical politics, and the destruction of bourgeois morality. Impressionism seemed to be the last art of mimesis, not essential for real expression. In his manifesto, "On Expressionism in Literature" (1917), the German writer Kasimir Edschmid wrote: "The world exists. It makes no sense to repeat it. To explore it in its every last tremor, in its innermost core and to create it anew—this is the greatest mission of art."[4]

The Introspectivist manifesto echoes the initial assumption of this statement, opposing mimesis as the principle of art, but seeks its object elsewhere: "The world exists and we are part of it. But for us, the world exists as it is mirrored in us, as it touches *us*. It becomes an actuality only in and *through* us." They promoted "Introspectivist" poetry as an intellectual insight into one's self, as a personal reflection of an internalized social world, rather than as a mere vehicle for the expression of a *Zeitgeist*, a political mood, the "essence" of the world or of "Man" in general. The poet's major concern was to express the organic relationship between outside phenomena and himself and to do so in an introspective and individual manner. "*In an introspective manner* means that the poet must really listen to his inner voice, observe his internal panorama—kaleidoscopic, contradictory, unclear or confused as it may be."

This was not an escapist, ivory tower poetry, however. A major antinomy of Introspectivist theory is between the emphasis on individual experience and the range of the world it reflects. A key passage in the "manifesto" reads:

For us, everything is "personal." Wars and Revolutions, Jewish pogroms and the workers' movement, Protestantism and Buddha, the Yiddish school and the Cross, the mayoral elections [in New York] and a ban on our language;

4. Kasimir Edschmid, *Über den Expressionismus in Der Literatur und die neue Dichtung* (Berlin: Erich Reiss, 1919), 56.

all these may concern us or not, just as a blond woman and our own unrest may or may not concern us. If it does concern us, we write poetry; if it does not, we keep quiet. In either case, we write about ourselves because all these exist only insofar as they are in us, insofar as they are perceived *introspectively*.

The list of thematic domains in this statement represents an Expressionist grasp of political and cultural realities, though observed as they become part of the personal world of a modern man or woman. It mixes religious attitudes and daily politics, world events and personal emotions, universal history and Jewish news in one kaleidoscopic whirl. One must not be misled by the individualism of the label "Introspectivism." Theirs was a poetry acutely attuned to the historical and political world, however personally internalized by each poet.

The major influence of Anglo-American poetry on the New York Yiddish poets lay in the tone of understatement and irony typical of Glatshteyn, the Leyeles of *Fabius Lind*, or the early Halpern, as opposed to the noisy screams of the Yiddish "big-city" poets in Europe. Thematically, the poets often guarded the autonomy of the individual and his idiosyncratic private world against the uniformity of leftist ideologies—but that too is a political stance. The Introspectivists were essentially political poets, although, in a "party-line" sense, they were the most apolitical poets in Jewish New York.

Thus, the Introspectivists met the challenge of Expressionism to find a response to the political and social realities which, in this age, entered personal life as never before and certainly determined the personal lives of Jews on the move, whose very channels of existence depended on the political climate. This conception also abolished the simplistic opposition between "Jewish" and "universal" topics, and put an end to the escape of the "Young Generation" poets from national themes for the sake of pure poetry. It also prepared the Introspectivists—Glatshteyn, Teller, Minkov, and Leyeles—to react naturally, as poets and as individuals, to the Holocaust, and to grasp it in their individual poetic language, as part of their personal experience.

The Introspectivists fought an ongoing battle against accusations that they were "knowledgeable" but cerebral poets. (Leyeles "knows" how to make poems, therefore he is not a poet. . .) The distinction between "poetry of feeling" and "poetry of thought" was meaningless for them ("there is no boundary between feeling and thought in contemporary man") as it was for T. S. Eliot. Those who adhered to either were "dualists" (compare Eliot's "dissociation of sensibilities") who created monotonous rhythms. Just as for other Expressionist or post-

Symbolist trends, for the Introspectivists, "everything is an object for poetry": "There is no ugly or beautiful, no good or bad, no high or low." This opening of all thematic boundaries did not, however, imply an atmosphere of laissez-faire; they proposed a specific theory allowing the inclusion of all elements in a poem, under the slogans of "chaotic" and "kaleidoscopic."

The idea that poetry should present "the chaotic" rather than neat, well-made poems was in the air. For the Expressionists, this meant being truthful to the real world. The Yiddish Expressionist, Uri Zvi Grinberg, a soldier and deserter in World War I, wrote in the manifesto of his journal, *Albatross* (Warsaw, 1922):

This is how things are. Whether we want it or not. We stand as we are: with slash-lipped wounds, rolled up veins, unscrewed bones, after artillery bombardments and cries of "Hurrah," after gas-attacks; after bowls filled with gall and opium and the daily water: disgust. And the foam of decay covers our lips.
   Hence the atrocious in the poem.
   Hence the chaotic in the image.
   Hence the scream in the blood.
   [. . .] *It is imperative to write such poems.*
Atrocious. Chaotic. Bleeding.——

The translation of this ideology into the actual language of poetry meant promoting a chaotic composition, avoiding any continuity of time and space in a poem ("death to time and space," proclaimed an Italian Futurist manifesto), showing defiance to overt coherence and closure, and constructing a random collage of discordant elements in one text. Moyshe-Leyb Halpern is an extreme example of such a poet: after his first book, he abandoned the Impressionist poetics and the well-rounded poem of the Young Generation and became increasingly demonstrative and whimsical in his disordered, chaotic compositions, especially in his rambling dramatic monologues.

The Introspectivists found "chaos" in their own psyches: "If the internal world is a chaos, let the chaos be manifested [in the poetry]." Chaos is not merely—and not primarily—the chaos of the modern world breaking out of all rationality, but the chaos of our personal stream of consciousness. "The human psyche is an awesome labyrinth." A person's "I" is subject and object at the same time, present and past, part and whole; his present life and the metamorphosis of previous lives all exist in him simultaneously. "He is simultaneously at the Ganges and at the Hudson, in the year 1922 and in the year when Tiglathpilesser conquered and terrorized a world. Therefore, the Introspectivist is chaotic and kaleidoscopic" (A. Leyeles, see "Chronicle of a Movement: Excerpts from Introspectivist Criticism," No. 11, AYP, pp. 785–804). Hence their opposition to the Imagist ideal of "concentration." Concentration and well-roundedness create a poem and a mood that is isolated and cut off from any context, and this is simply a "lie," the artificiality of art in relation to real "life," because the impact of any phenomenon on the human psyche stimulates a whole galaxy of moods, feelings, and perceptions.

The basic idea is similar to the concepts of "simultaneity" and "intersecting planes" in Italian Futurist plastic art, as the following passage from the Introspectivist manifesto shows:

When the poet, or any person, looks at a sunset, he may see the strangest things which, ostensibly, have perhaps no relation to the sunset. The image reflected in his psyche is rather a series of far-reaching associations moving away from what his eye sees, a chain of suggestions evoked by the sunset. *This*, the series of associations and the chain of suggestions, constitutes *truth*, is life, much as an illusion is often more real than the cluster of external appearances we call life.

In Leyeles's "Autumn," "Symmetry," and other poems, we find motifs of this perception, which often contain elements of Freudian psychoanalysis and of Oriental mysticism and Ouspensky's "fourth dimension."

The poetic equivalent to this psychological conception lies in the theory of kaleidoscopic art. Rather than mere "chaos," as embraced by the Expressionists and, instinctively, by M. L. Halpern, the kaleidoscopic vision is an organized presentation evoking elements from various discordant situations. Instead of the single image of the Imagists, the poem has many faces; instead of similes, it has colorful splinters of direct images. As N. B. Minkov pointed out in an essay on the poetry of A. Leyeles (1939), this resulted in an inherent contradiction: while introspection itself is analytical, the kaleidoscopic method is synthetic. The excellent poet Minkov was biased himself, always tending to the first option, immersed in a mystifying Introspectivism; but the analogy between the kaleidoscopic principle and Synthetic Cubism (as opposed to the earlier, Analytical Cubism) was apt: the idea was to present, like Picasso, a conscious construct of broken pieces simultaneously representing several discordant aspects or points of view. Whereas the Expressionist chaos found a unifying force in its loud, Whitmanesque voice, or in political pathos, Leyeles was looking for a unifying force in an all-pervasive rhythm which constituted the "soul" or the "essence" of the poem. As the kaleidoscope is opposed to the single image, so—in Leyeles's theory—the "fugue" of a free rhythm is opposed to the monotonous operatic "air" presented by one meter.

The concept of the kaleidoscopic method thus brought together several modern principles: the psychology of the stream of conscious-ness, the multidimensional nature of modern life, simultaneity of ex-perience, representation through splinter elements rather than through a full description, and the conscious organization of a poem as a "fugue" or a "symphony" of heterogeneous elements playing together in a single integrated whole. This concept describes the art of T. S. Eliot in "The Waste Land" and "Ash Wednesday" or Pound's "Cantos" better than do the Imagist theories stressing the "thing," the individual "image," or "concentration."

In their actual praxis, not all Introspectivist poets implemented the kaleidoscopic principle with full vigor. Glatshteyn used it in poems like "1919" (see chapter 9) but mostly preferred to base the com-position of a poem on a particular, unrealistic situation. Leyeles, after using it in such texts as "January 28" and some of his city poems, found a new solution in the poetic cycle, such as "The Diary of Fabius Lind" or "To You—To Me." Though each individual poem of a cycle centered on one mood, scene, or situation (to be sure, with associa-tions to other moods), the cycle as a whole contained a conscious kaleidoscope of heterogeneous topics—erotic, political, urban, and so on—presented in an intentional rainbow of rhythmical forms. Thus, the cycle "To You—To Me" has a framework written in a special eight-line strophe, in precise meter and rhyme; it is, however, interrupted in mid-strophe and mid-line—where a number of greatly varying met-rical and free verse poems are inserted—only to be resumed thirty pages later in the middle of the interrupted line and completed in a formal closure. On a higher level, the whole book, *Fabius Lind*, is just such a kaleidoscopic diary of a contemporary, in which the personal and the social, the trivial and the metaphysical alternate—matched by an ostensibly random alternation of a broad spectrum of formal and free verse—to present a kaleidoscope "of metamorphoses, pain, trans-formations, elation, and achievement over a range of a lived piece of life," as Glatshteyn described it. "In this book, ten years in the life of a highly cultured, unsettled, searching, refined Jew were fixed forever:

hence, *ipso facto*, for me, Leyeles's ten years are also—and primarily—ten Jewish years." (See "Chronicle," No. 25.)

The second principle accompanying introspection was the *individuality* of expression. According to the Introspectivist manifesto, "because we perceive the world egocentrically and because we think this is the most natural and therefore *the truest and most human* mode of perception, we think that the poem of every poet must first of all be *his own* poem." This principle is applied equally to content and form: "We insist that the poet present the authentic image that he sees in himself and present it in such a form as only he and no one else can see it." Each poet must develop his own poetic language and his own poetics, which may eventually subvert any principle of the group.

Here again, there is a paradox: by individuality, the Introspectivists did not mean relativism in value judgments. They insisted that the poet should not only be a "person" in his own right but an "interesting," "contemporary," "intelligent, conscious person capable of expressing the seen, felt and understood in his own, internally true, introspectively sincere manner." By means of association and suggestion—that is, through deliberate discontinuous composition and alogical devices of poetic language—the poet must "express the complex feelings and perceptions of a contemporary person." "Verslibrism," as Leyeles put it, is not just an innovation in form but an expression of a new content. "The new content is the modern life of the modern man, who is breaking away from the old idyllic world, from the old provincialism and small-town atmosphere" ("Chronicle," No. 10). When, like Eliot and Pound, the Introspectivists stressed that poetry should use the spoken language, it was "the spoken language of the more intelligent, more conscious part of the Jewish people" they had in mind ("Chronicle," No. 7).

Thus the poetic theory of the Introspectivists is based on several antinomies: introspection—but reflection of the social and political world; individual poetic language—but expression of "modern man." We may add a third pair: art for art's sake—but art as an "authentic" expression of "life." Answering the critic Nigger's demands for a "Jewish art," Leyeles claimed: "Literature is *art*. And art has its own laws, the highest of which is—art itself." But he immediately continued: "Art is *only* an expression of life" ("Chronicle," No. 5). In another context, Leyeles explains the formula, "art for art's sake": "Armed with his intuition, the modern artist does not want to know any tasks or goals other than art"; but here, too, he adds: "Because he knows that, for him, art is the only road to arrive at the truth, to see the world in its real light and to understand his own relation to the world" ("Chronicle," No. 15).

These antinomies catch some of the central contradictions and polemics of Modernist poetry since Symbolism. They do not offer an uneasy marriage of opposites but a conjunction of two contradictory poles, making the one stronger when it is expressed through the other. Introspectivist value judgment seems to require that both poles be expressed in each of the dilemmas.

From this conception, several additional antinomies can be derived. The Introspectivists did not impose on poetry any "Jewish" or other social mission but, "because it is art, it is Jewish anyway" ("Chronicle," No. 5). In their most experimental poetry, the Introspectivists invested "Jewish" elements; the Jewish experience was always part of their personal, "universal" experience. For them, Jewishness was a language rather than a mission: "A Jew will write about an Indian fertility temple and Japanese Shintoists as a Jew" (the Introspectivist manifesto). Not just as human beings but *as poets, as an essential aspect of their poetics*, they developed antennae sensitive to the political climate surrounding them and wrote about it rather than about conventional poetic topics. This is as true for their intense Americanness as for their deeply felt Jewishness. The Introspectivists were the first Yiddish poets who enthusiastically accepted the magnificence of the big American city, "the relation to the big city, to the Woolworths [Tower], the Empire States, the total gigantic rhythm of the Metropolis New York or the Metropolis Chicago" (A. Leyeles, *In zikh*, October, 1935). Yet even before the Holocaust, they shifted their emphasis to Jewish topics as central to their personal experience: "The same writers who perceived America and expressed it in poem, novel, drama, turned to Jewish history and sought characters and situations there for their contemporary and even 'American' ideas," wrote Leyeles in 1935 ("Chronicle," No. 22). That is why they were prepared to face the oncoming Holocaust and respond to it in poetry.

Similar antinomies obtain in the perception of poetic form. The Introspectivists paid attention to the details of form and language. The individual image, the right word in the right place, no superfluous similes or adjectives, and the liberation of the word as the material of art from the conventional ballast of centuries—all these seem to have been influenced by Italian and Russian Futurism. At the same time, for them, enhancing the art of language meant enhancing true expression. For example, Leyeles repeatedly emphasized that "rhythm is what actually makes the poem," that "words, ideas, content, images by themselves have no independent meaning in the poem. They exist only to serve. They help to create rhythm." For Leyeles, however, "rhythm" has no value when it is rhythm only rather than the "soul" of the poem, its metaphysical "essence," something that transcends the trivial and accidental "content."

Free verse appeared as a conscious tendency in French Symbolism in the last third of the nineteenth century and can be traced back to Goethe, Novalis and Coleridge. At the beginning of the twentieth century it moved from the periphery to the center of poetic theory. In 1905, F. T. Marinetti launched an international referendum on free verse, in which many important European poets participated. Published as a book in 1909 (with the Italian *Futurist Manifesto*), the *Enquête international sur le vers libre* may be considered a landmark that transformed one late French Symbolist technique into a central hallmark of Modernism. Free verse became a central principle of most Modernist trends in poetry: Imagism, Futurism, Expressionism, and Acmeism all felt it to be a crucial issue for the nature of the new art in language. However, the rationalizations of the theory of free verse as well as the actual forms it assumed differed widely.

Scarcely any free verse poems appeared in Yiddish before World War I. The Introspectivists were the first to make this a cardinal issue dividing the new poetry from the old. It was a genuine revolution since it is not easy for a poet raised on metrical verse to free himself from the automatized habit of falling into scansion. The Introspectivists may have received the green light from Anglo-American Imagism for this move, but they had a different conception of the problem. They emphasized not so much the aspect of freedom from tradition as that of individual expression and deliberate orchestration of a richer, rather than a more prosaic, rhythm. For them, free verse demanded "an intense effort" in coordinating and subordinating all aspects of sound patterning in the poetic texture. Free verse was to be an expression of individuality on all levels: of the poet, of the poem, and of the individual verse line. It was to express both "the natural rise and fall of a mood" and "the new music that stirs the world," the irregular tempo of the big city and the "disharmony" of the "contemporary psychic experience." Hence the emphasis not on uniformity or prosaic tone but on the interaction of many shifting rhythmical devices and the symphonic nature of a free rhythmic poem. Since individuality of rhythm, rather than freedom of verse, was the issue, this could be accomplished in regular meters as well, provided the variety of selected forms guaranteed the uniqueness of each poem. In sum, free verse in Yiddish poetry was a departure from the dominant, conventional form of a symmetrical, four-line, rhymed strophe and it worked in two opposite directions: of less and of more structured texts.

Monotony was death to poetry. Glatshteyn understood this in his own way when he denied the musicality of Edgar Allan Poe's "The Raven" (arguing against Leyeles, who translated it twice, in 1918 and in 1945!). He used the term again when he exposed the danger of a whole literature becoming "monotonic and monothematic" in "wailing together" after the Holocaust. Glatshteyn himself tried to save the individuality of the poem, even in that age of "collective stammer." As he put it: "Our word is our weapon and we must not let ourselves become primitive [in wailing over the destruction]." Glatshteyn cites as an example the prophet Jeremiah who, when a whole people was enslaved, "played" with the art of language and sought perfection in his "Jeremiads" ("May One Enjoy Elegies?" *Sum and Substance*, pp. 428–434).

The Introspectivist poets themselves were aware that their poetics was part of an international trend: "Certainly, there is a more direct relation between an Introspectivist and a German Expressionist or English Vorticist than between us and most Yiddish poets of the previous periods" ("Chronicle," No. 14). For the outside world, however, the Yiddish poets were isolated in a sealed ghetto. A telling example was the letter of the editors of the English-language *Poetry*, asking whether the language of *In zikh* was "Chinese" (see the *In zikh* reply in "Chronicle," No. 18 and also Nos. 24, 26). In the Jewish domain itself, there was a chronic scarcity of readers (see "Chronicle," Nos. 8, 19, 23). Of course, English poets also had relatively small circles of readers at the time, before Modernist poetry was introduced into college curricula, but Yiddish poets never enjoyed that canonization. Only the common national tragedy brought them back to the center of Jewish society and made them into social bards, sometimes at the expense of their poetic quality. Then it became clear what immense work had been done in the development of a new poetic language in Yiddish in New York between 1919 and 1950.

9

The End of a Language

nakht. in di tunklste ERTER finklen VERTER.
s'geyen op gantse SHIFN mit BAGRIFN.
un du, bapantsert mit shvaygn un klugzayn,
viklst op vort fun meyn.

Night. In the darkest places sparkle traces
Of words. Loaded ships with ideo-glyphs
Sail away. And you, armored in silence and wisdom,
Unwrap word from sense.
—J. Glatshteyn, "We the Wordproletariat," AYP, 274

The young Introspectivist Jacob Glatshteyn (1896–1971) felt that one could not make sense of the *velt-plonter* ("tangle of the world"), when shiploads of ideas sail away incomprehensibly. The Introspectivist poet wears the armor of personal wisdom and silence vis-à-vis the shouting, politicized society, observes his own consciousness ironically, and tries to liberate words from the burden of sense. In the poetry of the early Glatshteyn, there is no denial of his Jewishness but it is actually irrelevant for the human condition he represents. Jewish traces are simply part of his "impulses of memory," flashing suddenly in his field of consciousness like the strange word *tirtle-toyben* from his early childhood, in the poem "Turtledoves" (AYP, 214).

In his poem "1919," a date in history filled with red headlines of the Red Revolution and the rivers of blood from pogroms in the Ukraine, the protagonist is running around in New York, a latter-day Jacob son of Isaac, comically reduced to the familiar and childish "Yankl, son of Yitskhok," a tiny round dot that rolls crazily through the streets with hooked-on, clumsy limbs:

1919
di letste tsayt iz keyn shpur nit mer geBLIbn
fun yankl bereb yitskhok,
nor a kleyntshik pintele a kaylekhdiks,
vos kayklt zikh tseDULterheyt iber gasn
mit aROYFgetshepete, umgeLUMperte glider.
der oyberhar hot mit dem himlbloy
di gantse erd aRUMgeringlt
un nito keyn retung.
umeTUM faln "ekstras" fun oybn
un tsePLEtshn mayn vaserdikn kop.
un eyner mit a langer tsung
hot mit a shtik royt mayne briln oyf eybik bafLEKT
un royt, royt, royt.
ir hert:
ot di teg vet epes aZOYNS in mayn kop platsn
un mit a tempn krakh zikh ontsindn dort
un iberlozn a kupke shmutsiklekhn ash.
un ikh,
dos kaylekhdike pintele,
vel zikh dreyen in eter oyf eybikeytn
mit royte vualn aRUMgehilt.

Lately, there's no trace left
Of Yankl, son of Yitskhok,
But for a tiny round dot
That rolls crazily through the streets
With hooked-on, clumsy limbs.
The lord-above surrounded
The whole world with heaven-blue
And there is no escape.
Everywhere "Extras!" fall from above
And squash my watery head.
And someone's long tongue
Has stained my glasses for good with a smear of red,
And red, red, red.
You see!

One of these days something will explode in my head,
Ignite there with a dull crash
And leave behind a heap of dirty ashes.
And I,
The tiny dot,
Will spin in ether for eternities,
Wrapped in red veils.

—AYP, 209

The Yiddish expression "dos pintele yid" ("the Jewish dot") refers to the most elementary, irreducible point of identity of a Jew. It derives from the tiny but obligatory dot on top of the smallest Hebrew letter, and alludes to the name "Jew" (in some dialects: YID), to the initial letters of God's name, and to the names of the fathers of the nation, Isaac and Jacob, which are also the names of the poet and his own father. But in the poem, the epithet "Jewish" is not mentioned. Only the dot remains, a hard core, the tiniest visible existence, rolling in the streets. Both the dot and the secularized biblical names constitute anti-allusions, that is, allusions evoked to cancel the validity of the allusion. Yankl's limbs do not belong to him but are somehow hooked on, haphazardly attached to his body, clumsily irrelevant, as the stylistically outstanding long words (six and five syllables) expressively convey: *a-royf-ge-TSHE-pe-te* and *um-ge-LUM-per-te* ("hooked-on, clumsy"). *"Extras!"* (special editions of newspapers) fall everywhere from above, presumably from the El running above the streets of New York; but he cannot comprehend a thing and they squash his dumb, "watery head."

There is no single specific reference in the poem to any political event, though the time was filled with them; just the character's myopic eyeglasses get smeared with red and he is condemned to spin, lost in ether for eternities, with red before his eyes. Of course, this is New York. Glatshteyn's contemporaries in Europe filled their Expressionist poems with direct descriptions of the horrors of World War I and the pogroms of 1919. His experience is only a reflection of the European world, of news reports about it that fall absurdly in rapid succession onto his uncomprehending head. But the chaos of the modern world and the noisy metropolis are expressed just as strongly through indirection and understatement.

Glatshteyn's "1919" is a self-ironic, kaleidoscopic poem and, at the same time, an inverted statement about the political world and the mess it is in. The direct, coarse, juicy, rich, spoken language, with its diminutives, allusions, stylistic clashes, and ironic twists, is as Jewish as Yiddish lyrical poetry ever was before, even though thematically it is a cosmopolitan poem, smelling of New York confusion. Its conversational markers and precise sensibility for the effects of spoken intonations and sound relations in free verse demonstrate what the "Young Generation" missed with their exact meters and Symbolist poeticalness. There is also a direct jibe at neo-Romantic poetics in proclaiming that there is "no escape"—not from politics, its "Extras!" and red colors—but from the color "heaven-blue," a Symbolist poetic cliché externalized in nature: "The lord-above surrounded/ The whole world with heaven-blue/ And there is no escape."

Two poems from *Credos* (1929), "Autobiography" and "Jewish Kingdoms" (AYP, 246–7), again exhibit Glatshteyn's rich Jewish language of situations coupled with an ironic distancing from the old Jewish world. Like the Austrian Jewish novelist, Joseph Roth, in "Autobiography" Glatshteyn suspects that he is a lapsed Gentile and grotesquely demystifies the whole issue of history and roots. "Autobiography" may not be as coarse or as inwardly "anti-Semitic" as some of Halpern's poems about the old country, but it is as antinostalgic. In "Jewish Kingdoms," strange names of Polish towns float up in Glatshteyn's memory like dry leaves in a bath but he is incapable of longing for them.

Gradually but persistently, the rhyme ERTER—VERTER ("places—words"), emerges in Glatshteyn's poetry, as in the epigraph to this chapter (from *Exegyddish*, 1937, a book immersed in listening to the secrets of the Yiddish language). As the rhyme itself suggests, words (vERTER) contain places (ERTER). The names of Polish towns are mere names but they also recall a warm, early-erotic childhood experience. In the poetics of the early Glatshteyn, places occupy a central position. Though a master of the kaleidoscopic technique, he is uneasy about it. Glatshteyn is a talker, a narrator, and he prefers to locate his speakers in dramatized fictional situations. In the early poetry, the situations are mostly antirealistic, historical, or legendary: Gaggie the bear-trainer with his five wives, the poet's two-hundredth birthday, the Proud King, or Abishag. The Baron, an incorrigible liar, invents places with his words. Only in *Credos* (1929) does a more political realism enter his work and, even so, the basic technique is neither kaleidoscope nor metaphor but re-created fictional situations. Poems are anchored in places where characters are situated to enact their desentimentalized roles.

At least since Glatshteyn's poems about Nakhman of Bratslav, the connection is thematized: on the way to heaven, Nakhman becomes "everythingless in the world" and loses all his places and all his words, because there are no words (VERTER) without places (ERTER). Glatshteyn keeps repeating this persistent pair; in itself, it is a trite, obvious rhyme but it becomes the focus of a central theme, underlined by the spare and sporadic use of rhymes in his poetry. The theme is central even when the rhyme itself is absent. "Wagons" or "On the Butcher Block" are fictional places in which individual characters are located, expressing the horror of the impending Holocaust (rather than talking about it in general or attempting direct, realistic descriptions).

In the chilling poem of 1939, "A Hunger Fell Upon Us" (AYP, 308), the speaker may be in the same suburban home and garden as in the early poem of 1926, "On My Two-Hundredth Birthday" (AYP, 220), but there are also indications of a panhistorical space: "You touch your figtree,/ Stroke the bricks of your house." The safety of well-built bricks and of the biblical allusion ("everyone under his figtree") are both undermined with beautiful understatement: "Maybe nobody's come yet,/ But my bones already ache/ With the dampness of the Jewish weather." Hence, when the first news of the Holocaust arrives, he places the experience in space: "Here I have never been" (coupled with an anti-déjà vu, "This I have never seen"). The metaphor of space, embodying a "world" of experience and meaning, is central to Glatshteyn's thematics, poetic language, and fictional constructs.

But after the Holocaust, the relation is inverted as well: in Glatshteyn's early poetics, places carried words; now the words are the carriers of a lost world. When they lose their meaning, we lose our world:

All the existing words,
The expressed,
The understood,
Lie in their dumbfounded clarity.
Their sucked-dry meanings dozing off.
It is our world.
Soon it will lower the curtain.
—"We of the Singing Swords," AYP, 336

When Glatshteyn tries to understand the Holocaust, he conjures up a place, a tiny dot, from which he re-creates a lost world:

I shall stubborn myself,
Plant myself
In a private, intimate night
That I totally invented
And wondered-in on all sides.
I shall find a spot in space
As big as a fly,
And there I shall impose,
For all time,
A cradle, a child,
I shall sing into it a voice
Of a dozing father,
With a face in the voice,
With love in the voice [. . .]
And around the cradle I shall build a Jewish town.
                    —"I Shall Transport Myself," AYP, 340

These were words that carried in themselves the memory of places;
you could conjure up whole Jewish worlds from them. (Did these
worlds ever exist? Is he inventing them now?) But when the immediate
pain of the Holocaust was somewhat subdued, a new pain arose, the
pain of losing hold of the words themselves. The rhyme, ERTER—
VERTER ("words"—"places"), is back:

As to sad synagogues,   vi tsu troyerike shuln,
To doorsteps of belief—   tzu shveln fun gloybn,
How hard to come back   azoy shver iz tsuRIKtsukumen
To old WORDS.   tsu aMOlike VERTER.
I know well their PLACES.   baKANT zenen dir zeyere ERTER.
I hear their humming.   herst zeyer brumen, vey mir.
At times I get close, I look   kumst amol noent, kukst farBENKT
  longingly
Through the windowpanes.   durkh di shoybn.
—"Without Offerings," AYP, 361

Can we imagine the tragedy of writers—H. Leyvik, Jacob Glatshteyn,
A. Leyeles, and others—who felt such a mission of beginning in their
own lifetime and stood before the abyss of the end, losing first their
readership, then their source, their people in Europe (along with their
own parents), and finally the very language they had made into such
a fine instrument?

   Here stands the aging Glatshteyn, holding a handful of water in
his palm:

A few trembling lines on the palm of my hand.
I held them long
And let them flow through my fingers,
Word by word.
                              —"A Few Lines," AYP, 363

And again:

Soon we'll have lost all the words.
The stammer-mouths are growing silent.
The heritage-sack is empty. Where can we get
The holy prattle of promised
Joy? A child's grimaces
Are an alien spite-language.
In the dark we compose
Lightning-words, fast extinguished.
   And ash becomes their meaning.
   And ash becomes their meaning.
                              —"Soon," AYP, 363

This is a very private, very final Holocaust, for someone who was not there, who lived through it here, in America.

Index

Yiddish Scientific Institute. *See* YIVO
YIVO (Yiddish Scientific Institute), 67,
 80, 83, 87
"Young Generation," ["Di Yunge"], 140,
 146, 148, 159, 173, 176, 190; contributions of, 171–172; European
 counterparts of, 171; founding of,

170; Introspectionst revolt against,
 172

Zeitlin, Aron, 168
Zelig (film), 135
Zionism/Zionists, 84, 125, 131, 158
Zohar, 10, 83

CONTRAVERSIONS

JEWS AND OTHER DIFFERENCES

Lightning Source UK Ltd.
Milton Keynes UK
UKHW011239290821
389562UK00009B/378